Dalits and Upper Castes

DALITS AND UPPER CASTES

Essays in Social History

A. Satyanarayana

KANISHKA PUBLISHERS, DISTRIBUTORS
NEW DELHI-110 002

KANISHKA PUBLISHERS, DISTRIBUTORS
4697/5-21A, Ansari Road, Daryaganj
New Delhi -110 002
Phones : 2327 0497, 2328 8285
Fax : 011-2328 8285
E-mail : kanishka_publishing@yahoo.co.in

First Published 2005
Second Edition 2014

ISBN: 978-81-7391-703-5

PRINTED IN INDIA

Published by Madan Sachdeva for Kanishka Publishers, Distributors, 4697/5-21A, Ansari Road, Daryaganj, New Delhi-110 002, Typeset by Sunshine Graphics, Delhi, and Printed at Rajdhani Printers, Delhi.

Dedicated

to

Professor Dietmar Rothermund

Extraordinary Scholar and Great Humanist

Foreword

Professor A. Satyanarayana's book on *Dalits and Upper Castes* contains valuable historical material on the caste system with an insightful analysis into history of caste. Though most of the historical material for the rich research papers that he wrote for highly valued national and international journals and edited volumes published by eminent academicians is drawn from historical developments of the Telugu country, the book as a holistic reading draws lessons from a pan-Indian context. It makes an excellent history of caste in India. Satyanarayana's book breaks new ground in writing Indian history by evolving a historiography that treats caste as an historical category.

His first essay "Caste and Class in Rural Andhra 1947-1967" gives a glimpse of the historical linkages between caste and class as two intertwined social institutions. The discourse whether India is a caste centered country or class centered country is a basic debate in the Indian context. In this paper. Satyanarayana shows that by 1947 the landed property in Andhra transformed from Brahmins to Sudra upper castes and the agrahara landholders—the Brahmins—shifted to the urban employment sector. The coastal Kammas, Reddys and Raj us began to emerge as the political elite by using their landlord status in the agrarian economy. He very appropriately gives the example of Jagariamudi Kuppusway Choudhary, belonging to Kamma family of Guntur district, who owned about 24,000 acres of land. With vast data base he shows that by the early 1920s the Brahmins of Andhra had migrated to Madras in a big away and about 60 per cent of college graduates were Brahmins themselves.

By and large, the Sudra OBC castes and the Dalits had remained as tenants or agrarian labourers. He shows how caste feudalism destroyed the upper castes and the lower castes as both of them remained in the feudal superstition. The upper castes—particularly Brahmins—were spending the Agrahara feudal incomes on extravagance and wasteful ritual practices and consumption. The labouring and artisanal masses, on the other hand had no food to eat. Satyanarayana's study shows that in terms of land-holding, the Dalits were the poorest while the OBCs by and large were landless labourers or tenant farmers in the process of transition.

Having examined the caste relationships in the immediate post-Independence period in the second chapter—"Caste and Entrepreurship in Colonial Andhra, South India 1900-1947"—he examines the immediate period of pre-Independence in the context of the kind of caste relations existing among the people. The late nineteenth century and early twentieth century was the period of the beginning of entrepreneurship in the Telugu country. The historical Vaisyas had transformed into Komatis in this region and by and large controlled village, town, and urban business. One of the main characteristics of Komati business was avoiding tax payments and hiding that wealth underground. This wealth is historically known as *Guptadhana.* Because of this concealment of wealth underground, the historical formation of *Gupthadhana* (underground wealth) took place. This was slowly converted into Black money. This process has stalled the formation of progressive industrial capital. Because of the caste system, progressive dynamic entrepreneurial castes have not been formed. The Brahmins for a long time did not enter into business as they used to think that it was against their varna dharma. But the Brahmin-interaction with the British forced them to take up business and entrepreunerial activity. Satyanarayana's paper shows that the Brahmins began to share business with the Komatis in the late nineteenth century and early twentieth century. He says "the twice-born castes (Bramins, Kshatriyas, Rajus and Arya Vaisya Komatis) and the non-Brahmin upper castes (Reddis, Kammas, Naidus, Velamas, Lingayats etc) became the entrepreneurs." From the lower castes there was no entrepreneurial class that emerged and transformed the social mass into a market oriented people. This chapter of Satyanarayana will be very useful for future scholars to studying the relationship between caste, industrial production and the market.

The third chapter "Growth of Education" reviews the whole

history of education. This chapter deals with the position of education in modern Andhra from 1893-1947. India is one country where education—reading, writing of the book—is caste centered. The notion that only Brahmins should read and write and while others follow the intellectual leadership of Brahmins destroyed all possibilities of change. Satyanarayana tries to examine this fundamental issue and its historical implication. The point that the Brahmins have been the most autocratic suppressors of the spread of education among the productive communities is well brought out. It is also a known fact that the Dalit-Bahujans have been fighting for that single right with all the strength at their command. However, they did not succeed in getting education till alternative religious schools which made the book the link between God and people made their way into India.

Though the entry of Bible into India took place in the first century, it was not possible to touch a spiritual book as touching of a book is a banned within the Hindu realm of thought and civil society. The Bible was the first spiritual book that became touchable for those who were born within the Dalitbahujan castes. However, in the early period, the Bible was introduced only in small geographical zones like Kerala and as it was in Roman script, not many could read it. But the text as such was considered to be holy and it was very much touchable by all. The Hindu Vedas, Puranas and Upanishads were not touchable. Ramayana, Mahabharata and the Bhagavad Gita were also not touchable. Many hands seem to have been cut for touching them and many toungues were cut having read them.

The fact that a holy text was touchable had given a sense of liberation in spiritual terms. Nationalism in way is a text centered mass mobilization process. Only during the colonial period was the Bible translated into the mass languages of India through missionary activity. The missionaries as committed people in the divine cause believed in spreading the word of God. With the Bible getting translated into English the notion of God understanding all languages came into practice. In India before Christianity became a visible religion Islam had been a visible religion. But by and large the Quran remained in the confines of the Masque. The Quran was not made a book of education among non believers. Though Sufi saints propagated the greatness of Islam as a religion, the Quran as a book was never circulated among the non believing mass. In one of his chapters Satyanarayana discusses how Christianity provided the early education to the Dalitbahujans using Bible as a readable text. The second stage of mass education became possible with the Quaran making an entry into India. But the Quran remained for a long time inaccessible to the Indian masses as it was available only in Persian, Arabic and Urdu. Slowly when the Dalitbahujans embraced Islam and began to learn Urdu, they began to acquire literacy through religious means. But the state never got positively involved in providing literacy to the Dalitbahujans till the British initiated some schools and colleges. The secular educational institutions were in a way started by the British themselves.

Satyanarayana's study shows that even then the educational graph was showing a vast disparity between the upper castes and Dalitbahujans. By 1931, the education level of Brahmins was 51.1 per cent whereas the Madigas had a literacy level of 1.6 per cent and Malas had a literacy level of 1.9 per cent. The corresponding data for the Sudras, particularly the OBC castes, is not available but by any stretch of the imagination the literacy level of many OBC castes would be much less because in the Telugu country the OBCs had not embraced Christianity. The Dalit literacy rate had began to register because of the church institutions.

In his next chapter Satyanarayana examines the historical process of emergence of the Dalit protest literature in the Telugu country. The whole process of emergence of the Dalit protest literature in the late nineteenth century and early twentieth century was a process of liberation from British colonialism as well as caste colonialism from within. He reviews the entire literary movement emerging from Dalit struggles. In the former Nizam's State, Bhagayareddy Varma, a social reformer, established an Adi-Hindu association and started educational activity. In the Andhra region Kusuma Dharmanna, Vemula Kumaraiah, Nakka China Venkaiah, Jala Rangaswamy and so on created a condition of cultural revolution. Prof. Satyanarayana examins the writings of Gurram Jashuva in detail. Gurram Jashuva, the most powerful Dalit writer of the modem age, interrogated the cultural negativism of the Hindu social system through poetic writings in Telugu. He challenged his contemporary Brahminical writers and constructed literary texts that built an alternative idiom. Because of Gurram Jashuva, a large school of Telugu Dalit writers emerged.

Dalit protest literature has created a consciousness that gave rise to self-confidence among the Dalit masses. The written text has its own historical role. Dalit literature created tension and social friction because Dalits started asserting their social position. In Andhra Pradesh two major incidents at Karamchedu and Chundur occurred where several Dalits were murdered. Dalits who asserted their rights were made the targets of the attack. Whenever such attacks took place the Dalit-leadership mobilized the social mass into protest movements. After Satyanarayana wrote this paper a whole lot of new literature has been written depicting the living conditions, the day to day life struggles, the problems of child education, the maintenance of old aged Dalits, and on the adivasis and Backward class masses. The creation of Dalit literature is an ongoing process. The mass productive life of Dalitbahujans in its multi dimentional form and content has not come into literary textuality. Satyanarayana's writing of caste history from a multi-dimentional point of view is going to enrich Indian historiography.

The next chapter deals with "Dalit Identity and Consciousness in Colonial Andhra 1917-1947." The Dalit consciousness in the immediate context of pre-Independence India operates in a dual way: (1) It is a conditioned consciousness that gives consent to the process of exploitation by the upper castes as the large number of Dalitbahujans think that their social status is God given and (2) there is also an emerging new consciousness that keeps rebelling against caste exploitation as a small section of Dalitbahujan intellectual forces emerged to conscientize the conditioned consciousness and rebel against the oppressor.

The pre-Independence era has produced a small group of organic intellectuals who began to conscientize the consciousness of Dalitbahujans. Mahatma Phule, Savitribai Phule, Narayana Guru, Periyar Ramaswami Naicker etc., influenced the national psyche towards a process of social liberation from caste oppression. Apart from such national voices, there were many regional voices who began to articulate the liberation ideology of the productive masses. Satyanarayana has been examining the historical process of that protest consciousness. In the Andhra context, he examined the efforts made by Bhagya Reddy Varma, Kusuma Dharmanna and so on. Based on the new consciousness, there have been efforts to mobilize Dalitbahujan masses. Several caste organizations emerged during that period. Satyanarayana shows how various castes and occupational groups were mobilized to fight for their rights.

The following chapters are titled "Against Social Imperialism," "Swaraj yam/Swatantryam: Dalit Visions of Freedom," "Religion of the Poor: Dalits and Christianity in Colonial Andhra," "Upper Caste Violence against Dalits in Andhra Pradesh, 1947-1985," and finally, "The Birds ofPasage: Migration of South Indian Labourers to South East Asia" which was published in *Critical Asian Studies.* This final essay indicates the merit of this volume. By writing and publishing it in *Critical Asian Studies,* Satyanarayana has put the Department of History, Osmania University, on its academic legs and on the global map.

I leave to the readers to judge how Satyanarayana worked out an alternative historiography in these essays. In my view he created a new historiography that makes the anti-caste struggles as part of historical consciousness. Writing Indian history from caste point of view has been an unknown phenomenon in the course of writing of Indian history.

There are three contending historiographies in the so-called mainstream history of India: (1) The Hindu nationalist historiography (2) Secular nationalist historiography and (3) Subaltern nationalist historiography. The writers of all these three modes of histories came from a Brahmanical background. Even the Marxist, Muslim and Christian historians broadly fell into the trap of Hindu Brahminical historiography. The Muslim and Christian historians never realized that their self is either non-existant or totally marginalized. After class centred historiography emerged, with the introduction of Marxist methodology, the upper caste historians saw to it that caste never entered historiography. For them caste as an institution that created conditions of hegemony and subordination was seen as an institution of no historical consequence. All the Brahminical books from Rig Veda to Bhagvad Gita, their translations and interpretations all of them became a part of history. For them a historical culture means the culture that was constructed around the Brahminical books. But leather tanners, shoe makers, pot makers, shepherds, Iron Smiths, carpenters, or the tillers of the soil have not been seen as cultural constructors.

A pot, a shoe, a table, or a plough may be reflectors of our civilization. But civilization has its inter-relationship with culture. Even while writing economic history, the grain figures as a cultural and economic product. But the producer of the grain is never brought into history as a social being who was dehumanized by a social institution called caste. Writing about caste has been considered uncivilized. But living in caste, maltreating other beings as less than dogs and donkeys was considered necessary. A historian consciously or unconsciously lives in caste but does not want to historicize that living process. The historian does not even think that what he is doing is injustice to history. Silence on structured oppression is seen as a historical necessity. In fact such a silence is seen as history itself. That is the reason why the productive people's history has been a silent spectator of all the historical brutalities of the Brahminical people and their historians. No Brahminical historian realized that the silent watching of the suppression, of social beings who were producing food for the daily consumption of the supressors, and also the historians who glorified these suppressors, is huge crime. If the suppressor commits a crime one can understand it but if the historian remains silent about the crime, it has be dealt with more seriously.

In India, class brutalities have been talked of but caste oppression was never brought up about by historians. One of the reasons for class exploitation being discussed and caste atrocities not being talked about was that an oppressor himself/herself can be defined as being a part of the oppressed in terms of class. The notion of class in the Indian context is a fish in water, one need not labour much to catch it. Caste on the other hand is an institution that operates on the ground as an everyday reality. This everyday reality was also everyday history. But that everyday history of untouchability, cutting of tongues for reading the letter, the cutting of hands for writing the letter were never seen as historical facts. In contemporary history the discourse about humiliating the Daitbahujans on the question of reservations is not seen as historical humiliation of a social mass.

In a way Satyanarayana changes the course of that history writing. He examines the history of caste in a systematic manner. It is the history of the everyday life of Dalitbahujans. Their struggles, their relationship to the land, water and production needs to become part of living history. More than anythingelse, writing the history of caste relations and the conspiracy of Brahminism that worked throughout history to keep Dalitbahujan struggles out of history needs to be written as the history of this nation. Writing such history is not an ordinary task. Satyanarayana has made a serious beginning in the writing of such a history and many such historians have to come forwardand write regional histories and also national histories. Telling the truth in its true form alone becomes true history. Caste, class and gender oppressions are absolute truths and writing that history is the main role of the Truth Seekers whom Mahatma Phule calls the Satyashodhaks. Let there be many more Satyashodhaks in this country.

Dr. Kancha Ialaiah
Professor and Head
Department of Political Science
Osmania University
Hyderabad-500 007

Preface

The essays on *Dalits and Upper Castes* incorporated into the present volume were presented in various seminars and most of them were published in scholarly journals and edited books. They indicate my research interest pertaining to the social history of modern Andhra. They touch upon different aspects of caste-class relationship at the micro-level. In 1994, I published an essay on "Caste and Class in Rural Andhra" in which I analysed the dynamics of social transformation during the colonial and post-colonial period. Subsequently, I wrote many articles on dalits focusing on the evolution of dalit-bahujan identity and consciousness, a theme which has not been adequately dealt with by the historians of modern Andhra.

In recent years aspects of caste, class, agrarian social structure, dominance and resistance have attracted scholarly attention. Some studies have been carried out in this area. Yet the existing works on social history of modern Andhra do not adequately explain how upper caste dominance was constituted and sustained. What was the social/institutional basis of upper caste dominance? What was the relationship between land control, material production and caste system? How were caste relations constituted and articulated at the grass roots level? What are the social roots of caste violence? How does one account for growing atrocities on dalit bahujans? In the existing historical literature, the emergence of a dalit consciousness and of a distinct dalit sensibility also did not receive adequate attention. Similarly, what the dalits thought about their conditions, in their own terms, has not been properly analysed by scholars. The fact that dalits have the intellectual ability to creatively reflect on their conditions, in their own language, both historically and sociologically, has been missed out.

The essays presented in this volume will attempt at providing answers to some of these important questions. An understanding of such questions itself is crucial to unravel the complexities of caste system in modern Andhra. Taking caste as the central problematic of historiography, this study views caste as a dynamic, historically evolved structure of power relations of domination and subordination. The historical trajectory of the evolution of caste system is sought to be examined not merely in terms of its materiality, but also in its dialectical inter-relationship with the social, cultural and ideological-intellectual domains. Hence this study, instead of viewing caste as a cultural construct by the Brahmanical forces seeks to unravel the dynamics of Indian social system by viewing it as determined by the dialectic of upper caste dominance and lower caste resistance.

The present volume is expected to fill in the gaps in the existing studies by updating our knowledge, besides providing a new dimension to the study of the caste question in modern Andhra. It is also expected that the essays in this volume will help in developing an alternative methodological framework to understand the nature of caste system in south Indian society.

In the course of my research on modern Andhra I have been fortunate to have the support of a number of institutions and individuals. I received help from several quarters, and my debts of gratitude have indeed piled up. I am indebted to the authorities of Osmania University, who provided me ample opportunities for my teaching and research activities during the last two decades. I was fortunate to receive financial assistance from the Indian Council of Historical Research and the University Grants Commission, New Delhi, for my research projects. I am also thankful to the authorities of Japan Foundation and the German Academic Exchange Service for awarding me post-doctoral fellowship.

I am deeply indebted to Professors S. Bhattacharya, V. Ramakrishna and A. Bobbili for their help and encouragement. I owe a special debt of gratitude to Prof. Kancha Ilaiah for writing foreword to his volume. I also thank all my colleagues in the Department for showing interest in my work and helping me in many ways. I am thankful to Dr. I. Thirumali and Dr. Y. Chinna Rao, for their warm friendship.

I am extremely grateful to Professor Dietmar Rothermud, my Ph.D. Supervisor, at South Asia Institute of Heidelberg University, Germany, for his concern towards me, and my work. I dedicate this volume to him as a token of gratitude for all that he has done for me.

During the course of my research I have visited various archives and libraries for material collection. The authorities and staff members of the Library of South Asia Institute of Heidelberg University, Germany; the Library of Oriental Institute, Tokyo University, Japan; Library of the Modern Oriental Studies, Berlin. Germany; Francke Foundation Library, Halle, Germany; Library of the International Institute of Social History, Amsterdam, The Netherlands; National Archives of India, Nehru Memorial Museum and Library, New Delhi; A.P. State Archives and Research Institute, Tarnaka, Hyderabad; Tamil Nadu State Archives, Chennai, Osmania University Library, Hyderabad, have been very helpful. I thank them all.

How can I forget to thank Seeta, my wife, who shared all my troubles and stood by me through the difficult period of research trips abroad and silently encouraged my academic endeavours. My dearest children, Uma and Jaswanth cheerfully bore my frequent and prolonged absence from home.

Finally, I am grateful to M/s Kanishka Publishers, New Delhi, for bringing out this volume in record time.

Hyderabad **A. Satyanarayana**

Contents

Contents

1

Caste and Class in Rural Andhra, 1947-1967: A Historical Perspective

In a recent article, Rajni Kothari observed that the 1967 elections represented the "first major assertion of rural India," and "highlighted the power of locally entrenched elite within the Congress."[1] He also maintained that it marked a "watershed in India's political development." He noted thus:

> "The institutionalization of adult franchise since 1952 and the generally faithful implementation of the democratic process under Nehru (e.g., through a massive programme of rural development and the introduction of 'democratic decentralization' through panchayati raj) gave considerable power to party leadership at lower levels who could deliver the votes and who controlled local institutions, exercised leverage at higher levels and in course of time got elected to state and national bodies. All this led to a significant shift of power from the middle classes to the rural, 'vernacular', middle castes."[2]

Further, it has been pointed out that "the unfolding of the democratic process in the first fifteen years had led to a challenge to the hegemony of the educated urban middle classes from a political elite that drew its power from the "control of rural institutions and the rural vote."[3] The objective of this chapter is to discuss the origin and crystallization of the rural elite in Andhra over a period of time. It attempts to analyse the dynamics of the formation of 'rural elite' or what we call the rural rich[4] in the Andhra countryside during the first two decades of the post-Independence period (i.e., 1947-1967). The central focus is on the changing caste-class composition of the rural rich in Andhra over time. The formation and crystallisation of the rural rich is discussed in terms of an examination of the evolution of the rural political economy in Andhra. That is to say, the economic foundations of the rural rich will be discussed with special reference to the control over land, expansion of commodity production and the (agrarian) market. An attempt will also be made to relate the socio-economic position of the rural rich to its hegemony over political power at the local level. The exercise of power by the rural rich will be analysed in terms of its access to the local institutions of power and authority, viz., the panchayati raj and the co-operative societies.

The chapter is divided into four sections. While the first section discusses, in broad terms, the relationship between land and caste during the colonial period, the second section examines, on the basis of micro-level data, the changing caste-class composition of the rural rich in Andhra. The articulation of political power and its various forms will be explained in the third section. Section four contains a summary and conclusion.

I

Land, Caste and Power: The Colonial Background

During the colonial period, the agrarian social structure in Andhra closely corresponded to the structure of land ownership, power and authority. Although the British abolished the existing caste-defined position over land and other resources, and imposed juridico-legal relationships of land ownership (property right, private property in land, etc.), the caste hierarchies continued to exist and often overlapped with the hierarchies of economy and power. The socio-economic transformation during the colonial period (1802-1947) resulted in the formation of new classes, formally separated from the traditional caste system. Yet the categories of caste and class were, to a large extent converged, and continued to be interlinked. Broadly speaking, the fusion and convergence of caste and class in the colonial context contributed to the emergence of two distinct groups of people, namely, landlords (*zamindars*) and peasants/tenants.

The first group, consisting of the minority sections of society, though owned and controlled land and other resources, but did not participate in the process of production. The second group, though heterogeneous in terms of caste, constituted the majority section, comprising mainly of the tillers of land. In most of the cases and for a long time, the cultivators who tilled the land and harvested its yield, had no rights over the land.

As a result of the British colonial policies in the nineteenth century, with respect to the structure of landholding and as a consequence of the impact of new economic forces, Andhra districts (coastal Andhra and Rayalaseema) evolved a distinct system of land tenures, viz., *zamindari* and *ryotwari*.[5]

> "Intermediaries with control over land had been a historical phenomenon in coastal Andhra... colonialism for its sheer survival had propped up these rent-squeezing intermediaries and for a century and half yielded to their pressure tactics."[6]

Big landlords considered the *zamindari* system as an important characteristic feature of the agrarian structure in coastal Andhra. Under the *zamindari* system, the concentration of land in some districts[7] was as follows :

Table 1
Total Cultivated Area
(in per cent)

	Ryotwari	*Zamindari and Inam*
Ganjam	55.1	44.9
Vishakhapatnam	9.4	90.6
East Godavari	59.1	40.9
West Godavari	59.7	40.3
Krishna	45.7	54.3
Guntur	70.6	9.4
Nellore	49.8	50.2

The *zamindars* in Andhra were basically the parasitic rent-receiving landholders who exercised ownership rights in land and other resources without undertaking supervision and cultivation of land. But, by virtue of their 'proprietary rights', they could and did burden the tenantry with heavy taxation (rack-renting), unauthorized and illegal extractions and squeezed out as much surplus as possible.[8] Control over the means of production (land) enabled the landlords to exercise unquestioned power and authority over the peasantry. In terms of caste, the *zamindars* in Andhra were a mixed lot. The landlord class in coastal Andhra primarily consisted of the non-Brahmin upper castes, viz., the Kshatriya, the Velama, the Kamma and the Reddy. There were few Kshatriya *zamindars*, mainly found in the Vishakapatnam district; the Maharaja of Vizianagaram and others. The important Velama *zamindars* who controlled extensive areas included the Rajas of Panagal, Bobbili, Venkatagiri, Pithapuram, Mirzapuram and Nuzvid; estate holders of Challapalli, Vuyyuru, Muktyala, etc., were Kammas, while the Munagala *zamindar* belonged to the Reddy caste.

Generally speaking, landlordism was closely associated with the permanent settlement. However, in the *ryotwari* areas also, big pattadars owned vast landed properties. The landlords of the *ryotwari* region overwhelmingly belonged to the non-Brahmin upper castes: Reddies in Rayalaseema, and Kammas, Rajus and Reddies in coastal Andhra. In Rayalaseema especially, the village officers' families held considerable acres of land and controlled other economic resources in the countryside. Their wealth and richness enabled them to exercise power and domination over the dependent peasantry. Since they occupied village offices (Patel, Munsab, etc.) and positions, it was possible for them to command respect and authority.

Below the landlords were a large peasant community comprising owner-cultivators, occupancy tenants and various types of under-tenants. The tenant-cultivators in the *zamindari* and *ryotwari* areas also belonged to the Sudra *varna* which included peasant castes as well as artisan castes, viz., the Reddy, Kamma, Kapu, Raju, Telaga, Balija, Saale (weaver), Chakali (washerman), Mangali (barber), Viswabrahmin (goldsmith), Goundla (toddy tapper), Yadava (shepherd), Kummara (potter) and Uppara (mason). Strictly speaking, in Andhra, landlords belonging to the Velama, Kamma and Reddy castes had a Sudra status, nevertheless they maintained their ritual distance from their dependents.

The Brahmins were the highest caste in the traditional Hindu society. During the pre-colonial days, they held landed property and monopolized learning and administrative positions. The Brahmins in Andhra primarily possessed *inam* lands, also known as *agraharms, shrotriyams,* etc., granted by the rulers. The British colonial government also confirmed and conferred 'proprietary rights' to the owners through the *inam* settlement (1859-61).[8] Although the *inam* land consisted of different varieties (*amaram, kattubadi, sarva, shortrium,* etc.), the biggest beneficiaries were undoubtedly the Brahmins. It has been estimated that between six and fifteen per cent of the total cultivated area in the Andhra districts was under *inam* tenure.[9] By and large, in many *inams* there had been a separation between ownership and cultivation. That is to say, because of the considerations of tradition and pollution, the Brahmin landowners did not till the land themselves, but leased-out to non-Brahmin tenant-cultivators. Therefore, in Andhra, we find the widespread prevalence of absentee landlordism in *agraham* villages. The tenants of the *inam* lands had no ownership rights and were subjected to rack-renting.

The Vaisyas (Komati), third in the *varna* hierarchy, were essentially a mercantile community. Very few of them owned lands and cultivated with the help of farm servants. There were some Komati families such as the Motheys in Ellore (West Godavari) who held vast landed properties (estates). But this was an exception. The Komatis in Andhra were actively engaged in their traditional occupation of trade, moneylending and business.

The artisan and service castes like the Saale, Kamsali, Goundla, Mangali, Chakali, etc., did own some land but it was too meagre to depend upon for their livelihood. Since many of these castes witnessed the destruction of their traditional occupations (de-industrialisation), they swelled the ranks of the rural poor. Consequently, they constituted a large part of agricultural labour, next only to the untouchables. Many micro studies reveal that the artisan castes gradually lost their landed property in favour of other dominant castes and thus became landless.[10]

The untouchables (Harijans), who are the lowest caste, performed occupations like scavenging, leather work, etc. Under colonial conditions, they constituted the bulk of the agricultural labour force and worked as farm servants and casual labourers. Very few (less than 10%) Harijan families possessed agricultural land. The main source of their livelihood was manual (menial) labour. They had no right to own land, nor were they considered to be peasants or tillers of soil. The colonial land regulations never granted them the status of an occupancy tenant, though they might have cultivated lands as tenants and sharecroppers. In the case of untouchables, therefore, there was a clear correspondence/correlation between social and economic status.

Having described the position of different castes in terms of landholding, we shall now turn to the interrelationship between caste, land and power in rural Andhra during the colonial period.

The evolution of the land tenure system under colonialism strengthened the position of *zamindars* as well as the big *ryotwari* landlords in terms of their control over land. It may be pointed out that for years the *zamindars* had been able to command and exercise immense power and authority in the countryside mainly on account of their grip over land. The *zamindari* agrarian structure enabled the landlord class as a whole to appropriate a larger share of agrarian surplus by means of extraction of exorbitant rents. The landlords' authority was, in fact, maintained on the basis of rack-renting. The *zamindars* in Andhra held vast estates and obtained unfettered access to communal, waste, forest lands and other resources. It may be noted that they exercised rule and control over not only land and forests but also over ponds, sources of irrigation, etc. Thus, the *zamindars'* power was further reinforced since they acquired enormous wealth and affluence based on rack-renting and illegal cesses. Acquisition of wealth and control over resources enabled the landlords to maintain their higher status. It also sustained their hold and hegemony over rural society, economy and polity.

On the basis of the available evidence, it can be said that besides controlling vast areas under the permanent settlement, the *zamindars* also possessed private (*seri*) lands running into thousands of acres. It has been found out that some *zamindars* like Challapalli owned about 17,000 acres as private land. Others like the Raja of

Bobbili 1,000 acres, Raja of Pithapuram 2,000 acres, Raja of Vizianagaram 1,454, acres and the Raja of Munagala owned more than 4,000 acres of land.[11] The *seri* lands were extended over time by the occupation of relinquished and evicted lands bought from the *ryots*. It has also been established that the private lands were enlarged by illegal occupation and encroachment of communal lands.[12] The *zamindars* employed farm servants and wage labourers to cultivate their personal lands. But, in most of the estates, private lands were leased-out to middlemen and under-tenants/tenants-at-will. The possession of vast estates and private lands helped the landlords to exercise control over their tenants.

As we have noted above, big landlords were not only confined to the permanently settled areas, but were also found in the *ryotwari* system. One of the notable landlords of the ryotwari areas in Andhra districts was Jagarlamudi Kuppu Swamy Chaudhary who "owned 2,400 acres of agricultural land and 2,000 acres of plantation and paid Rs. 8,000 in *kist* and Rs. 480 as income tax."[13] He was one of the biggest landowners-moneylenders in Guntur district. Ethirajulu Naidu was another leading landowner and tobacco merchant in Guntur; K.V. Reddi Naidu (Kapu) held lands worth Rs. 75,000; Dandu Naryana Raju and P. Reddi Raju (Kshatriyas) owned extensive lands in West Godavari district; Kasu Reddi of Guntur belonged to the family of village officer and held extensive lands. In the Rayalaseema region, too, many village officer families possessed vast landed property. Thomas Munroe's *ryotwari* settlement did not completely eliminate the big landed properties owned by the village officer (Patel, Munsiff, etc.) families in the ceded districts.

Thus, the landlord class in the Andhra region consisted predominantly of the non-Brahmin upper class, viz., Kshatriya, *Velama*, Kamma and Reddy. Though it was numerically insignificant (less than one per cent of the total population in 1931), yet it controlled the rural economy, society and polity during the colonial period. Most of the big *zamindars* like the Rajas of Bobbili, Venkatagiri, Pithapuram, Mirzapuram, Chellapalli, and Vuyyuru were also moneylenders. By leasing out lands and advancing money they were able to tighten their grip over the dependent tenantry. As creditors, the landlords always commanded authority over debtors. By virtue of 'proprietorship' over land, the *zamindars* could lease out lands to whomsoever they wanted and displace the tenants-at-will at their will and pleasure. The threat of eviction coerced despite granting the tenantry into submission. The colonial land legislation, certain rights of occupancy, on the whole failed to protect the tenants. The growth of population and land hunger further strengthened the hold of landlords over the rural population. In caste terms the vast mass of the tenantry, both in the *zamindari* and *ryotwari* areas, consisted of the peasant and artisan castes. Particularly the lower castes among the backward communities such as Goundlas, Yadavas, and Telagas used to lease in lands from landlords. They were the most exploited lot as they were subjected to frequent rack-renting and illegal exactions.

Control over land and acquisition of wealth and affluence helped the landlords to exercise power and authority. The growth of the non-Brahmin movement and the establishment of the Justice Party led to the rise of landlord power in Andhra. The opportunities provided by the colonial state in terms of local self-government and 'diarchy' were utilized by *zamindars* to their fullest advantage. Their ability to extend patronage and exercise control and domination over their dependents contributed to the monopoly of power by them. As a matter of fact, the working of diarchy (in the 1920s) witnessed the emergence of landlords as 'political bosses' in the Madras Presidency. Due to colonial patronage, between 1921-36, out of four chief ministers, three belonged to the *zamindar* class.[14]

The legislative council and the local board elections provided opportunities for the landlords to emerge as the dominant political elite. An examination of the electoral data (of the mid-1920s) reveals the fact that landlords successfully competed with the professional elites (lawyers), occupying positions in the Madras Legislative Council. The strength of the landlords in the council increased from twenty-eight in 1920 to thirty-eight in 1926; whereas the representation of lawyers declined from forty-eight to thirty-six during the same period.[15] Some of the *zamindars* in Andhra like the Rajas of Bobbili, Pithapuram, Venkatagiri, Mirzapuram were active and took a leading part in the Justice Party as well as in local and provincial politics. They held positions (chairmanships) in the district and taluk boards. A perceptive scholar remarked that: "Landlords with local influence discovered that as presidents and members of local boards, they could wield a large amount of influence in their locality, and exercise greater power over their neighbours."[16] Being powerful men in the countryside they could and did command the votes of their creditors and dependents. Therefore, between 1920-40, many local boards were controlled by landlords belonging to the *zamindari* and *ryotwari* areas. The landlords' control over provincial politics remained unchallenged till the late 1930s. However, it is not suggested that agrarian society below the landlords remained static and undifferentiated. What is stated here is that as a social class the landlords exercised both economic and political domination over the peasants in Andhra during colonialism.

Although the Brahmins were the highest caste and enjoyed unchallenged high ritual status, in terms of economic status they were to the landlords. Of course, the *agraharamdars* as well as major *inamdars* who held vast landed properties could be considered as rich landholders. But, in general, the Brahmins in Andhra as a whole were not considered landed gentry. Initially, they were dependent on land for their livelihood and the revenue derived from the lands was the major source of income. However, the opportunities provided by the colonial regime enabled them to opt for new pursuits of life. More importantly, the Brahmins as a whole had occupied very important and 'unnaturally prominent' places in the fields of education and public service. Therefore, it was rightly pointed out that educationally the Brahmin was the leader of South India."[17] Among the college graduates of Madras University (in 1920-21), sixty-four per cent came from the Brahmin caste, though Brahmins comprised only around three per cent of the total population.[18] Thus, they successfully utilized the opportunities presented by the British, and many Brahmins in Andhra had taken up new occupations like law, journalism, medicine, teaching, etc. They entered the colonial administration and newly created urban professions in disproportionately large numbers. A recent study concluded that under colonialism (in south India) "urbanization and Brahmin dominance were interrelated features of social change."[19] Besides education and public services, the Brahmins in Andhra also controlled the Congress party and dominated public life.

As an enlightened social group, the Brahmins were also in the forefront of political organizations and the nationalist movement. During the pre-independence period, in terms of the relationship between caste, rank and politics, the Brahmins dominated the political arena. The nationalist movement and the Congress party were controlled by the Brahmins, at least till the late 1940s. Especially in Andhra, the urban professional elites like Konda Venkatappaiah, Pattabi Sitaramaiah, Tanguturi Prakasam, Ayyadevara Kaleswar Rao (all Brahmins) had played a very significant role in politics. Therefore, it can be concluded that the advantages of landed property, education, public service and political power contributed to the emergence of Brahmins as a privileged elite group in Andhra society.

Since they had free access to the new opportunities created by the colonial state, they enjoyed a higher status even in terms of economic position and hence could be termed as the upper class of Andhra society. Nevertheless, the source of their prestige and status was not entirely the possession of landed property. They occupied a prominent socio-economic position by virtue of their access to education and employment.

It has been pointed out earlier that the peasantry beneath the landlord predominantly belonged to the Sudra varna. Of course, the peasant society (both in the *zamindari* and *ryotwari* areas) was stratified and differentiated in terms of caste and class. There were rich, middle and poor peasants as well as upper and lower (or forward and backward) castes among the peasants in Andhra. However, compared to the lower caste peasants/tenants, the peasants/tenants (the peasantry) belonging to the upper castes (numerically preponderant Kammas and Reddies) enjoyed certain advantages. Within the constraints of colonial agrarian legislation they were able to secure occupancy rights and were protected from rack-renting and arbitrary eviction. The Kamma, Kapu and Reddy peasantry in Andhra were/are known for their hard-work and enterprising nature. The *ryotwari* land tenure, the widespread prevalence of peasant proprietorship and the development of irrigation system contributed to the rise of a stable middle level peasantry in coastal Andhra. Furthermore, commercialization, commodity production and agrarian trade led to the emergence of a fairly prosperous peasantry. Elsewhere we have explained the process of the emergence and crystallization of 'nascent peasant-bourgeoisie' in rural Andhra towards the end of colonial rule.[20] It has also been noted that certain peasant castes such as the Gowaras in Vishakhapatnam district and Kapus, Kammas and Reddies in the delta districts of Krishna, Godavari, Guntur and Nellore were market-oriented, dynamic and acquisitive. Because of their overall dynamic nature, these communities became an assertive social class and set a new trend and direction in rural Andhra.

The emergence of a dynamic social class within the peasantry manifested in the rise and growth of the Kisan movement in Andhra during the 1930s. The peasant proprietors in Andhra who belonged to these dominant castes provided leadership to the agrarian movements and challenged the authority of the feudal landlords.[21] They took an active part in the development of the anti-*zamindari* movement and other agrarian struggles. The growth of the Left Movement (between 1934-47) which weakened the authority of the landlords in Andhra also benefited the upper echelons of the peasant proprietors.

However, the lower sections of the backward castes like the Yadavas, Goundlas, and Telagas as well as the artisan castes continued to remain poor peasants and under-tenants. They did not benefit from the opportunities provided by the colonial situation.[22] In most of the cases they tended to lose their lands and join the ranks of the rural labour force. Micro-level village studies clearly indicate the process of the decline of the artisan castes.

II

Land, Caste and Class

By the end of the colonial rule there emerged a situation in which the hitherto dominant social groups, i.e., the landlords and Brahmins tended to lose their pre-eminent position in the realm of economy and polity in the countryside. Various factors were responsible for such a decline:

(*a*) The abolition of the *zamindari* system and other land tenure systems.

(*b*) The shift of landholding from Brahmins to non-Brahmins and migration of Brahmins from rural areas to towns and cities.

(*c*) The crystallization of a dynamic agrarian entrepreneurial class, which had taken advantage of the new economic opportunities of the post-1947 years, and consolidation of it's position as a dominant social class.

Although the landlords exercised authority over the village community for a long time, they did not remain unchallenged. Especially during the 1940's, strong anti-*zamindari* movements tended to undermine and weaken their authority and domination. The rich tenants belonging to the upper non-Brahmin castes were at the forefront of these struggles. It has been observed that the growth of left and radical peasant movements were largely responsible for the enactment of agrarian legislation, which drastically curtailed the powers of landlords over time.[23] On the eve of independence, the Rent Reduction Act (1947) and the Madras Estates Communal, Forest and Private Land Act (1947) were passed as a result of the aggressive peasant struggles in Andhra. These legislations together with the anti-*zamindari* movement brought about the drastic decline of landlords power over the tenantry. The *zamindars* could no longer freely resort to rack-renting, illegal exaction and encroachment. The cumulative effects of these legislations was disastrous, since it crippled the financial resources of the landlords. Thus, the economic basis of the foundation of the landlords' power and authority was badly shaken by these Acts. Finally, the Estates Abolition Act of 1948 gave a death-blow to the crumbling *zamindari* institution. Although the abolition of *zamindari* did not result in the radical redistribution of land, it certainly weakened the authority of landlords to a considerable extent. The ex-tenants in the permanently settled areas could acquire occupancy rights. At least a section of the ex-*zamindari* tenants substantially benefited from the legislation. Some of the big tenants and leasees of the *zamindars* were able to buy lands and acquire ownership rights.

Ample evidence is available with regard to the decline of Brahmins, *insofar* as their landed status is concerned. As we have noted earlier they held considerable *inam* lands. But due to urbanization and migration to cities they were forced to dispose of their lands to the non-Brahmin tenants. Various studies clearly indicate that there was a shift in the economic power from the Brahmins to the tenants. The Brahmins who were the original landowners (in the *agraharams*) sold their land to the hard-working Kammas and Kapus.[24] A study of an *agraharam* village in Krishna district highlights that there was a significant shift in the land ownership pattern over the period between 1930 and 1982. The Brahmins who owned seventy-seven per cent of the total land in 1930, were left with only three per cent by 1982.[25] Similarly, another study of a village in the Rayalaseema area shows that the ownership of land by Brahmins declined from thirty-six per cent in 1891 to only three per cent in 1982. It has also been observed that "the caste-wise ownership of land clearly shows that the Brahmins were the single largest landowning caste in 1891, but by 1948 they had lost their supremacy."[26] Village surveys in some other districts of coastal Andhra (Vishakhapatnam, Guntur and West Godavari) also confirm that "land has been rapidly passing from the Brahmins.... The *inam* lands of the Purohits and the Pujaris are being disposed of frequently."[27] The Brahmins lost lands not only to finance the education of their young family members and make a living in the urban areas, but also due to their conspicuous consumption and extravagant expenditure on rituals and ceremonies. There is sufficient evidence to suggest that many Brahmin families were ruined as a consequence of extravagance and wasteful expenditure. The decline and disintegration of absentee landlordism paved the way for the crystallization of a dynamic rural rich in the countryside. Undoubtedly, the post-colonial economic and political developments also facilitated the emergence of the new rural rich. The implementation of the *zamindari* Abolition Act and other tenancy legislations, though slow and halting, during the 1950s and 1960s contributed to the decline of the power of the non-cultivating landlords. The agrarian legislation thus laid the basis for the rural rich to emerge as the main landholding class. In caste terms, it consisted primarily of the Kamma, Kapu, Velama and Reddy castes. The evolution of the agrarian economy during the post-1947 period also contributed to the emergence of these dominant peasant castes.[28]

The various village surveys conducted during the post-independence years indicate that a significant section of landholders from among the Kamma, Kapu and Reddy castes emerged as the dominant peasantry. In the districts of East and West Godavari, Krishna, Guntur and Nellore in particular, peasants have emerged as the substantial landowners. Gradually, over a period of time, peasants in these castes have increased their landholdings by purchasing land sold off by other people. It has been observed that the Kammas could maintain and improve upon their lands mainly because of their 'attachment' to land as well as 'the extraordinary care' they take in agriculture. In areas where they were numerically greater they emerged as a socially and economically dominant caste. It was reported in a village survey that, "due to the possession of more than ninety per cent of the entire cultivable land in their hands, Kammas hold all the other castes in position of economic subordination."[29] A study on the pattern of land concentration in a village (in Krishna district) concludes that:

> "Fifteen families—eleven Kammas and four Brahmins—hold about sixty per cent of the land though they account for less than five per cent of the total households... But caste-wise analysis of data on landownership clearly establishes the fact that 96.49 per cent land is still in the hands of Kammas and Brahmins (Kammas 84.25 per cent and Brahmins 11.80 per cent)."[30]

Another study of a village in East Godavari district also shows that "2.3 per cent of families owned sixty-one per cent of land."[31] In areas where the Kapus and Balajis were numerically strong, they emerged as the dominant castes. It has been pointed out that as far as the Kapu caste was concerned, "their economic position, social standing and the numerical strength have made it the dominant caste in the village."[32] In the tobacco-rich Malkapuram village (Guntur district), "the Kammas dominated all fields, *viz.*, social, economic, political by virtue of their riches."[33]

Similarly, where the Reddies were more in number they too emerged as an economically powerful peasant group. According to the survey of Sayana in Tamballapalle village (Chittoor district), there was "a high concentration of land commonly found in some of the *ryotwari* villages in the districts of Bellary and Nellore. Most of the land is locked up mainly with the three Reddy houses of families."[34] Also, in another village of Chittoor district, "where the Reddies constituted 5.6 per cent of the total population but held 43.4 per cent of landed property."[35] In Yelamanshipadu village (Nellore district) where the Reddy caste is predominant, "almost all the Reddy households hold lands and every year they add something to the already existing land."[36] In terms of capital formation, "out of the forty-seven households surveyed, as many as twenty-six households invested money for the purchase of land: if it is analysed according to community it can be seen that there are ten Reddy households which invested Rs.10,46,000 for the purchase of land."[37] Likewise, in Karada village (Vishakhapatnam district) where the *Velamas* were a predominant community, the larger part of the cultivable land was possessed by them.[38]

The hold of the dominant castes over the village economy can also be confirmed by the pattern of capital formation and family budgets. A village survey (in 1961) in West Godavari district concludes thus:

> "If one enquires into the family budgets of different castes one is sure to come to the conclusion that family economy of the Kammas, the principal land proprietors in the village, is sound. Further, among the various capital formation activities the investment on land is important both from the point of view of the number of households that invested therein. Among the different castes that invested on land, Kammas rank first. They tried to augment their land resources during the past ten years. They rank first with respect to the amount of capital invested."[39]

In a prosperous village in Guntur district, "out of the total value of Rs. 1,43,365 worth of assets purchased, the share of Kammas is very large, being in order of Rs. 1,28,800 (89.8%)."[40] Similarly, in a village in Krishna district, "out of the total capital formation of land goods worth Rs. 1,98,050, as much as Rs. 1,82,200 was made by eleven households of Kammas caste only."[41] In a delta village of East Godavari district, the dominant peasant castes (Kapu and Balija) contributed around seventy-nine per cent of the capital formation in 1961.[42] The fertility of soil and secured irrigation were the most important factors for the increasing investment in land in the 1960s.[43]

Various village studies have also brought out another significant fact, i.e., the majority of village population belonging to the backward castes and the Scheduled Castes does not own much land. A considerable majority among them was found to be landless. A noteworthy feature of the distribution of land in a village in Rayalaseema was that:

> "Majority of Harijans do not own even a small piece of land. The percentage of landless Harijans is 63.4. The backward castes are at par with the weaker sections, 55.6 per cent of the households of backward communities are landless."[44]

Similarly, in an *agraharam* village (in Krishna district), it was found that the Scheduled Castes who constituted about thirty per cent of the total population held around twelve per cent of the land. The percentage of landless among them was seventy-six.[45] Another village survey in Chittor district has also shown that the Harijans, who constituted around twenty-three per cent of the district's population, did not own land as the sole means of their livelihood.[46] Insofar as the landholding pattern was concerned, the position of the artisan and other lower castes was also similar to that of the Scheduled Castes.

A study of the pattern of land concentration in some delta villages of the Krishna and East Godavari districts concluded that the Scheduled Castes who constituted around one-third of the village population have not been able to acquire any land.[47] This generalization is also applicable to other lower castes. The agricultural census data (of 1980-81) also indicates that the Scheduled Castes which constitute around fifteen per cent of the total population held only seven per cent of the operated area.[48]

From the above presentation, it is clear that insofar as the backward castes and Harijans are concerned, there was no perceptible change in their position with respect to the ownership of land. In the case of Scheduled Castes, they could possess some land as a result of land redistribution. But the artisan communities and the lower backward castes owned small holdings. Their holdings were neither viable for efficient farming nor sufficient to meet even the subsistence needs of the peasantry. Therefore, the smaller peasantry among them had to depend on casual labour for their livelihood. Many of the backward caste peasants possessing small holdings were forced to pledge their lands to the upper caste well-to-do families in order to finance cultivation. There was also a tendency on the part of the artisan castes and others to lose lands to others. It has been found that among the artisans, "the goldsmith, the carpenter and the blacksmith who constitute the bulk of artisans are losing land... The potter, it may be said, is gradually going to the well."[49] In caste terms, land had been rapidly passing off from the Brahmins, artisans and Harijans. Broadly speaking, "the depressed classes, as a whole, like the Harijans, are being systematically robbed of the small properties of their lands."[50] A detailed survey of some villages in coastal districts reports:

> "The most striking feature is that the rate at which land is passing off from the groups of small economic status to those of big economic standing is almost, on the aggregate, more than twice the rate at which land ownership is passing off in the opposite direction, namely, from the big to the small. Thus, the small owners are bought up by the comparatively bigger people, and this process of swallowing up is found to be a common phenomenon in many parts of the province."[51]

The reason why the upper caste peasantry became dominant, was, besides their 'cultural ethos', 'acquisitive nature,' etc., due to the expansion of the agrarian economy since 1947. Given the advantages of land ownership and access to market, the rural rich were able to produce more remunerative and commercial crops. The growth of cash crops such as tobacco, sugarcane, cotton, etc., facilitated the accumulation of surplus by the rural rich. Since they were not burdened by heavy taxation and indebtedness, they benefited from the rising agricultural prices. The growth of internal trade in paddy and export trade in cash crops provided immense opportunities for the rural rich to hasten the accumulation process. Especially in the delta districts of Godavari, Krishna, Guntur and Nellore, the rich Kamma and Reddy peasantry benefited enormously by taking up commercial agriculture.

The strategies for rural development during the early decades of the post-independence period also provided ample opportunities for the rural rich to augment resource mobilization and accumulation. In his field notes (late 1960s), Daniel Thorner observes that "there are millionaire cultivators" in coastal Andhra who "invested their gains from agriculture in trade, transport, moneylending and industry and dominated the villages economically, socially and politically."[52] It has been noted that the developmental activities undertaken by the panchayati raj and other rural institutions benefited them enormously as they possessed "much land and good connections." They could take advantage of the rural co-operative credit societies to finance their enterprises. Since credit was linked to landed assets, the rural rich not only cornered a larger share but also commanded control over financial institutions. Whereas, the majority of the middle and poor peasantry of the lower castes were virtually excluded from the benefits of the rural credit societies. We are told that "the ordinary small and middle peasant did not benefit much from them."[53] The rural rich were also able to utilize the institutional credit to finance their agricultural enterprise as well as other business. It has been said that loans taken by the rural rich

> "ostensibly for agricultural purposes may not be spent on that...instead, agricultural credit is being diverted to water, transport, mica, cattle, or other business...to start or to expand their private, non-agricultural business, the bigger people form... a co-operative rural bank."[54]

Evidence from other village surveys also confirms this observation.

The rural rich have not only taken advantages of the credit institutions but have also dominated the rural credit market. Since they own substantial holdings and have accumulated surplus they could diversify their economic activities into trading, business and moneylending.

In addition to institutional credit, the rural rich was also benefited from the new agricultural technology as well. The *panchayat samitis* encouraged the big cultivators to use fertilizers and improved seeds.

They also supplied high yielding varieties, pesticides and other chemical fertilizers to the well-off peasants. During his tour in coastal Andhra villages, Daniel Thorner came across the 'well-to-do peasants', who obtained foreign power-cultivators, threshers, pumpsets, tractors etc., through government loans at low interest rates. The rural rich was thus in the forefront of agricultural modernization. As 'progressive' and 'enlightened' cultivators, they took advantage of the available new technology and adopted several of the latest methods of farming to improve the agricultural yield in their farms.

The possession of landed property and accumulation of surplus by the rural rich further intensified the process of differentiation within the peasantry. Although the process of proletarianisation in agriculture of the small and poor peasantry has been a slow one, it resulted in the alienation of iand for the lower castes and artisans. A recent study on labour relations in Andhra noted that

> "the proportion of the agricultural labourers in the total agricultural population had increased steadily and continuously from twenty-seven per cent to fifty-three per cent between 1951 and 1981."[55]

It also pointed out that marginal cultivators tended to lose their lands and thus become labourers. It has earlier been pointed out that the available evidence from micro-level studies reveals that considerable sections of the lower backward castes, artisans and the Scheduled Castes do not possess land. Thus, a major section of the backward and lower castes constituted the rural poor in Andhra.

Our data also indicates that even when these groups of people possessed land, it was too meagre to become a source of livelihood for them. It may be noted that since they did not acquire any 'special skills' or 'master any craft', they had no other alternative in case they lost their land. A village survey (in 1961) has pointed out that "casual labour is the second major occupation providing employment for a majority of the poorer sections of the population. People belonging to castes like Christian, Golla, Goundla, Madiga, Uppara, Yanadi and Yerukala usually eke out their livelihood by working as casual labourers."[56] Therefore, it is clear from the above discussion that the rural poor in the Andhra countryside was a severely divided lot in caste terms. Just as the emerging rural rich *out cross* caste lines, so do the rural poor.

III

Caste, Class and Power

The emergence of the rural rich as the dominant land owning class enabled it to exercise power and authority in the countryside. Though the ownership of land alone was not sufficient to acquire power, nevertheless it was an important means for its achievement. Various micro-level studies have pointed out that in coastal Andhra, where the Kammas were wealthy and more influential, they could wield power because of their control over land. Along with it, numerical support was also an important basis of their power. Hence, in Andhra, after 1956, the dominant castes like the Reddies, Kammas, Velamas and Kshatriyas emerged as the most powerful political elite.[57] Rajni Kothari observes thus:

> "Representation of Reddies and Kammas in Andhra politics is higher than their proportion in the population and increases at higher levels of politics. At twenty-five per cent of the population in 1962 they occupied thirty-nine per cent of the legislative assembly seats, fifty-three per cent of the ministerial posts and the presidencies of the Congress, Communist and independent parties. The increasing predominance of these castes at higher levels is also evident in *panchayati raj* institutions. Across the state, the Reddies held thirty-nine per cent of the samiti presidencies and fifty-five per cent of the *zilla parishad* chairmanships."[58]

The Congress leadership at the grassroot levels was predominantly rural in nature. The rural rich became the 'backbone' of the Congress Party, especially since the 1940s. Historically speaking, the rise of the rural rich as the politically dominant class meant the displacement of traditional leadership, *viz.*, the feudal landlords and Brahmins. It should be pointed out that prior to independence the Congress Party was dominated by the educated urban professional elites who were mostly the Brahmins, whereas the *zamindars* enjoyed the privileges bestowed on them by the colonial state power, in terms of occupying ministerial positions under diarchy. However, the integration of the emerging rural rich into the political field occurred towards the end of colonial rule. In fact, in order to widen the scope of the Congress Party and the nationalist movement, the Brahmin political elite secured the help and support of the rising rural rich.[59]

After the formation of Andhra Pradesh and with the introduction of *panchayat raj* and rural co-operative societies, the rural rich could really become politically powerful. In addition to their numerical strength, their property and social status reinforced the power and authority of the dominant peasant castes in the countryside.[60] A study on Congress leadership in Andhra Pradesh noted that:

> "Between 1956 and 1972, three principal castes had an upper hand (Reddies, Kammas and Kshtriyas) in party politics. They constituted more than sixty per cent of the Congress Legislature Party, seventy per cent of the cabinet positions and ninety-five per cent of the *zilla parishad* chairmanships....The caste alignment at the lower level...reflects itself in the party organisation. This process is further promoted by the local *panchayat raj* functionaries who usually belong to the dominant castes and who wield powerful influence in local power politics."[61]

The available evidence from village studies reveals that a majority of the presidentships of local bodies were occupied by members of the dominant castes. For instance, Kammas in coastal Andhra and Reddies in Rayalaseema overwhelmingly controlled the rural institutions of power. "The panchayats have not usually represented the ordinary people of the village. Rather, they have been an instrument of a majority, the most powerful group in the village",[62] remarked a perceptive scholar. Various studies of village panchayats in Andhra have indicated that the rural rich were able to exercise power over the local bodies, because of their ability to extend patronage to lower castes. It is stated in a village survey that:

> "Kammas, being economically dominant, enjoy social prestige much beyond the traditionally highly placed Brahmins in the society...Kammas wield power just by the grip of economic control over the rest of the people in the village, as they possess about ninety-

> five per cent of the total village lands...Almost all the Christians and the other people are depending upon Kammas for their livelihood in one way or other."[63]

An analysis of the socio-economic background of the rural leadership also shows that it mainly comprises the dominant peasantry, viz., 'big landowners' and 'sophisticated cultivators'. The new leadership belongs to the dynamic rural rich who possess substantial landholdings and new technology. They are capable of diversifying their surplus profits into various fields moneylending, trade, business, agro-industries, etc. Thus, it is clear that over a period of time, rural power has shifted more decisively from the traditional elite of the village into the hands of the new leaders. A study of the pattern of leadership in the co-operative societies shows that the upper caste peasantry cornered a major share of the available credit. Insofar as the positions in the co-operatives were concerned, the economically powerful castes dominated the rural credit societies. It was observed that "the formidable combination of cultivating moneylender-cum-trader dominates the co-operatives."[64] An analysis of the caste composition of co-operative societies in the countryside indicates that there is much less representation of the lower castes.

An examination of the data about village leadership also confirms that the upper caste peasantry monopolized the positions of power in various local institutions. It is observed in a village survey: "Though all castes are represented in the panchayat, the only decision-makers are Kammas and the others just obey their verdict without any sign of protest."[65] Although the backward castes and the Scheduled Castes were the majority in the countryside, they did not have any effective participation or say in decision making. Lack of unity among the lower castes and their economic dependence on the rural rich made it impossible for them to exercise decisive control over the panchayat raj institutions. The backward castes and Scheduled Castes could participate in these institutions simply because the rules necessitated it. Otherwise their representation might not have been there. However, in the local institutions of power, their voice carries no weight unless supported by the members of the dominant castes.

It is clear from the above analysis that political power and power structure in Andhra rural society is decidedly influenced by landownership, social status and economic dominance. In other words, the political leadership in rural Andhra predominantly emanates from the rural rich of the forward castes. The social character and composition of the political institutions reveals that they are controlled by the landed interests drawn from the dominant peasant castes. Thus, there is a convergence of political and economic power. It should be pointed out that the emerging leadership at the local level belongs to the class of owner-cultivators.

IV

Summary and Conclusions

Our analysis of the changing relationship between caste, class and power in rural Andhra during the colonial and the post-colonial periods indicates a gradual decline of the power and authority of landlords as a whole. The traditionally dominant social groups in the rural society, viz., the *zamindars* and Brahmins (insofar as they were landholders) have lost their hegemony since the post-1956 years. During the colonial period, the landlords and the Brahmins formed the dominant political elite, and the emerging rural rich from among the dominant peasant castes were subservient to them. The peasantry belonging to the non-Brahmin upper castes was not able to compete or challenge the entrenched groups during the colonial rule. The Brahmins, because of their landed property, education and employment, occupied pre-eminent position in the Congress party and colonial bureaucracy while the *zamindars*, as they were rich and influential in the countryside, monopolized the higher level of politics. Therefore, there was a clear convergence of control over land and political power. By virtue of the possession of vast estates the landlords (both in the permanently settled and *ryotwari* areas) exercised dominance and power in the countryside. The vast majority of the peasantry had to acknowledge their supremacy.

Nevertheless, during the late-colonial period and around the beginning of the post-colonial period, there emerged a rural rich peasantry. But they could consolidate their position only after the abolition of the *zamindari* system. The upper caste peasants, who were the ex-tenants of *zamindars*, purchased lands from the landlords as well as from the small lower caste peasants to enlarge their landholdings. Moreover, the post-colonial land reforms further strengthened their position by eliminating the intermediaries. The evolution of an agrarian economy during the post-independence period also provided opportunities for the rural rich to emerge as an important economic power in the countryside. Since they became substantial landholders, they could benefit from the changing economic conditions, i.e., growth of commercial farming, internal and external trade in agricultural commodities, etc. While the peasants belonging to Kamma, Kapu, Velama and Reddy castes emerged as the dominant peasantry, the vast majority of peasants from the lower and backward castes, artisans and Scheduled Castes remained poor and subservient. In the process of economic transformation the small peasants of the lower castes were expropriated by the rural rich. Today, substantial section of the backward castes and Harijans a constitutes the rural poor. The upper caste peasants who replaced the feudal landlords have thus become the main exploiter class in the countryside. The contradiction between the rural rich and the rural poor has manifested in terms of caste conflict. This clearly demonstrates the fact that the proletarianisation of agrarian social classes cuts across caste lines.

The emergence of the rural rich as a dynamic class has brought about a change in the social basis of rural power structure. The post-independence developments such as adult franchise, *panchayat raj* institutions, etc., have enabled the upper caste dominant peasantry to exercise control over the rural institutions of power and authority. Thus, there is a shift of power from the landlords to the rural rich. Two factors have contributed to this change in a significant way: (a) the decline of the influence of the old feudal system, and (b) the growth of an elaborate political machinery which links the village leadership to the provincial and the national leaderships. This has made it possible for the rural rich to acquire power. The power of the rural rich is based on control over land and their preponderant numerical strength within the village. By and large, these two factors tended to reinforce each other. However, it should be pointed out that although political power has shifted from the landlords to the rich peasants, it has not gone into the hands of the backward sections of society.

REFERENCES

1. R. Kothari, "The Rural Urban Cleavage" in *News Time*, 12 July 1987, p. 2.
2. *Ibid.*
3. *Ibid.*
4. 'Rural Rich' in this paper refers to a dynamic social class which is economically, socially and politically dominant in the countryside. It is located within the production process and relations of production. It has been identified as a class which participates and/or takes active part in the agrarian production. The absentee landlords of feudal type are not included in this category.
5. The permanent settlement was introduced in the Northern Circars (Coastal Andhra) during 1802. The *ryotwari system* had come into being during 1820-40. See, M. Pattabhi Ram Reddy, *Peasant and State in Modern Andhra History*, Kavali, 1986.
6. G.N. Rao, "Dimensions of Land Control in Coastal Andhra: A Historical View", in *A P Economic Association Conference Papers*, Warangal, 1984.
7. *Ibid.*, p. 61.
8. *Ibid.*, p. 65. Also see *K.S.S. Seshan*, "The Problems of Inam Tenures in an Andhra Zamindari—Punganur", in *A P Economic Association Conference Papers*, Anantapur, 1987; R.E. Frykenberg, "The Silent Settlement in South India, 1793-1853: An Analysis of the Role of Inams in the Rise of the Indian Imperial System", in R.E. Frykenberg (ed.), *Land Tenure and Peasant in South Asia*, Delhi, 1977, p. 39.
9. Percentage of Inam are to total area in Andhra : 1. Ganjam (11.8); 2. Vizagapatnam (12.4); 3. East Godavari (5.8); 4. West Godavari (10.1); 5. Guntur (6.2); 6. Krishna (10.1); 7. Nellore (8.3); 8. Chittoor (15.7). Source: *Statistical Atlas of the Madras Presidency*, 1931.
10. See G. Slater, ed., *Some South Indian Villages*, Madras, 1918.
11. *Madras Legislative Assembly Debates*, Vol.VI, 1947, p. 114.
12. C.J. Baker, *The Politics of South India, 1920-37*, Delhi, 1976, p. 113.
13. For an analysis of the Non-Brahmin movement and Justice Party

in South India, see. E. Irschick, *Politics and Social Conflict in South India; The Non-Brahmin Movement and Tamil Separatism, 1916-1929*, Berkeley, 1969; M.R. Barnett, *The Politics of Cultural Nationalism in South India*, Princeton, 1976; C.J. Baker, *The Politics, op. cit.*

14. They were the Raja of Panagul 1921-26, The Zamindar of Kumaramangalam (Dr Subbarayan) 1926-30; The Raja of Bobbili, 1932-36.
15. Baker, *op. cit.*, p. 155.
16. M.Venkatarangaiya, *Local Boards*, p.67, cited in C J Baker, *op. cit.*, p. 112.
17. Y. Vaikuntham, *Education and Social Change in South India: Andhra*, 1880-1920, Madras, 1982, p. 167.
18. Baker, *op.cit.*, pp. 46-47.
19. Barnet, *op.cit.*, p. 16.
20. A. Satyanarayana, "*Agrarian Relations Under the Impact of Colonial Rule in Madras Presidency 1900-1940: A Case Study of Andhra Districts*", unpublished D.Phil. Thesis submitted to Heidelberg University (West Germany), 1983, Chapter V.
21. In an earlier study it has been shown that the rich peasant class belonging to the non-Brahmin upper castes was mainly responsible for the growth of Kisan Sabha Movement in Coastal Andhra. See my "*Kisan Movement in Madras Presidency, 1928-42: A study of the Anti-Zamindari Agitation*", unpublished M.Phil Thesis, Jawaharlal Nehru University, Delhi, 1979, Ch III, IV and V.
22. The lower castes did not benefit very much by education and employment opportunities during colonialism. For the details of literacy among castes, See, Y. Vaikuntam, *op.cit.*, p. 168.
23. A. Satyanarayana, "*Agrarian Legislation and the Peasantry in Andhra*", 1946-48 (mimeographed).
24. Detailed survey of a village in West Godavari district over a period of 50 years is made in *Census of India*, 1961, Village Monographs (Unagatla), Hyderabad 1961, p.20. "Changes in the ownership of land which was responsible for the shift in the economic power from the Brahmins to Kammas and Kapus. Among the Brahmins, who were the original landowners, the present position stands as a marked contrast to their past status. Only 5 households own land and the maximum size of the holding remains between 10-15 acres. This clearly indicates the gradual decline in the economic power of the community", p. 19.
25. G. Nancharaiah, "Land Legislation and Changing Agrarian

Structure", in *A P Economic Association Conference Papers*, 1987, p. 171.

26. D. Raja Sekhar, *Land Transfers in Andhra: A Case study of a village*, *Ibid*., pp. 142 and 115.
27. V. V. Sayana, *Land Sales, Land Values and Land Transfers*, Delhi, 1952, p. 21.
28. During the late-colonial period the non-Brahmin upper caste peasantry had a solid land base (peasant proprietorship, occupancy rights etc.) and thus had a "head-start" over others. They also acquired a "cultural ethos" which suited the rural rich classes. Within the limits of colonial economic framework the upper caste peasantry slowly but steadily entrenched in the rural economy. They have also played an active role in the peasant economy by positively responding to the market. Since the turn of the present century commercialization of agriculture, expansion of commodity production, agrarian trade and market contributed for the transformation of agrarian relations which resulted in the emergence of a substantial section of the rich peasantry.
29. *Census of India*, Village Survey Monograph, Maredumaka Village, Krishna District, p. 96.
30. B.A.V. Sharma (ed.), *Political Economy of India*, New Delhi, 1980, pp. 507 and 510.
31. *Ibid*., p. 506.
32. *Census of India*, 1961, Village Survey Monograph, Pasarlapudi, Lanka (East Godavari), p. 70.
33. *Census of India*, 1961, Village Survey Monograph, p. 114.
34. *op. cit*., p. 11.
35. B.A.V. Sharma, *op. cit*., p. 522.
36. *Census of India*, 1961, Village Survey Monographs, p. 30.
37. *Ibid*., pp. 34-35.
38. *Census of India*, 1961, Village Survey Monograph, p. 33.
39. *Census of India*, 1961, Unagalta Village Monograph, p. 37.9.
40. *Census of India*, 1961, Malkapuram Village Monograph, p. 95.
41. *Census of India*, 1961, Maredumaka Village Monograph, p. 74.
42. *Census of India*, 1961, Pasarlapudi Lanka, Village Monograph, p. 34.
43. "Most of the people in the village are interested in investing their surplus earnings, if any, only in land and livestock and other tools etc., which are helpful in agriculture. As the lands are fertile and provided with regular supply of water for irrigation by canals... the turn-out of crops is generally high. In view of these advantages

everyone in the village usually thinks of improving his landed property..." *Census of India*, 1961, Maredumaka Village Monograph, p. 75.

44. Sharma, *op. cit.*, p.523, In a Reddy caste dominated village "Most of the Malas and Madigas are not possessing any land".
45. G. Nancharaiah, *op. cit.*
46. Raja Sekhar, *op. cit.*
47. Sharma, *op. cit.*, pp. 596-98.
48. *Agricultural Census*, 1980-81 (A.P.) cited in Nancharaiah, *op. cit.*, p. 169.
49. Sayana, *op. cit.*, p. 191.
50. *Ibid.*, p. 21.
51. *Ibid.*, p. 25.
52. D.Thorner, *The Shaping of Modern India*, Delhi, 1980, p. 203.
53. *Ibid.*, p. 74.
54. *Ibid.*, p. 190.
55. M. Atchi Reddy, "Labour Relations in Andhra Pradesh Agriculture, 1881-1981", in *Indian Journal of Labour Economics*, Vol.XXVI, 1983, No. 3, p. 164.
56. *Census of India*, 1961, Maredumaka Village Monograph, p. 64.
57. Rajni Kothari observes thus: "The pre-eminent position of the Congress party in the Andhra Pradesh, has been due to the development of support base, centred around the landed gentry... The medium-sized landlords and owner-farmers are dominant in the party and Government. While the leadership of the freedom movement essentially came from the upper castes, it has now shifted to dominant agricultural castes. All the Chief Ministers in Andhra Pradesh have been from the dominant castes of Reddy, Kamma and Velama... The composition of the Cabinet has reflected the same phenomena. Upto 1971 the Reddis had the single largest representation (28 to 38 per cent), together with Velamas and Kammas, the representation has varied between 45 to 58 per cent". B.A.V. Sharma, *op. cit.*, p. 7.
58. Rajni Kothari, (ed.), *Caste in India Politics*, Delhi, 1964, p. 132.
59. *Ibid.*, pp. 152-53.
60. A village survey noted thus: "The Kammas who come to the Scheduled Caste people numerically and economically well-to-do and socially occupying a high status. Thus is an important caste which occupies a vital position in the social organisation of the

village. All the other castes are so placed in the system that they subserve the best interests of this caste". *Census of India*, 1961, Marendumaka Village, Monograph, p. 111.

61. G. Ram Reddy and B.A.V. Sharma, (eds.), *State Government and Politics: Andhra Pradesh*, Delhi, 1979, p. 209.
62. Thorner, *op. cit.*, p. 164. "The Panchayat Raj, which was introduced in 1959 has been dominated by the dominat peasant castes. In the 1970 elections to the Panchayati Raj bodies in 15 out of 21 Zilla Parishads, the Reddy community captured Chairmenship. Out of 324 Samiti Presidents nearly half of them belong to the same Reddy Caste". Sharma, *op. cit.*, pp. 7-8.
63. *Census of India*, 1961, Maredumaka Village Monograph, p. 19.
64. Thorner, *op. cit.*, p. 173.
65. *Ibid.*, p. 89.

2

Caste and Entrepreneurship in Colonial Andhra, South India 1900-1947*

The main purpose of this chapter is to discuss the social background of commercial and industrial entrepreneurs of colonial Andhra in terms of caste/community composition. It proposes to analyse the nature and character of entrepreneurial response to the growth of medium and large-scale industries at the regional level under colonial conditions.

Studies on the growth of modern capitalism and industrial entrepreneurship during the colonial period have indicated regional variations. It has been suggested that in eastern and western India, the traditional merchant groups belonging to the Marwari, Parsi, and Gujarati communities dominated commerce and industry in the private sector; while in southern India, the Chettiars took a leading role in trade, commerce and industry.[1] However, these macro studies pay inadequate attention to pertinent issues related to the growth of capitalism and the rise of the capitalist class, and are thus unable to comprehensively engage with questions like:

(*a*) What was the inter-relationship between caste, capital and entrepreneurship i.e., what was the role of the caste system in the emergence of the capitalist class?

(*b*) What were the different processes of evolution of industrial capital and industrial entrepreneurship? and

(*c*) How did entrepreneurs belonging to the non-trading castes/communities emerge?

The multidimensionality of the formation of industrial capital and the evolution of the modern capitalist class can be better understood on the basis of detailed micro-level studies. It may be pointed out that such regional studies will clarify some of the issues raised above and provide insights into the specific character and form of the process of evolution of indigenous capitalism and the capitalist class in the colonial context. Hence, this Chapter will highlight the changing nature of the caste system and the disjunction between traditional occupation and modern entrepreneurial activities on the basis of empirical evidence at the regional level. Further, it will question the validity of certain assumptions made by Max Weber regarding the caste system. Weber believed that the Hindu caste system and the irrational doctrines of Hinduism were not conducive for the conomic and technological transformation of India. Moreover, he argued that the caste system, which reduces occupational mobility and prevents innovation, was not favourable for the emergence of a dynamic industrial capitalist class. He wrote:

> The core of the obstruction was rather imbedded in the spirit of the whole system [...] it must still be considered extremely unlikely that the modern organization of industrial capitalism would ever have originated on the basis of the caste system. A ritual law in which every change of occupation, every change in work technique may result in ritual degradation is certainly not capable of giving birth to economic and technical revolutions from within itself, or even of facilitating the first germination of capitalism in its midst.[2]

However, recent studies by some sociologists, economists, historians etc., have suggested that the dynamics of the Indian social structure did allow certain adaptive strategies towards occupational mobility and modernisation.[3] Nafziger remarked:

> "Despite the powerful socio-religious sanctions given to the caste system, there are several dynamic factors making fluidity and flexibility in occupational and caste structures possible."[4]

Moreover, "modifications of the caste system and the modernization of traditional occupational cultures have gone farther than Weber seems to have believed possible."[5]

In his analysis of the entrepreneurial activity in some industries in Tamil Nadu, Berna observed that, "sociological factors, such as caste, attachment to traditional activities, and approval or disapproval of the social group to which a potential entrepreneur belongs are less important than economic factors such as access to capital and possession of business experience and technical knowledge".[6] Baldwin's study indicated that, "in Indian industry, the caste system seemed to be considerably looser and more flexible than it often appears [...]. Its novelty, quaintness, and historical importance produce an exaggerated estimate of its present role in the cities, where disintegration may proceed rapidly."[7] Therefore, in this paper an attempt is made to explain certain aspects of convergence and divergence between caste system and class formation, viz., caste/class origins of entrepreneurs in modern Andhra.

The integration of Andhra's economy into the world market commenced in the late 19th century. It facilitated and accelerated commercialization of agriculture in terms of the export of raw materials like cotton, oilseeds, tobacco, jute etc., and the import of manufactured goods from England such as cotton-textiles, gunny bags and oil. Thus till about the depression years in the 1930s, Andhra economy tended to primarily cater to the needs of export-oriented foreign trade. The growth of trade and commerce in agricultural commodities necessitated the establishment of agro-processing small-scale industries such as rice mills, cotton gins, jute presses, and groundnut decorticating factories. The total number of such industries, which came under the Factories Act, increased from 11 in 1899 to 242 in 1920.[8] The following section will briefly examine the nature of industrial growth in colonial Andhra during the 1930s and 1940s.

I

The *laissez faire* policy of the colonial state in India, till about the end of the first world war was meant to facilitate the flow of surplus from India to England. However, due to certain changed circumstances in the international economic order and domestic compulsions a shift was noted in colonial India's fiscal, monetary and industrial policies. *The Report of the Indian Industrial Commission* provided the basis for the new industrial policies of the post-1920 years. Thus the inter-war period witnessed industrialization in terms of the development of import-substitution consumer industries in India. The Telugu speaking districts of the Madras Presidency[9] had also witnessed the rise and growth of several domestic-market oriented, medium and large-scale industries. Among them, agro-based industries like rice mills, oil mills, cotton mills, tobacco and sugar factories played a significant role. As the Andhra region was endowed with considerable natural and agro-economic resources, it offered much scope for the growth of such industries. For instance, the growth of modern rice mills was made possible because of the superior irrigation and canal system of delta districts like Krishna, Guntur, and East Godavari. Landlords, rich peasants and the local Komati merchants took an active part in facilitating this growth. It has been found that by the end of the 1940 rice mills, in numerical terms, accounted for more than half of the total industries in the coastal Andhra districts of Krishna, Guntur, East and West Godavari, and Nellore.

The growth of major agro-industries in the Andhra districts during the 1930s and the 1940s marked an important turning point with regard to capital investment in industry. The depression years, which changed the terms of trade between agriculture and industry in favour of the latter, brought about a significant shift of capital from agriculture and moneylending to industry.[10] The boom in investment in the local industries was also encouraged by the changes in the industrial policy of the Madras government, viz., tariff protection to sugar and cotton textile industries and the post-war development plans with regard to oil mills and cement factories. Certain other factors like the availability of abundant raw materials also accelerated the growth of the agro-based industries. The growth of sugar industry in Andhra was sustained by the increase in the sugarcane area over time, particularly in localities where sugar mills sprung up or where there was a prospect of their establishment.

Coastal Andhra districts, especially Vishakhapatnam, East and West Godavari, and Krishna, were eminently suited for the development of the sugar industry. Following the recommendations of the *Indian Sugar Committee* in 1920, and since sugarcane was one of the important each crops, the Madras government favourably considered the growth of the sugarcane cultivation and the sugar industry. But due to certain constraints like the ryots preference for paddy cultivation, insufficiency of irrigation system, high costs of cane cultivation, and the widespread prevalence of *jaggery* making the efforts of the government did not succeed. However, the passing of the Sugar Industry (Protection) Act of 1932 together with the effects of world economic depression caused a sudden growth of sugar industries in the Andhra region. It was found that a fall in the prices of paddy and other commercial crops led to the an increase in cane cultivation. Area under sugarcane cultivation expanded in the vicinity of sugar factories. Between 1934 and 1937 a dozen new sugar industries were established in the Madras Province, of which six were located in the Andhra districts. It is interesting to note that in the formation of sugar mills, landlords and rich peasantry played a significant role. Unlike in the United Provinces, most of the sugar factories in Andhra were formed by the sugarcane growers associations and co-operative societies.[11] It can be said that the growth of the sugar industry during the post-depression period was due to positive state intervention. By the end of colonial rule there were eight sugar mills in the Andhra districts with a daily crushing capacity of 5275 tons, and providing 20,744 tons of white sugar during 1948-49.[12]

The development of cotton textile mills in Andhra can be traced as far back as the 1870s. Three unsuccessful attempts were made by private capitalists to establish cotton mills in coastal Andhra between 1870 and 1920. In the mid 1920s in the East Godavary district, weavers of the Devanga/Padmasali caste and others made a modest beginning to start cotton mills which would cater to the significant demand in the district for cotton yarn, especially in the villages around the mills. Despite the fact that Coastal Andhra had many advantages for the development of cotton mills, such as adequate supply of raw materials, fuel, water supply, labour and market, only two small mills were established before 1930. This was due to several factors: lack of interest among investors in joint-stock enterprises, preference for investment in trade and moneylending, indifference on the part of the government to extend help and encouragement to local industries, etc.[13]

However, the grant of protection, effects of depression and subsequent changes in government policies led to the development of large-scale cotton mills in the Andhra districts. In fact, the provincial government had been frequently pressurised by political leaders and business communities to extend the necessary help and encouragement in establishing more cotton mills, particularly in the ceded districts. It has been suggested that Bellary, Kurnool and Anantapur districts fulfilled all the requirements for the successful working of a cotton textile mill, viz., proximity to raw cotton producing tracts, sufficient supply of labour and nearness to market. During the 1930s many official and non-official committees also recommended the establishment of cotton mills in the cotton growing areas of the Andhra region as well as the provising of financial assistance by the provincial government to them. Consequently, private investment in cotton mills was encouraged by the government in terms of extending, albeit limited, financial assistance, under the State Aid to Industries Act. The number of cotton mills in Andhra thus increased from two to five between 1924-46.[14] It should be noted that this was made possible both due to the changes in the policy of the government and the availability of private finance and enterprise.

Prior to the First World War a considerable quantity of groundnut produced in the Andhra districts was exported to foreign countries. It has been estimated that the quantity of such exports from Andhra ports increased from 60,000 tons to 2.06 lakh tons during the periods from 1925-26 to 1940-41.[15] Yet only a small percentage of the annual outturn of oilseeds was converted into oil within the province or region. Some enterprising merchants and rich peasants built small-scale oil pressing units to utilize the locally available raw material and cater to the growing market for oil. They proved to be moderately successful and obtained profits during the first quarter of the 20th century. But the economic depression of the 1930s caused dislocation of markets for both groundnut kernel and oil. It also caused a setback to the nascent oil crushing industry in Andhra. During the depression period and in the post-depression period, there was a growing demand from merchants, peasants, and nationalist forces for the development of oil mills with state aid and encouragement. The effects of depression, dislocation of foreign markets, changing official attitude and the need to develop domestic market for industrial crops prompted limited state initiative and intervention in the development of oil industry in the province. The ceded districts seemed to provide immense opportunities for the growth of oil milling industry. In accordance with the changing official attitude and the need to develop a domestic market for industrial crops prompted limited state initiatives and intervention in the development of oil industry in the province. The ceded districts seemed to provide immense opportunities for the growth of the oil milling industry. In accordance with the changing official attitude, the Industries Department and its director had been advocating the installation of vegetable oil and hydrogenation factories in select districts in the province. It has been suggested that the development of oil mills would not only bring down the large exports of groundnut kernel, but also help meet the local requirements of vegetable *ghee* and fallow. In order to accelerate the growth of oil mills, the Madras government granted financial assistance to some private capitalists and encouraged others to float more mills. As a result, during the post-second world war period *vanaspati* and oil refining industries witnessed a significant growth in Andhra.

II

From the discussion above, it is clear that during the post-depression period, Andhra districts witnessed a boom in investment in the modern agro-industries. These industries catered mainly to the home market. As stated earlier, this industrial boom became possible in the context of changing government policies and favourable economic and political conditions. In fact, since the late 19th century, expansion of commercial agriculture and trade provided immense opportunities for investments in the agro-processing industries. Elsewhere we have analyzed the process of the formation of the peasant bourgeoisie in Andhra and pointed out that it invested surplus capital mainly in land, money lending, trade, and small-scale processing industries.[16] The emergence and crystallization of the rural rich belonging to the dominant peasant castes like the Kamma, Kapu, Reddi, and Velama etc., played an important role in the formation of peasant capital.

Nevertheless, it was not until the depression years that major agro-industries developed in Andhra. As Baker pointed out, the depression [...] persuaded many of the rural wealthy to try and place their surplus funds in the town and it also created an impetus for a shift of capital, entrepreneurship, and artisan skills from country to the town.[17] This was true of Andhra as well as Table 1 below indicates, in the 1930s and 1940s there was a rapid growth of joint-stock companies and capital.[18]

Table 1
Joint-Stock Companies and Capital Mainly in the 1930s and 1940s

Years	*No.*	*Rs. in lakhs*
1919-20	37	47.74
1924-25	69	89.88
1933-34	47	72.66
1938-39	90	116.60
1945-46	178	217.01
1947-48	260	415.05

In contrast to the earlier period, investment during the inter-war period primarily went into the manufacturing sector. The aggregate capital investment in the 1940s in this sector in Andhra totalled Rs. 245.31 lakh. What is significant to note is the fact that the industrial structure of Andhra, during the inter-war period, was characterized by its diversity; whereas in the pre-depression years the small-scale agro-processing industries were predominant, the subsequent period saw the emergence of major enterprises of various kinds. After the grant of protection, local entrepreneurs took the lead in the development of agro-industries as well as others such as cement, ceramics, chemicals and fruit canning, which catered to the needs of the internal market. The participation of foreign capital in the industrialization of Andhra was negligible; it dominated the export-oriented industries like tobacco (Indian Leaf Tobacco Development Company) and jute (Macleod). Besides the manufacturing industries, new investments by the local capitalists were also made in various other commercial/business ventures.

An examination of the composition of the joint—stock capital in Andhra indicates that new concerns such as investment trusts, trading companies, film industry, and mica companies *registered significant growth*. Likewise, capital enterprises like electric supply companies were formed in almost all the important towns of Andhra in the 1930s. Electricity produced in the thermal power stations at Bezwada, Kakinada, Masulipatnam, Nellore etc., was supplied to many towns. The aggregate capital investment in the power supply companies in 1945 amounted to Rs. 29.57 lakh.[19] Profits generated in trade, commerce and commercial agriculture were channelled into such ventures as capital investment. Most of the investments in manufacturing industries were undertaken by merchants (who were actively involved in raw cotton and oilseeds trade), small and big landlords and substantial peasants (who made profits in commercial agriculture, rural credit, agrarian trade and processing industry). It seems that dislocation in export trade and decline in profit in money lending compelled many of them to seek investment in industries and other commercial enterprises. It was not as if capital had been "shy" of entering the industrial sector in colonial Andhra: rather, the indifference of the government and the lack of adequate official assistance, had, at least till the 1930s, confined local capitalists to more secure sources of profit, viz, moneylending and trade. But once new opportunities for industrial investment opened up, indigenous capital was increasingly channelled into manufacturing industries.

Therefore, we find the predominance of merchants and landlords in the establishment of large-scale industries in Andhra. It is generally admitted that merchants, being men in possession of capital and entrepreneurial skills entered the industrial sector, i.e., there was a conversion of merchant capital into industrial capital. Thus, in Andhra, merchants constituted the largest single occupation group which invested in industry. Studies on entrepreneurship in other parts of India[20] revealed that a negligible number of entrepreneurs are drawn from an agricultural background. It has been said that in most cases merchants first, then artisans, and finally professionals have been the principal groups from which capitalists have emerged. But the findings of this study show that the agrarian classes were as prominent as the traditional merchants and professionals in industrial development in Andhra during the period under study. An examination of the available data on the socio-economic background of the Board of Directors of various industrial/commercial concerns reveals that two groups, viz., merchants and landlords dominated the manufacturing sector. Let us look at the typical example of the *Rayalaseema Cotton Mills*, Adoni, Bellary:

> No. 1. Proposed Director is a Cotton Grower and owner of a cotton Ginning Factory. He was a member of the *Indian Central Cotton Committee* from 1938 to 1940 and was also a Director of the *East India Cotton Association*, Bombay. He has experience of Company Management as the chairman of the *Rayalaseema Bank Ltd.*, Bellary, Director of the *Cuddapah Electric Supply Co. Ltd* and *Prithvi Insurance Co. Ltd.*, Madras.
>
> No. 2. Proposed Director is the Chairman and Director of *Vahini Pictures Ltd.*, *Cuddapah Ceramics Ltd.*, Director, The *Cuddapah Electricity Supply Co. Ltd.*, and the *Rayalaseema Bank Ltd.* He has been running a cotton hand-spinning and weaving centre at Tadipatri, Anantapur district very successfully. He is the owner of a Cotton Ginning and Pressing Factory at Tadipatri. He is the Managing Director of *India Fruits Ltd.*, Kadiam and has considerable experience of Company management in several other companies.
>
> No. 3. Proposed Director is the President of the *Yemmiganur Weavers' Co-operative Production and Sale Society Ltd.* This society is the largest Handloom Weavers' Society in South India having more than 1,000 looms under its management, and as such he has considerable experience in the yarn and cloth business.
>
> No. 4. Director is one of the biggest cotton growers of Bellary District.
>
> No. 5. Proposed Director is a Cotton Merchant of over 25 years standing at Adoni.
>
> No. 6 is one of the big Cotton and Yarn Merchants of Adoni. His family has been supplying cotton to mills for the last 30 years and more.
>
> No. 7 is a Yarn Merchant and the owner of the Cotton Ginning and Pressing Factory at Adoni.

> Nos. 8, 9 and 10 are yarn, cotton, and cloth merchants respectively. They and their families have been doing this business for more than 30 years.[21]

Therefore, this company consisted of eight merchants and two Reddy landlords, including "one of the biggest cotton growers of Bellary District." This was also true of the *Bezwada Cotton Mill;* out of nine Directors, five were merchants and four were landlords. In another big cotton mill, *The Hemalatha Textile Mills Ltd.*, Guntur, merchants were predominant.[22] Similarly, in the development of oil milling industry it was merchants and big zamindars such as the Raja of Bobbili, who played a leading role.

In the case of Sugar industries it was mostly landlords and rich peasants who took the lead in establishing the co-operative sugar factories at Etikoppaka and Thummapala in Vishakhapatnam district and Vuyyuru in Krishna district; while big merchants dominated the sugar mills in the private and joint-stock sectors.

In the formation of chemical, pharmaceutical, ceramic and engineering industries, professionals played the pioneering role. About the *Andhra Pharmaceutical Works Ltd.*, Bezwada, it was mentioned that it was formed by "a number of medical men and medical stores people" and its "directors are mostly drawn from the Medical profession with a few directors from the business and legal profession."[23] Its Managing Director was a medical graduate. Likewise, the Managing Director of an engineering firm, *The Industrial Engineers and Merchants Ltd.*, Bezwada was "a foreign returned Mechanical Engineer"[24] and its Governing Director was a retired principal of an engineering college. The urban middle classes, white-collar employees and advocates seemed to have invested mostly in electric supply companies, as well as banking and insurance companies. But the artisans of Andhra did not seem to have fared well; there was only a small cotton spinning mill and a silk factory which belonged to the Devanga/Padmasalis, the traditional caste of weavers. Also, very few Muslim families (Nawabs and Sultans) had entered the industry.

It may be noted, however, that the category of "merchants" did not consist only of the Arya Vaishyas or Komatis—the traditional community of traders. Rich peasants belonging to the dominant castes of Kamma, Naidu, Kapu, Reddy, Velama and Lingayat who entered into business also became merchants. However, the leading Komati families in Andhra, viz., the Maddi and Majeti families in Guntur, the Mothey family in Ellore, and the Pyde and Neelam families in Kakinada, and Rajahmundry, were also prominent industrialists. Likewise, the category of "landlord" consisted of two groups (*a*) big zamindars like the Rajas of Bobbili, Venkatagiri, Chellapalli, Pithapuram, Mirzapuram, Nuzvid etc. and (*b*) small landlords who were also called "proprietors of villages" and substantial peasants in the ryotwari region. For example, the Etikoppaka Sugar Factory was dominated by such small landlords belonging to the (Kshatriya) Raju caste. Among the big landlords, the zamindars of Bobbili, Chellapalli and Nuzvid played a significant role in industrial entrepreneurship. The Raja of Bobbili was involved in grain and moneylending and later moved into business and industry. He also pioneered the sugar and oil mills in the Vishakhapatnam district; he was mainly responsible for the formation of three sugar mills and one vegetable oil factory in this district in the 1930s and 1940s. The Nuzvid zamindari family who owned vast mango gardens took an interest in the fruit canning industry, while the Raja of Chellapalli participated in a number of concerns: sugar, chemicals, banking, insurance, etc.

The Rajas of Pithapuram and Mirzapuram were involved in the cinema industry, and also lent money to fellow zamindars. The Raja of Venkatagiri invested in many enterprises in Madras; and he was the President of the Indian Chamber of Commerce in 1945. In terms of caste, the zamindars in Andhra belonged to the dominant non-brahmin upper castes: Velama, Kamma and Reddy.

The substantial Reddy and Naidu landholders (of the ryotwari area) of the ceded districts and Nellore, and the Kammas of Guntur and Krishna districts were also prominent in various agro-industries as well as in the mining and tobacco business. Mining in the Rayalaseema region and Nellore was almost the preserve of the rich Reddy landlords. It has been noted that a "[...] detailed description of the 146 working mines in Nellore in 1944, clearly shows a pattern - the predominance of the Reddies. As high as 55 per cent of total mining leases was with them. Further, most of the large mining leases were under their control. The next in importance were the Komati Chettis and Chettiars who had secured about 23 per cent of the lease. The rest, mainly Nayudus, Kammas and Muslims [...] even if one looks at the list of major mica exporters (who were also mine-owners) the dominance of Reddies is quite clear."[25]

In fact the first micanite industry in the Madras presidency was started by a Nellore Reddy mica-owner-exporter. A study on Kurnool noted that: "The rich farmers also invested in various joint-stock companies [....] During and after World War II, the opportunities for investment in non-agricultural activities such as mining transport and lift irrigation schemes were on the rise. Much of the rural surplus flowed into these ventures."[26] The entrepreneurs belonging to these dominant castes also invested their surplus capital in hotels, the cinema industry, transport, banking, real estate, etc. Further, in the 1940s, they entered in a big way into the contract business (both, the public works department and the railways). Thus we find the names of certain leading Kammas and Naidus as first class contractors: they included families like Devini, Yarlagadda, Yalamanchali, Kavuri, Surpaneni, Vallabhaneni, Oogineni, Kommineni, Chalasani, Kakani. Whereas, the Komatis were mainly found, besides in industry, in the wholesale business (turnover more than Rs. 2 lakh per annum).[27]

Therefore, it is clear that industrial enterprise in colonial Andhra, during the period under study was dominated by entrepreneurs drawn mainly, if not solely , from the twice-born castes (Brahmins, Kshatriya, Rajus and Arya Vaishya Komatis), and the non-Brahmin upper castes (Reddies, Kammas, Naidus, Velamas, Lingayats, etc). The participation of Brahmins in industrial activity was also significant; as they acquired skills and knowledge in technical and professional education, they ventured into industry. Whereas the Komatis had been involved in trade and commerce for a long period of time, and when the situation was favourable, had diversified their investment, the entrepreneurs belonging to the Kamma, Velama and Raju castes in coastal Andhra, and the Reddies, Naidus and Mudaliars in the ceded districts were conspicuous by their overwhelming presence on the Board of Directors of several companies. The predominance of entrepreneurs drawn from the dominant land holding castes/communities like the Reddy, Kamma, Naidu and Mudaliar was quite pronounced in certain industries, viz., cotton mills, oil mills, and sugar mills. For instance, the *Chittoor Sugarcane Growers Association*, which proposed to establish a sugar factory, consisted of 10 Reddy and two Naidu landlords.[28] *The Bank of Chittoor Ltd.*, was dominated by landlords of *Kamma-Naidu*, Reddy and Mudaliar castes.[29] The Kammas, a sizeable and prosperous cultivating caste primarily in the coastal districts, were, together with the Reddies and Rajus, among the economically dominant castes in Andhra.

The rich Kammas of coastal Andhra were very active in the establishment of many rice mills and sugar factories at Vuyyuru and Tanuku and in the tobacco trade at Guntur. Although the export trade of tobacco was dominated by the ILTD Company, rich and enterprising Kammas increasingly participated in it. Some of them also became big exporters of tobacco to foreign countries. The Kamma entrepreneurs also took a keen interest in establishing other medium scale industries such as tile and brick factories, fruit canning and ceramics. Interestingly, lower castes (i.e. backward and untouchables) were conspicuous by their absence in industrial entrepreneurship. Hence there seems to be a positive correlation between caste ranking, and representation in entrepreneurial activity. There was also a significant positive relationship between caste ranking, and education, income and occupational status. Available evidence indicates that the twice-born castes together with the non-Brahmin upper castes had educational advantages over the lower backward castes. This is confirmed by the literary rates of the different communities/castes in Andhra.

Consequently, this study suggests that the emergence of industrial entrepreneurship in colonial Andhra was conditioned by social as well economic factors. Accumulation and access to capital, possession of business experience, and the opportunity to acquire technical and managerial skills were far more important. Moreover, it should be noted that the prevailing social structure and the caste system in colonial Andhra had a profound influence in determining who acquired capital and obtained business and technical knowledge. It may also be noted that no single caste or community solely dominated the industry, rather, industrial entrepreneurs belonged to several castes with the exclusion of the lower castes. A perusal of the lists of the Board of Directors of several companies in Andhra indicates that Komati merchants, Brahmins, Kammas, Naidus, Reddies, etc., were the main shareholders. Most of them had either landed property and/or previous experience in commercial enterprise. It appears that initial capital accumulation by the entrepreneurs was obtained through profits in commercial agriculture and/or moneylending. Local officials like the Collectors commented that many of the Directors of industrial concerns were "men with considerable influence and good financial resources." Local merchants assumed an increasingly important role in industrial investment during the inter-war period; hence more persons of trading background entered the industry. Merchants the rural rich, qualified professionals, and white color employees of the upper castes were found side by side in many industries in Andhra. In terms of their caste background, they all belonged to the twice-born and Sat-Shudra communities.

To conclude, two interrelated aspects are highlighted in this paper, i.e., the growth of industries and the entrepreneurial response to it. The growth of agro-based medium and large industries characterized the evolution of industrialization in colonial Andhra. It was facilitated by changing government polices and economic conditions. The world economic depression and its effects, to a large extent, influenced entrepreneurial response to industrial development. It was found that diversion of surplus profits from commercial agriculture, rural credit, and trade into industrial investment was mediated by merchants and the rural rich communities. Thus, in the formation of industrial capital and entrepreneurship in the Andhra region, a significant role was played by the increasing participation of agrarian capital and the rural rich. Unlike the other parts of India, the traditional merchant communities, viz., Arya Vaishya/Komaṭi did not monopolise investment in the industrial sector. Instead, the capitalist class of

Andhra consisted of the traditional merchants and rich agrarian communities belonging to the dominant peasant castes of Kamma, Naidu, Kapu, Reddy, etc. Thus Bagchi's observation that, "there is little evidence that entrepreneurship in agriculture provided a stepping stone to industry"[30] is not applicable to colonial Andhra. It is also interesting to note that landed gentry, like the big zamindars of Bobbili, Chellapalli, etc., did play a notable role in industrial investment. Similarly, some of the Brahmin landlords/*agraharamdars* and professionals also participated in industrial enterprises.

Therefore, there was a clear-cut divergence between caste and occupation as far as the formation of entrepreneurship was concerned. The emergence of industrial entrepreneurs with a peasant background was also proof of this. Yet in caste/community terms entrepreneurial activity was confined to and the preserve of the dominant upper castes like Raju, Brahmin, Vaishyas, Kamma, Kapu, Reddy, etc. It meant convergence of caste and class status, i.e., the upper echelons of these castes evolved as the industrial class. Possession of landed property, economic wealth/resources, educational and technical qualifications, access to sources of power and patronage enabled them to evolve as the capitalist class. Caste/class convergence is also confirmed by the absence of entrepreneurs drawn from the lower Shudra and untouchable caste/communities. In other words, lower caste status, meagre landholding, poor economic position and literacy, etc., did not provide an opportunity for social mobility and the rise of entrepreneurs from among them; in spite of the fact that the caste system was dynamic and undergoing transformation. In this sense, caste status was a crucial determinant in the formation of entrepreneurship in colonial Andhra during the period under study.

REFERENCES

* This chapter is a part of my research project on "Caste and Dominance in Andhra Pradesh". I am grateful to Prof. H. Yanagisawa, Institute of Oriental Culture, University of Tokyo, Japan and Prof. D. Rothermund, South Asia Institute, Heidelberg University, Germany for their help and encouragement in writing this paper. I am also thankful to the authorities of the Japan

Foundation, Tokyo and the German Academic Exchange Service (DAAD), Bonn for providing financial assistance to my research project.

1. A.I.Levkovsky, *Capitalism in India*, Bombay, 1966; V.I. Pavlov, *The Indian Capitalist Class*, New Delhi, 1964; A.K. Bagchi, *Private Investment in India, 1900-39*, Cambridge, 1972; R.K. Ray, *Industrialization in India, 1914-1947*, Delhi, 1979; For regional studies: T.A. Timberg, *The Marwaris*, Delhi, 1978; D. Tripathi (ed.), *Business Communities of India*, New Delhi, 1978; D. Tripathi, *Business and Politics in India*, Delhi, 1991.
2. Max Weber, *The Religion of India*, Glencoe, 1958, p. 112 (emphasis in original).
3. See M. Singer (ed.), *Entrepreneurship and Modernization of Occupational Cultures in South Asia*, Durham, 1973; Morris D. Morris, "Values as an Obstacle to Economic Growth in South Asia: An Historical Survey", *The Journal of Economic History*, 27, 1967, pp. 588-607.
4. H.A. Gould, "The Adapative Functions of Caste in Contemporary Indian Society", *Asian Survey*, 3 (9), 1963, p. 429.
5. E.W.Nafziger, *Class, Caste and Entrepreneurship*, Honolulu, 1978, p. 47.
6. J.J.Berna, *Industrial Entrepreneurship in Madras State*, Delhi, 1960, p. 84.
7. Cited in E.W. Nafziger, *Class, Caste and Entrepreneurship, op. cit.* p. 47.
8. For details see, A. Satyanarayana, *Andhra Peasants under British Rule, 1900-1940*, Delhi, 1991, Ch. 5.
9. They were Ganjam, Vizagapatnam, East Godavari, West Godawari, Krishna, Guntur, Nellore, Bellary, Anantapur, Kurnool, Cuddapah and Chittoor. See O.H.K. Spate, *India and Pakistan. A General and Regional Geography*, London, 1960, p. 689.
10. For a detailed discussion on various aspects of the world economic depression see D. Rothermund, *India in the Great Depression*, 1929-39, Delhi, 1992; (ed.), *The Global Impact of the Great Depression, 1929-39*, London, 1997; C. J. Baker, *An Indian Rural Economy, 1880-1955*, Delhi, 1984.
11. For details, see A. Satyanarayana, "The Evolution of Agricultural and Industrial Entrepreneurs in Coastal Andhra: A Study of Sugar

Industry, *1932-1947,"* in *A.P. Economic Association Conference Papers,* Srikakulam, 1989; pp. 38-56.

12. Andhra Chamber of Commerce, *Silver Jubilee Souvenir,* Madras, 1953, p. 203.
13. A. Satyanarayana, "Industrialization in Colonial Andhra, 1914-47", pp. 23-30 (Mimeograph).
14. Andhra Chamber of Commerce, *Silver Jubilee 1953,* p. 211.
15. A. Satyanarayana, "Industrialization in Colonial Andhra," pp. 39-46.
16. A. Satyanarayana, "The Evolution of Agricultural and Industrial Entrepreneurs", *op. cit.* pp. 50-52.
17. C.J. Baker, *The Politics of South India,* Delhi, 1976, p. 85.
18. Report of the Joint Stock Companies in India for the years shown in table 1.
19. This is based on *Kothari Investors Encyclopaedia,* 1946.
20. *See* footnote 1.
21. Government Order (G.O.) Law (General), 3778, 28th Sep. 1945.
22. G.O. Development (Dev.) 1332, 10th September, 1926; G.O. Dev. 1644, 16th April, 1952.
23. G.O. Dev. 1613, 7th August, 1942.
24. G.O. Dev. 1308, 6th May, 1942, p. 190.
25. Keshabanada Das, "Growth and Decline of the Mining Industry in Nellore, 1911-1950", *The Indian Economic and Social History Review,* 28, 1991, p. 401.
26. G.O. Dev., 1927, 16th August, 1940; G.O. Dev. 3382, 1st September, 1945.
27. *Commercial Directory of Madras Presidency*, Madras, 1952.
28. G.O. Dev. 5426, 3rd November, 1948.
29. G.O. Dev. 2381, 23rd July, 1946.
30. A.K. Bagachi, *Private Investment in India,* p. 213.

3

Growth of Education Among the Dalit-Bahujan Communities in Colonial Andhra, 1893-1947

The objective of this chapter is to examine the social context of the educational development of the lower castes under colonial conditions in Andhra, which refers here to the Telugu-speaking districts of the erstwhile Madras Presidency. They are: Ganjam, Vizagapatnam, East Godavari, West Godavari, Krishna, Guntur, Nellore, Chittoor, Cuddapah, Kurnool, Anantapur and Bellary. In this essay the term Dalit-Bahujan is used as an inclusive category. It contains different castes, ranging from artisans to untouchables. Bahujan is refer to the lower Shudra orders who are actively involved in and form an integral part of the production process. By referring to them as Bahujans, their numerical strength, manual labour and involvement in the production of material wealth is emphasized. The term Dalit (meaning oppressed) has gained currency in recent times. In this paper it refers to the Madigas and Malas of Andhra, who are also known by the names Scheduled Castes, Depressed Classes, Panchamas, Adi-Andhras, Harijans, etc. All these terms are used interchangeably here.

Although Dalit-Bahujan communities consisted of numerous endogamous sub-caste groups, in terms of material conditions and literacy levels, all of them were placed, barring minor variations, in an identical position during period. Though there were colonial no socio-cultural interactions between the lower Shudra castes and the Dalit communities, there was a commonality of interests and aspirations for the acquisition of modern education among these castes. I use the term Dalit-Bahujan as suggested by Dr. Kancha Ilaiah in his book, *Why I am not a Hindu*.

It has been observed that "the education system is of crucial importance in [the study of] any society, and [that], at the same time, the system of education has to be examined within the context of the society in which it has developed."[1] This essay studies the relationship between the prevailing caste system and the educational progress of different communities in modern Andhra during the pre-Independence period. An attempt has been made to discuss the role of various agencies in the growth of education among the lower castes/communities, as well as of the downtrodden people. Despite the limitations imposed by the colonial government on the castes, prejudice, resistance and opposition of the dominant upper castes considerably hindered the progress of mass education in colonial Andhra. The nature of this upper-caste antagonism towards the educational advancement of Dalit communities is also highlighted in this chapter.

It is often assumed by scholars that the introduction of Western education by the British and the consequent flow of western ideas not only inculcated a 'new spirit' among the Indian people but also worked as a great catalyst of 'social change' in modern India. Thus, a study entitled, *Education and Social Change in Andhra,* noted: 'English-educated people were the pioneers in ushering in new ideas and thoughts. They attacked the social evils, initiated reforms and *strove to create a homogenous society*... There was an inter-connection between the growth of education and social change' (emphasis added).[2]

Such a sweeping generalisation ignores the complex nature of the inter relationship between education and the social structure/ caste system. It does not indicate the nature of the 'social change' brought about by the impact of Western education. It presumes a social consensus and harmonious relations with regard to the spread of modern education across different segments of Andhra society. What is missing are the notions of conflict and competition inherent in the process of acquisition and dissemination of knowledge in any society. While the privileged reproduce their hegemony/

dominance over the entire society, the underprivileged community's urge is to use education to acquire self-respect, equality and social prestige.

The above-quoted statement also ignores the fact that the social stratification defined by the Hindu caste system determines the general framework and structure of education by reinforcing caste/class distinctions and hindering rapid social mobility, particularly among the lower castes. In such a situation, education, far from being a means of rapid social transformation tends to reflect and perpetuate caste distinctions. Hence, it is necessary to locate the impact of education within the context of social stratification. As Stone pointed out, "It is important to remember that the relationship between social structure and education is a two-way feedback process, each affecting and acting upon the other". Furthermore, "Education is so powerful factor in preserving existing social distinctions that the change is always a highly explosive political issue and is always bitterly resisted and resented".[3]

As far as modern Andhra is concerned, it can be said that upper caste groups such as the Brahmins, for instance, who were enjoyed a monopoly of relatively key positions in the lower rungs of the colonial bureaucratic structure, were quite unlikely to welcome or favour the improvement and/or expansion of educational facilities for underprivileged communities. Members of the elite sections also tended to obstruct, both overtly and covertly, any advancement of educational facilities to the lower castes which would make the downtrodden their social equals and competitiors.

In a recent study, Aparna Basu remarked, "Few historians have ventured to examine education at the local level ... We need to know both the attitudes of the upper castes/classes towards it as well as the attitudes of those who benefit from it".[4] In this article an attempt has been made to analyse the impact of education on the caste structure at the micro-level, namely the Andhra region of Madras Province. It also addresses some specific questions: Who were considered the 'educated castes' in modern Andhra? Why did certain castes and communities advance more than others? Why and how did some castes respond more readily than others to education? From what castes and income groups did they come?

This chapter is divided into three sections. The first section contains a description of the caste system and the educational advancement of different caste groups in modern Andhra. The role of the colonial government and other agencies in the growth of education among the Dalit communities is discussed in section two. The third section provides details of upper caste discrimination against Dalits in the educational institutions in various Andhra districts, as well as the response and attitude of the colonial state.

Caste and Education

The growth of education among different castes in modern Andhra, as indicted by literacy rates, is presented in Table 1. In Andhra there is no real Kshatriya Varna, but the locally dominant landed gentry known as Raju claimed Kshatriya status. Similarly, the local trading communities called Komati also claimed twice-born status as Vaishyas. The upper Shudra category consists of groups considered as the dominant peasants castes in Andhra. Almost all the zamindars of modern Andhra belonged to these communities.

The dependent and begger castes of Andhra can be divided into two groups: (*a*) those who were dependent on the peasant castes, and (*b*) those who were dependent on upper caste elites and the aristocrats associated with temples. They were also semi-nomadic. he dependant castes in the former category were mostly illiterate and poor, while those in the latter category were well educated and reasonably well-off. Table 2 gives literacy rates of these groups as indicated in the 1921 census report.

Tables 1 and 2 show that the growth of education in Andhra closely corresponded to the prevailing caste hierarchy. That is to say, high and low caste distinctions in society paralleled the access of these caste groups to educational opportunities. Thus, the higher a caste stood in the social/caste scale, the better was its educational position. Hence, it can be said that caste, as an institution based on the concept of inherited inequalities, privileges and prestige, tended to give rise to still greater inequality in the distribution of educational resources. The data on literacy rates in Andhra during the pre-independence period confirms the common perception that educationally the Brahmin is the leader of south India, and that

Table 1
Literacy of Selected Communities
(Per cent of total population)

	1901	*1911*	*1921*	*1931*
I. Upper castes (Dwijas)				
1. Brahmin	35.5	38.9	37.5	51.1
2. Kshatriya/Raju	N.A	N.A.	11.4	20.8
3. Arya Vaishya/Komati	25.2	26.2	29.1	34.5
II. Upper/advanced Shudra castes				
1. Kapu/Telaga/Reddi	2.9	5.2	6.0	8.6
2. Kamma	2.5	6.5	7.6	N.A
3. Velama	1.3	3.2	4.2	N.A
III. Bahujan/productive castes				
1. Artisans				
(a) Kamsala (goldsmith)	8.3	13.1	15.0	17.4
(b) Sale (weaver)	2.5	6.2	8.7	N.A
2. Lower Shudras/other backward castes				
(a) Golla/Yadav (shepherd)	0.5	1.4	1.6	2.4
(b) Gamalla/Settibalija (toddy tapper)	1.0	1.9	2.6	N.A.
(c) Muttacha (hunter/cultivator)	1.0	2.0	3.2	N.A.
(d) Boya/Bestha (hunter/fisherman)	0.4	1.1	1.4	1.7
(e) Mangali (barber)	1.8	3.5	4.6	N.A.
(f) Tsakala (washerman)	0.3	0.6	1.0	N.A.
(g) Kummara (potter)	N.A.	N.A.	2.8	N.A.
(h) Odde/Uppara (earthdigger/mason)	0.2	0.6	1.4	N.A.
(i) Dependent and begging castes (see Table 2)				
IV. Dalits				
1. Madiga (leather worker)	0.1	0.4	0.5	1.6
2. Mala (field servant)	0.3	0.7	0.9	1.9

Compiled from the census reports of the Madras Presidency for the years shown (N.A. = not available).

the depressed class figure poorly in educational matters. Since the Dalit communities were at the lower level of the educational pyramid (with just 1% literacy), they naturally present a dismal picture in terms of educational achievement.

Table 2
Literacy Rates in 1921 for the Dependant Castes
(Per cent of total population)

Category A		*Category B*	
Viramushti	3.6%	Bhogam/dasi (dancer/musician)	23.5%
Pichchikuntla	1.75%	Bhattaraju (bards and panegyrists)	17.2%
Dommara	2.4%	Satani (temple servant)	20.4%
Budabhukkala	0.92%	Tamballa (Saiva temple priest)	15.2%
		Vipravinodi (dependent on Brahmins)	8.5%

It is only to be expected that the Brahmin (with more than 50% literacy) should be more literate than the rest of the communities, because for generations this caste has monopolized all knowledge. Brahmin intellectuals compiled and wrote *Shastras* which declared that an educated Shudra or Untouchable should be avoided like the plague. Moreover, the traditional Hindu notion that knowledge is sacred and therefore not to be imparted to the ritually impure lower castes worked in favour of the upper castes, who kept their hold on modern education. The Brahmin, therefore, stood far ahead of every other class or community as regards educational progress. The early migration of Brahmins to urban areas in pursuit of education and employment is clear proof of this. Available information on the educational progress of the Brahmins since the late nineteenth century indicates that they had the lead in acquiring an English education.[5] Since Western education had by then become a sort of *sine qua non* for public honour and social respect, the ritual superiority of the Brahmins was further reinforced and strengthened during the colonial period.

Communities connected with trade and commerce like the Komati and Balija had also begun to quickly respond to the new educational opportunities. Western education provided them with an opportunity to carry forward and expand their traditional occupational skills in the changing new colonial context. In fact, the caste association of the Komatis of modern Andhra, the Arya Vaisya Mahasabha, carried out systematic propaganda for the opening of schools, hostels and institutions of learning for students from their own community.[6] The Komati community even set up its own facilities, such as scholarships for poor Komati students, hostels, etc., to enable their children to acquire modern education, and through it, to compete for new positions of power and prestige as well as to enhance their chances of success in the growing competitive market for jobs and occupations.

Thus, the upper caste communities in Andhra were quick to see the utility of the modern education introduced by the British government, and sent their children to urban centres for study and employment. The costs of education and living could be borne by the wealthy sections among them; for example, most Brahmins were landholders and the Komatis were rich traders. Thus, during the period, the majority of the student population had arisen from among these castes. For the upper caste, education had become a means of acquiring the modern skills valued by their colonial masters who, after all, set the standards of 'merit' and 'efficiency'. 'Government service is the most respectable employment a man can obtain. Those who gain its prizes are leaders in native society', remarked a British official.[7] The colonial education system, despite its constraints and limitations, had begun to be prized as a scarce, valuable commodity by the upper castes. Given their social standing and material resources, they certainly gained a disproportionately higher share of the allocation of educational and employment chances during the colonial period. The traditional or ritual superiority of these castes was thus reinforced in the secular hierarchy of the modern period through the instrument of English education. Hence, Western education, though open, remained basically exclusive and biased in favour of the upper castes/classes.

Among agricultural castes such as the Kapu and Kamma, with less than ten percent literacy, educational progress was slow but steady. Unlike the Brahminic upper castes, they lacked a tradition of learning and the aptitude for modern education. Generally speaking, the peasant castes were not as quick as the Brahmins in appreciating the advantages of modern secular education and culture. They also did not have the hereditary intellectual base, which for thousands of years, had been the preserve of the

Brahmins. A Telugu proverb says, '*Kapula chaduvu kasula chettu* (educating the Kapus is a waste of money).'

Notwithstanding such disadvantages, the agricultural castes proved capable of the highest intellectual training since the early decades of the twentieth century. Although Table 1 indicates that literacy among the cultivating castes was far below that of the Brahmins and Komatis, the rate of growth is significant. Literacy rates among them tripled, and in some cases, quadrupled during the first quarter of this century. The Census Commissioner remarked in 1921 that there had been 'a very large increase in literacy among Velamas, who now have 70 males and 15 females per mile literate, as against 36 males and 5 females in 1911'.[8]

A similar rapid educational progress was made by the Kamma community of coastal Andhra, mainly due to the sustained propaganda of their caste association, the Kamma Mahajana Sabha.[9] The reasonably well-off sections of this community could afford to send their children to schools and obtain entry into modern education and employment. Kinship networks and caste-centred educational institutions, hostels, etc., greatly facilitated the educational progress of the Kammas.

In the early decades of the twentieth century, the non-Brahmin upper caste elites from the Kamma, Reddy, Kapu and Velama castes began to demand that educational facilities be extended to their communities as well. The growth of the non-Brahmin Justice movement and other socio-cultural and caste movements facilitated the gradual spread of literacy among them, which in turn enabled them to gain reasonable access to education and employment. Perceptive colonial officials also observed that the pre-eminent position of Brahmins in the educational and employment fields was being threatened by the emergence of non-Brahmin elites. They noted that the cultivating castes and Brahmins were rivals in government employment, the professions, etc. The educated representatives of the agrarian castes were found to be quite equal to the Brahmins in ability as well as numbers in these pursuits, denoting the increase of higher education among them. A study on Andhra mentioned, "the growth of consciousness among the non-

Brahmin classes due to the growing importance of English education became a threat to Brahmin domination."[10]

With regard to the Bahujan communities, the data presented in Table 1 shows that artisans were relatively better educated than the other lower Shudra castes. The Kamsali and Sale castes had a higher level of literacy than the cultivating non-Brahmin castes. The Kamsalis occupied a fairly high position with about 18 per cent literacy. They are also said to have had an advantage in female education and in literacy in English. From the medieval period the five artisan castes called Panchanamvaru have repeatedly waged a cultural and ideological battle for a higher place in the caste system than the one allotted to them by the Brahminical authorities. They also defied Brahminical supremacy and donned the sacred thread of the Dwijas. They styled themselves as Viswabrahmans and added the suffix *achari* (religious teacher) to their names. Communities who donned the sacred thread, but were linked to Pothuluri Veerabrahmam, who condemned the caste system and asserted social equality?[11]

The occupations of the Kamsalis required them to acquire knowledge of the classical scriptures related to architecture, sculpture, carpentry, jewellery, etc. Though they were considered as lower Shudras in the ritual hierarchy, they had the benefit of education in the indigenous schools which pre-dated the Western education system.[12] This, as a skilled community well-versed in textual and scriptural knowledge, its members, particularly in the urban areas, were able to gain entry into institutions of English education. During the early decades of the twentieth century, their caste association, the Vishwabrahmana Mahasabha, worked for the educational and social uplift of the community. It held annual conferences in various towns of coastal Andhra and propagated the need for the educational and occupational advancement of the community as a whole.[13] It repeatedly pleaded with the government to encourage the traditional crafts and technical education among their community members. It maintained that a liberal education would strengthen the craft skills of their community; and it contributed to the spread of vocational knowledge in order to facilitate economic development. The activities of the Mahasabha contributed considerably to the growth of educational awareness among the members of this community. In order to sustain educational activities in the community, it mobilized financial resources through donations and subscriptions, and awarded annual grants to eligible poor students of the community.

In various conferences held by the Mahasabha, resolutions were passed urging the Madras government to introduce compulsory education for children below twelve years of age. The need for the growth of education among its members and their entry into public employment was also emphasized. It is significant to note that this caste association consistently pleaded for the growth of women's education, and awarded scholarships for Kamsali girls from its education fund. It also organized competitive examinations for girls and awarded them prizes with a view to propagate educational ideas among the women of the community. Community-oriented publications, such as the journal *Sriviswakarma*, played a notable role in motivating the Kamsali to pursue modern education.

Other than the Viswabrahmans, the weaving communities too organized into a caste association in north coastal Andhra. It was known as the Pattusale Jateeya Mahasabha, and it too propagated the need for western education.[14] In its first conference, held on 21 May 1934, the importance of English education was stressed. It was resolved to organize village committees for the spread of elementary education in the community as well as to mobilise funds by way of donations from the rich people of the caste. The urge for modern education and an awareness of the need to modernize occupational skills were displayed by members of this community.[15] An activist of the Mahasabha said, 'just as oxygen is essential for the human being, so is education. Education is an equal to oxygen. It is also essential for livelihood. Wake up at once, my caste brethren. Organise caste meetings in your respective villages. Propagate the need for modern education among your children'[16] (my own translation). Similar sentiments were articulated by enlightened members of the community in the course of caste meetings held in different parts of Andhra.

Among the village service castes, the Mangalis, though not

usually held in high social esteem, maintained an appreciable percentage of literacy. Toddy and fishing communities also strove hard to propagate the idea of Western education through their respective caste associations.[17]

However, the marked awareness of the utility of modern education and the desire for educational achievement displayed by various organizations of the lower castes could not, and did not, contribute substantially to the spread of mass education among them. Factors like the inability and unwillingness of the colonial government to provide adequate facilities for the extension of popular education, and the inability of the majority of the rural poor to spare their children for school, significantly to the educational backwardness of these lower castes. The very nature of the colonial education system, with its irrelevant curriculum and inadequate or inaccessible institutional set-up, did not motivate them to pursue a Western education.

Another contributory factor was the destruction of village-based handicrafts, with severe economic consequences for the artisans. The dislocation of traditional occupations and loss of patronage forced many members of the artisan communities to move to other occupations. Census data and various village surveys indicate a gradual shift of the artisan communities from non-agricultural to agricultural and other sectors.[18] In the Andhra districts, by 1921-22 per cent of the Boya, 31.9 per cent Golla, 20.3 per cent Sale, 22.5 per cent Mangala, 11.8 per cent Tsakala and 6.2 per cent Kamsala worked as ordinary cultivators.[19] In pursuing their respective occupations, the members of these occupations were not inclined to send their children to school, considering that there were few adequate educational facilities available in the rural areas, where the majority of them lived, and particularly when the younger ones could be economically helpful to the family. Even when these communities were forced to migrate to urban areas (where educational facilities were available), they went as a result of the loss of livelihood in the villages, not because they could benefit from the educational facilities. This was in contrast to the urban migration of Brahmins and other upper castes, who went to the urban areas for the sake of an English education and not for the sake of a livelihood.

By the very logic of their socio-economic situation, the lower caste groups were, to a very large extent, forced out of the modern education system. Furthermore, and unlike the upper caste groups, the lower castes could not visualize in education any relevance or hope for the betterment of their traditional skills. This has been amply indicated by the views expressed by the leading members of various caste associations. The Viswabrahman Mahasabha, for instance, deplored the irrelevance and unsuitability of a liberal English education for their occupational and professional advancement. It sought the development of vocational and technical education as a suitable measure for the economic upliftment of the artisan communities. Such opinions were also expressed by the caste associations of the Sale, Gamalla, Boya, etc.[20] These communities desired an educational system that emphasised vocational training. The toddy tappers pleaded for an education which would provide them with knowledge regarding the production of jaggery from date-palm juice. Likewise, the weavers aspired to upgrade their traditional skills with the aid of vocational and technical training to be provided by the government-run educational institutions. But the colonial state preferred and largely encouraged non-technical education, and failed to provide the necessary incentives to the vast majority of these communities. Even when a few technical/vocational schools and colleges did get established, the members of the lower communities could not utilize the opportunity, because they required a certain number of years of prior schooling. The immediate and practical utility of an English education was not appreciated by a majority of the lower caste groups, for the simple reason that they did not see in it any relevance to the direct expansion of their traditional skills and occupations. To a very large extent the new educational system was, in fact, distanced from their immediate practical needs. Therefore, to them agriculture and wage labour, rather than education, provided the immediate alternative for meeting the challenges of the loss of livelihood based on handicrafts. Thus, the colonial educational system seriously failed to meet the aspirations of the lower castes for socio-economic advancement. Although they displayed a new consciousness for acquiring access to English education, the socio-cultural environment was not conductive. Unlike some agrarian castes such as the Kammas and Velamas, the majority of the lower Shudra castes did not achieve any economic progress. The insensitivity of the colonial educational system to the vocational needs of the lower castes, aggravated by their dire economic circumstances, acted as a serious deterrent to the lower castes, who could not benefit out of it. The modern secular education, instead of providing opportunities for occupational and social mobility, facilitated the continuation and perpetuation of social hierarchy and inequality.

Education of Dalits

The untouchable communities, who occupied the lowest position in the traditional caste hierarchy of Andhra, were as a rule denied the right of education and excluded from certain other occupational privileges. Unlike the other lower Shudra castes, they did not have the benefit of an indigenous educational system, such as the pathasalas which were prevalent in the Andhra region prior to the advent of British rule.[21] These indigenous schools were mostly attended by children of Brahmin and other higher castes/classes. The rigid hierarchical system of castes and social discrimination, which pervaded the school environment, deprived the children of Untouchable communities of a stimulating educational environment, considered a prerequisite for the development of a human being. Unequal treatment was meted out to them, and they were collectively discriminated against by the higher castes. These communities occupy the lowest position in the caste and occupational hierarchy, and have suffered many social disabilities for centuries. The stigma of untouchability had deleterious effects on the personality and behavior of the members of these communities.

Nevertheless, the struggle against caste discrimination and efforts to eradicate untouchability have occupied an important part of the social reform movements and ideologies of Andhra since the beginning of the modern period.[22] It is difficult to find any clear or authentic historical evidence regarding the Untouchables' own attitude to their status or internalization of caste ideology, as well as any information about mass-based self-motivated resistance movements against the caste system. Although it is possible to suggest that attempts by individual members of the lower castes have been made to protest against caste discrimination and also obtain social advancement, it is the advent of Christian missionaries into Andhra districts that heralded a new epoch in the emancipation of the Dalits from caste oppression/tyranny.

During the early decades of the nineteenth century, Christian missionaries were the pioneers of Western education in Andhra.[23] Several missionaries worked among the Untouchable communities, mainly the Malas and Madigas, and carried out proselytising activities. In the process of religious conversion, the spread of education became an important instrument. Hence, the Untouchable communities for the first time began to enjoy the benefits of education. The Christian missionaries were thus responsible for imparting an identity to these people by extending educational facilities to the lowest rungs of Andhra society. Conversion to Christianity enabled the Untouchables to obtain noticeable gains in education and employment. The establishment of missionary elementary schools in different districts of colonial Andhra not only facilitated the education of converts, but also that of other sections of Hindu society. The Untouchable communities, in particular, gained admission into the schools without any discrimination. Therefore, it is mainly due to the activities of the missionaries that the Dalit communities got the benefits of modern education. The educational endeavors of the missionaries contributed significantly to a new awakening among underprivileged groups of Andhra society, inducing them to gradually claim equality and social respect.

The colonial state remained indifferent to the education needs of the natives for a long time. The efforts of Thomas Munro in the Madras Presidency in the 1820s did contribute, albeit in a very insignificant way, to the establishment of government schools in the smaller towns and villages of various Andhra districts.[24] The Macaulay's Minute formed the basis of a nation-wide educational programme in colonial India, but it did nothing for the education of the depressed classes. The theory of downward filtration became the greatest stumbling block to the spread of education among the lower castes and communities. The Wood's Despatch of 1854 made some provision for the education of the depressed classes, but official neglect and apathy continued to deny the benefits of modern education to the lowest rungs of society.[25] The educational ideal of the colonial state was that no boy should be refused admission to Government College or school merely on the grounds of caste, but this was not fully implemented in practice, in spite of specific orders being issued from time to time. Also, the principle of openness and equality of treatment for all castes admitted inside the school, as enunciated by colonial educationists, was undermined by prejudice and resistance from the upper castes. Instead of pursuing its stated policies with strict adherence to the principles of liberalism and humanism, the colonial government succumbed to the pressures of upper caste prejudices and made compromises under the pretext that no principle, however sound, could be forced upon an unwilling society in defiance of social and religious sentiments. These upper caste 'sentiments' were certainly quite detrimental to the educational needs and progress of the lower castes. Thus, the social and religious prejudices of upper caste elites obtained the subtle consent of the colonial rulers.

To avoid difficulties arising from caste prejudice, it was considered necessary to start low caste schools. Subsequently, the Hunter Commission of 1882 recommended the establishment of separate schools for the children of Depressed Classes in India. The deplorable position of the Depressed Classes was more due to the prevalence of untouchability and caste discrimination than to any inherent inability of the classes themselves. To avoid difficulties arising from caste prejudice, it was considered necessary to start low caste schools. Subsequently, the Hunter Commission of 1882 recommended the establishment of separate schools for the children of Depressed Classes in India. In pursuance of the recommendations of the Hunter Commission, the Madras government provided a number of concessions and incentives in order to spread Western education among the Untouchable communities. They included: the opening of special schools, financial assistance through the grant of stipends, allotments of public lands to Panchama schools, fee exemptions, and grants-in-aid.[26] The Madras government also found it necessary to offerinducements to the parents to persuade them to send their children to school, rather than to earn.[27]

By the end of the nineteenth century, the Madras Presidency had opened 2,934 institutions 'intended chiefly for Panchamas', of which, 6 were run by the government, 491 by local boards, and 1,1612 were aided institutions.[28]

The Educational Reorganization Committee of Madras opined:

> The education of depressed classes became a matter of national duty, and public funds should in justice be available to all reasonable extent in serving their interests.[29]

During the first quarter of the twentieth century, the Madras government initiated various policy measures to augment educational facilities for the Untouchable communities. Through successive orders issued in 1919, 1920 and 1922, it emphasized the necessity of admitting low caste children to schools under public management.

The most noteworthy measure of the local government was the creation of a labour Department, which was made responsible for the educational progress of Dalit communities. Thus, separate Labour Department schools were set up throughout Madras Presidency, and the total number of public institutions chiefly intended for the Depressed Classes increased gradually. As Table 3 shows, the number of special schools for Untouchable communities increased by 42.2 per cent between 1919-1920 and 1936-37, while the strength of Depressed Class students went up by 180 per cent during the period 1919-20 and 1948-49. Although this appears impressive, it must be remembered that compared to the total population, only 7.52 per cent of boys and 1.65 per cent of girls belonging to the Untouchable communities had the benefit of school education in 1928-1929. In the same year, Scheduled Caste students consisted 11.6 per cent of the total school population. It was also found that the number of male Dalit students tended to decrease as they went up to the higher classes. They constituted 6.6 per cent of total students at the primary level (Class V) but declined to 2.8 per cent, and 0.89 per cent respectively, at the

Table 3
Public institutions for the Depressed Classes in Madras Presidency

Year	*No. of Schools*	*Student Population*
1919-20	6438	1.75 lakhs
1920-21	7007	1.93 lakhs
1921-22	8045	2.22 lakhs
1922-23	8575	2.38 lakhs
1924-25	9086	2.54 lakhs
1925-26	9413	2.63 lakhs
1931-32	10215	2.92 lakhs
1936-37	9151	3.29 lakhs
1948-49	N.A.	4.90 lakhs

Compiled from the annual reports on public instruction in Madras Presidency for the years shown.

secondary and high school levels in 1928-29. In other words, the number of Scheduled Caste students in the higher classes became quite negligible.[30]

The social background of college students in Andhra districts also confirms the fact that Dalits were effectively excluded from higher educational institutions. This is demonstrated in Tables 4 and 5. Available information regarding the economic background of the student community of these colleges also clearly indicates that the majority of them were drawn from the rich and middle classes. Almost all of them happened to be the children of officials, traders and landholders. Undoubtedly, Dwijas and Shudra upper castes constituted the majority students community in these colleges. Needless to say, very few students belonged to the lower Shudra, artisan or Dalit communities.

In addition to separate schools, the children of the Depressed Classes were also admitted into common public schools. Apart from the missionary schools, local board and government schools increasingly catered to their educational needs in the Madras Presidency. Scholarships and other incentives provided by the government from time to time contributed to a modest growth in

Table 4
Caste composition of the students of Ceded Districts College, Anantapur

Community	*1921*	*1923*	*1924*	*1925*	*1928*	*1935*	*1936*	*1937*	*1938*
Brahmin	127	131	135	138	156	107	125	150	143
Non-Brahmin	23	33	63	75	92	122	99	123	145
Mohammaden	05	09	18	18	19	15	17	14	24
Christian	Nil	01	02	04	05	03	04	06	03
Dalit	Nil	Nil	Nil	Nil	Nil	Nil	03	02	03
Total	155	174	219	236	272	247	248	295	298

Compiled from the Annual Admission Reports of the College for the years shown.

Table 5
Caste Composition of the Students of Government Arts College, Rajahmundry

Community	*1924*	*1926*	*1935*	*1936*	*1938*
Brahmin	221	257	170	172	201
Non-Brahmin	99	120	70	79	83
Mohammedan	18	15	10	13	11
Christian	06	04	03	02	01
Dalit	Nil	Nil	02	01	0
Total	344	396	256	267	296

Compiled from the Annual Admission Reports of the College for the years shown.

lower caste literacy during the first quarter of the twentieth century. The grants-in-aid policy also encouraged many local boards in the Andhra region to admit the children of Dalit communities into their schools.

After 1919, the educational progress of Dalits in joint schools was helped when the government ordered the removal of schools from rented buildings, temples, *chavadis* and *agraharams*, the owners of which objected to the admission of Untouchables to their premises, otherwise accessible to all castes/classes. In order to ensure that public funds were not expended on buildings from which Panchamas were likely to be excluded, the government ordered in April 1920 that before any new building site was selected or constructed, a certificate should be obtained from either the Collector or Inspector of Schools to the effect that the site or building would be accessible to all classes of the community, including Panchamas.[31] Further, wherever new school buildings were constructed by local boards, the principle of locating them in places freely accessible to all classes of pupils was carefully observed. Some District Education Councils also increased teaching grants to those aided elementary schools under their jurisdiction, which freely admitted pupils of the Adi-Andhra communities. In pursuance of the policy of the Madras government in the matter of the admission of children belonging to the Depressed Classes into all schools under public management, several Cheri schools, meant exclusively for Untouchables, were amalgamated with joint schools under local boards. It was observed that progress, though slow, was being made in enrolling Panchama children into joint schools under public management. The Director of Public Instruction, in his report for the year 1935-36, wrote thus:

> "Progress during the past few years in the matter of admissions of pupils belonging to the Scheduled Classes into common schools has been so slow that, during the year under report, Government decided to take the drastic step of imposing on the managements of elementary schools, as a condition of recognition, the duty of enrolling pupils belonging to these classes.[32] The newly framed rules under the Madras Elementary Education Act have given a wider interpretation of 'accessibility': under these new rules a school is treated as inaccessible and is liable to loss of recognition if no pupil belonging to the Scheduled Castes is found on the rolls. It is hoped that these rules will strengthen the hands of the inspecting officers and enable them to record greater progress in the admission of the Scheduled Castes into general schools for communities."[33]

The educational policies of the Madras government during the 1920s and 1930s should be viewed in the context of the growing demand from those groups which had so far been denied education. The growth of the non-Brahmin movement, the rise of the Dalit movement, the formation of associations by various low caste groups and their socio-political mobilization, as well as changing constitutional and political developments exerted considerable pressure on the colonial government to provide educational opportunities to the hitherto neglected groups and communities.[33] Education and the employment of non-Brahmin communities were two key issues that consistently emerged in the political sphere of the first quarter of this century. There was a growing realization among the lower castes that the key to their socio-economic upliftment and future development lay in education. The leaders of these communities became all the more aware of the urgency of their need for Western education due to constitutional reform and devolution of political power, which, they realized, would benefit those with an English education, professional qualifications and administrative experience. Among the Untouchable communities as well, there was a growing urge for modern education, as they became aware that it would enable them to raise their socio-economic status and make political power accessible.

The educational aspirations that were initially fostered by Christian missionary institutions became sharper and better articulated in the early decades of the twentieth century. Besides Christian missionaries, other social reform organizations in Andhra, like the Brahmo Samaj, also aided the growth of educational consciousness among Dalit communities.[34] By the 1920s, there was widespread awareness of their condition among the Untouchable communities, as was indicated by the activities of the Adi-Andhra Mahasabha. In fact, the first generation Mahasabha leadership was drawn mainly from educational institutions organized by the Christian missionaries and Brahma Samaj.[35] This generation pressed for a more vigorous campaign for the spread of education, and argued consistently for educational progress of the Dalits. They were endowed with a clear vision regarding the emancipatory role of modern education in the future development of the community. The Adi-Andhra movement decided to end the humiliating discrimination imposed on the Depressed Classes through Western education; and thus obtaining political power, they intended to achieve social equality and dignity. In conference after conference, the Mahasabha passed resolutions urging the government to introduce free education for the children of Untouchable communities.

The movement for educational advancement by the Adi-Andhras in the 1930s received much encouragement from the activities of the Andhra Provincial Harijan Sevak Sangh, which was established in 1932. It carried out programmes like cleaning Dalit localities, establishing separate schools and hostels for Dalit students, digging drinking-water wells for Dalit communities, facilitating temple entry for Dalits, etc. Between 1932 and 1934 the Sangh established as many as 41 night schools, 11 day schools, 19 hostels and 20 libraries for the benefits of Dalit students, and incurred a total expenditure of Rs. 22,000. It also established a few vocational training schools and administered various scholarships. During the first half of 1935, it incurred an expenditure of Rs. 4,778 towards the maintenance of hostels, which accommodated 215 boys and 18 girls, and Rs.1, 963 towards the establishment of 6 new schools in various districts of Andhra. The Sangh mobilized donations and used the funds to award scholarships to girl students of the vocational schools. The leadership of the Sangh also persuaded the provincial government to reimburse the local boards for meeting the school fees of Dalit students during the academic year 1934-35.[36]

The activities of the Adi-Andhra Mahasabha and the Harijan Sevak Sangh, together with the positive attitude of the Justice Party government of Madras province in the 1920s and 1930s generated renewed enthusiasm for modern education among the Dalit communities. The changing attitude of the British towards the conflict between the Brahmans and Non-Brahmins also contributed to the formulation of new policies, like those which led to more facilities for Dalit students in the joint schools under public management.

Nevertheless, whenever the local government tried to help the downtrodden communities through its Labour Department, it met with a good deal of active opposition from the upper caste elites. The Madras government was thus compelled to open separate schools for the Depressed Classes, realizing they could not easily enroll in ordinary schools. The establishment of a large number of such schools itself indicates that resistance to mixed-caste education was extremely powerful. Thus, a British official noted:

> Government activities in aid of these unfortunates have met with some lip sympathy but a good deal more practical opposition... The tale of minor disabilities and annoyances is long, and the end not in sight. The share taken by far-from-exalted communities in maintaining disabilities and resisting amelioration is one of the most noteworthy and most depressing features, and apt to encourage misanthropy in the observer, who is given wide illustration of how unpleasant a creature man can be.[37]

However, it seems to have been realized by the Madras government that its separate schools for the Untouchables were not particularly efficient, for the reason that there was genuine difficulty in obtaining good teachers for them, as high caste teachers did not wish to serve in them and the depressed communities had been able to produce only a few teachers. There was, therefore, a tendency on the part of the government to discard the system of separate schools. Thus, in the 1920s, the Madras government deliberately rejected any demand of the Untouchable communities for such schools, on the ground that it was 'neither educationally sound nor practically feasible'. For example, in response to a representation made by the Andhra Provincial Adi-Andhra Association for the opening of free and separate educational institutions for the spread of education among the children of the Depressed Classes, the Madras Government replied thus:

> The ideal to be aimed at has been held to be admission into all schools on an equal footing, in other words a modification of the conditions and social structure of Indian society rather than emphasizing social barriers by the establishment of separate high schools. In the eye of the government and the law, *your people possess the same rights and privileges as other citizens but what you propose would tend to accentuate a distinction, which it is our object to eradicate.* (Emphasis added.)[38]

Conflict Over Education: Evidence of Caste Discrimination Against Dalits

The provincial government of Madras encountered stiff resistance to its policy of providing educational access to Dalit students in the common schools. The opposition of the higher castes was particularly strong in several municipal and Taluk board schools of Madras Presidency. This upper caste resistance to the spread of elementary education among the power castes and communities in the districts of Andhra seems to have been spearheaded by the local zamindari class.

> The higher classes and the zamindars were not very much in favour of the education of the masses. The British government was advised mostly by zamindars, and the same zamindars who controlled villages became a great hindrance to the spread of mass education in spite of the growing demand for knowledge from the masses and the efforts of government and local bodies to spread it. Naturally, the spread of primary education was unsatisfactory in Andhra.'[39]

The ambitious and ruthless Andhra landlord class, primarily drawn from the Shudra upper caste communities, wanted to keep the lower castes ignorant in order to maintain its dominance over them, and were perhaps apprehensive of having to deal with educated peasants, artisans and labourers. Similar instances of caste discrimination in public schools were also reported from other provinces of British India, like Bengal and Bombay.

Various reports of the educational officials of the Madras government mention the 'existence of deep-rooted caste prejudice' particularly in the rural areas, as one of the reasons for the slow progress in enrolling Depressed Class students into the common schools. Whenever the government insisted on strict implementation of the principle, upper caste resistance was expressed in the form of withdrawal of their children from schools that had been opened to the Untouchable communities.[40] For instance, in 1920, the Amalapuram taluk board in Godavari district disregarded government policy and passed a resolution, on the petition of certain villagers that 'the admission of Panchamas in public schools was undesirable, as it led to caste friction.'[41] Similar instances were also reported from other taluks of Andhra districts. Reviewing the situation, the Secretary to the Education Department of the Madras government noted:

> *This evidences unjustifiable weakness on the part of local bodies in carrying out the policy.* If a firm stand is taken and the pupils of the Depressed Classes are kept on in such schools, castemen will soon reconcile themselves to the situation ... Where caste children are withdrawn as a result of the admission of the Depressed Class pupils, the vacancies should be filled up as far as possible by other Depressed Class children and no compromise allowed.[42] (Emphasis added)

In order to increase the admission of Untouchable children in the joint schools, the government followed a policy of shifting schools that were located in places inaccessible to all classes, including Panchamas. Thus, over the years many schools running in temples, chavadis, private rented buildings, etc. were relocated. During 1921-22, it was observed that in the taluks of Bandar and Vijayawada in Krishna district, Bhimavaram in Godavari District, and Koilkunta and Nandyal in Kurnool district, several schools remained in private buildings whose owners did not agree to the admission of Adi-Andhras.[43] The number of such schools in the Ramachandrapuram taluk of Godavari district was 'rather high' Difficulties were also experienced by the education department and local board officials in procuring suitable buildings.

Even when Untouchable students were admitted into the common schools, they were made to sit outside the buildings or on separate benches, despite the fact that the teachers had been warned against such practices. Some Brahmin teachers who had been transferred to Adi-Andhra schools declined to join and even resigned from the service. In some instances, as in the Ganjam and Bellary districts, separate sections for students of the Depressed Classes were opened in caste Hindu Schools. Although the government did not accept this as an 'ideal arrangement' and requested the local bodies to consider the 'desirability of amalgamating the sections gradually'[44] such practices persisted.

Available evidence suggests that in districts such as West Godavari, Krishna and Guntur, the disparity between number of schools made accessible to pupils of the Scheduled Castes and the number in which they were actually admitted was very great. During the academic year of 1935-36, in the entire Madras Province Dalit students were admitted into only 55.8% of the schools under the public management. This means that nearly half of the common schools were still out of their reach. This discrepancy was attributed by officials to the apathy of local bodies and to caste opposition. The Director of Public Instruction remarked in 1937 that the progress of the common school system was *'far behind the expectation.'*[45] Many presidents and chairmen of local bodies reported that the children of Adi-Andhra did not generally seek admission into caste Hindu schools under public management because they had separate aided missionary institutions under both public and private management. It was also noted that the Adi-Andhra did not use the schools declared to be accessible to them because they were very poor and quite dependent for their livelihood on the higher caste peasantry of the village and hence did not wish to incur the displeasure of their masters by acting against their sentiments. The officials also note, 'The scheduled caste people were afraid of sending their children to school on account of the aggression of caste people.'[46] Caste discrimination was not confined only to elementary schools. It also prevailed in private institutions. In fact, the managements of private schools negated Madras government policy on this matter without any serious consequences because the admission of Adi-Andhra had been left as an opinion.

The response of the Madras government to upper caste resistance was neither unambiguous nor consistent. The persistent refusal of the local board leadership, private management and teaching community, all primarily drawn from the higher castes, to comply with government orders often left the government helpless. The inspecting staff of the Education Department repeatedly drew the attention of the provincial authorities to the indifference and uncooperative attitude of local board officials and teachers towards the implementation government policies. Although the government sometimes responded by threatening to withdraw grants and refusing or delaying recognition of defiant school board managements, such warnings did not yield any results. The upper castes dominated local government and private institutions, and they systematically subverted the ideals of the colonial education policies in practice. Some upper caste elites felt that the government was taking sufficient care of the interests of the Adi-Andhras, and therefore, if they could help it, did not wish to admit Untouchable children to their schools. Upper caste prejudice and apathy could not be overcome by the colonial government precisely because of its dependence on the social support of these classes in maintaining the system at the grass roots level. British pragmatism also prevented them from taking any drastic action against upper caste-dominated institutions. That the colonial state was not prepared to vigorously pursue its own policies with regard to free access to educational institutions irrespective of caste and creed was indicated when the Sanskrit College at Tirupathi refused to teach *vyakaranam* (grammar) to non-Brahmin students under the pretext of 'protecting the principles of tradition, custom and orthodoxy.' When the government insisted, the manager of the college asked, 'Why not penalize the college by the withdrawal of recognition to it?' The government vacillated and compromised.[47]

Contrary to the attitude of the government, the leadership of the Adi-Andhra Mahasabha was very critical of upper caste attitudes. To the extent possible, Dalit representatives in local bodies successfully insisted on the implementation of the equality principle.[48] When it could not be helped or where they were strong and great in numbers, Dalits sought the establishment of separate schools for themselves. This was mainly intended as on assertion of their willingness to face difficulties and progress. It was particularly satisfying to them when they got members of their own communities posted in these schools. The efforts of Dalit organizations also tended to neutralize and soften caste pupils joined the separate schools meant for Untouchables. Likewise, some Adi-Andhra teachers were accepted in caste Hindu schools. Although these are rare instances, this was a positive indication.

It is interesting to note that the upper caste nationalist intelligentsia, particularly under the influence of the Gandhian 'Harijan upliftment programme,' though sympathetic to the cause of Dalit education, was not entirely free from caste prejudice. A few glaring instances of caste discrimination in the 'nationalist' educational institutions of coastal Andhra can be cited. The reputed Andhra Jateeya Kalasala Industrial School, which was under caste Hindu management, is a case in point. Its aims were stated to be to impart 'literary, scientific and technical education on national lines, under national control and directed towards the realization of the nation's highest destiny.'[49] Nearly 100 boys lived in its hostel, and about half of them were Brahmins. There were only 3 or 4 Panchamas, and they were 'housed in a separate shed'. So much for the 'realisation of the nation's highest destiny'!

Similarly, caste discrimination against Dalits in the recruitment to teaching posts in the Hindu High School at Bandar, Krishna district, was reported in the press.[50] The management of this school, which was dominated by Brahmins and advanced Shudras, are alleged to have denied appointment to a Dalit trainee teacher candidate 'on the ground of caste.' This was a recognised institution getting public funds, but it refused to implement government policies regarding the appointment of teachers from Dalit communities. This incident should be viewed in a large context: no Dalit teacher was to be found in the high schools of the Krishna and Godavari District Boards. The reporter, who seemed to be a Dalit himself, lamented, 'Even in these days of spread of Harijan upliftment, that too in towns and public schools, if caste discrimination is practiced, what will be the fate of villages?' (My translation).[51] He also remarked sarcastically that the upper caste management of the Hindu High School, due to its caste prejudice, was of the opinion that Dalits were unfit to be appointed as teachers.

The feelings of educated Dalits against caste discrimination can be found in abundance in vernacular writings. Dalit literature of the pre-Independence period in Andhra depicted innumerable examples of caste relations. The educational aspirations and perceptions of Dalit communities occupied an especially prominent place in the short stories, plays and novels written by Dalit scholars.[52]

To conclude, an attempt has been made in this paper to analyse the role and problems of Western education among the lower Shudra and Untouchable communities. It is observed that modern education had a differential impact on the various segments of Andhra society. Its benefits were not shared equitably by all castes, as the prevailing social structure exerted a decisive influence in determining access to it. Compared to the upper castes, the access of Dalit and Bahujan communities to educational opportunities was severely curtailed due to widespread caste prejudice and discrimination. As a consequently, the educational achievements of the lower castes were quite insignificant. The advantages in terms of family, literary tradition and economic resources of the privileged castes like the Brahmins greatly facilitated their absorption of modern education, and contributed considerably to their upward social mobility.[53] Modern education enabled the upper castes to further strengthen their *ascriptive* status and continue their dominance. Although the lower castes became increasingly aware of the utility of a Western education, they could not achieve any noticeable upward mobility. Western education thus tended to reinforce the existing *ascribed* status rather than facilitate or promote achieved status through social ascent. In other words, the shift from *ascription* to achievement as a basis of social mobility did not take place in Andhra. In a sense, instead of giving rise to a secular society, education tended to perpetuate the traditional social hierarchy based on caste.

The upper caste elites, who benefited immensely from modern knowledge, consciously opposed its spread among the lower caste groups. The leadership of the local boards and the teaching community in the elementary schools acted as important agencies in blocking the educational opportunities and advancement of the Dalit and Bahujan castes. As a result, the growing aptitude, zeal and enthusiasm of various lower castes for educational progress could not translated into reality. Even the limited chances made available by the colonial educational system were effectively denied by the intolerance and contempt of upper caste elites. The upper caste elites resisted any expansion of mass education by wrecking the system at the grassroots level. It was not only among the Brahmin elite that the greatest intolerance was found; the recently promoted upper Shudra castes were even more severe on the 'underdogs.'

It is often said that due to poverty and indifference, the lower castes could not gain easy access to modern education. Although this is partly true, it was in fact caste prejudice more than their disinclination for schooling which kept the under privileged lower communities educationally backward. It is interesting to note that in colonial Andhra, upper caste resistance was more fierce and bitter in those taluks which were relatively educationally advanced. In areas where there was comparatively higher literacy among the upper castes, antagonism to mass education was more intense and widespread, as for instance in the prosperous villages of the Krishna-Godavari delta of coastal Andhra. This was also the region where the socio-political mobilization of the Dalit and Bahujan castes was better organized and their educational aspirations more sharply articulated. This perhaps, threatened entrenched upper caste interests and thus aroused their jealousy. Especially, the attempts to improve the conditions of the Dalit communities caused bitter resentment among the upper caste elites, who preferred to keep them under their control. This resentment often found expression in intensified caste hatred. In spite of upper caste resistance, however, the Dalit-Bahujan communities of colonial Andhra managed to achieve some sort of 'sponsored' vertical mobility, mainly due to state patronage in the form of scholarships, hostels, special schools, etc. These limited education and occupational changes did not substantially alter their material conditions; in fact, the social world of the lower orders remained the same as it had in the past.

REFERENCES

1. A. Basu, *Essays in the History of Education,* Delhi, 1982, p. 91.
2. Y. Vaikuntham, *Education and Social Change in South India: Andhra, 1880-1920,* Madras, 1982, p. 1.
3. L. Stone, "Literacy and education in England, 1640-1900," in *Past and Present,* No. 42, February 1969, p. 71.
4. A. Basu, *Essays in the History of Education,* op. cit.
5. V. Ramakrishna, *Social Reform in Andhra,* Delhi, 1983.
6. For more details about Komati caste organizations, see Government Order (G.O) (LSG) 8 September, 1928, cited in Washbrook, "The development of caste organizations in South India, 1880 to 1925", in Baker and Washbrook, *South India, Political Institutions and Political Change, 1880-1940,* Delhi, 1975.
7. *Census Report,* 1871, Madras, Vol. 1, p. 191.
8. *Census Report,* 1921, Madras, Vol. 1, p. 119.
9. For details see K. Bhavaiah Choudary, *A Brief History of the Kammas,* N.P. 1954.
10. Y. Vaikuntham, *op. cit.,* p. 167.
11. Ramakrishna, *op. cit.,* p. 45. Also see Reddy, "Social Awakening among Certain Oppressed Communities in Andhra during the later

Vijayanagara Period", in *Ithihas*, Vol. XIX, No. 182, Hyderabad, Jan-Dec. 1993, pp. 55-56. Y. Chinna Rao, "Education and Identity Formation Among Dalits in Colonial Andhra", in S. Bhattacharya (ed.), *Education and the Disprivileged* (New Delhi: Orient Longman, 2002).

12. Dharmapal, *The Beautiful Tree: Indigenous Indian Education in the Eighteenth Century*, New Delhi, 1983.
13. The activities of the Sabha are reported in *Krishna Patrika (KP)*, Oct. 27, 1991; *KP*, Jan. 5, 1912; *KP*, Jan. 26, 1912; *KP*, Jan 4, 1913; *KP*, Jan.1915; *KP*, Sep. 29, 1917; *KP*, Feb. 6, 1926.
14. *KP*, Sep. 4, 1915 and Sep. 25, 1915.
15. *KP*, Jun. 9, 1934.
16. *KP*, Sep. 25, 1915.
17. *KP*, May 12, 1912; *KP*, Apr. 12, 1913; *KP*, Dec.3, 1921; *KP*, June 14, 1924.
18. *Census Report 1871*, Madras Vol. 1, pp. 151-59.
19. Calculated from *Census Report 1921*, Madras, Vol. II.
20. See above, F. No. 13, 14 and 17. For details about the fishermen's caste association, *Agrakula Kshatriya Mahasabha*, see *KP*, June 15, 1918; *KP*, Oct. 22, 1921; *KP*, Oct. 20, 1928.
21. Dharmapal, *Beautiful Tree, op. cit.*
22. Ramakrishna, *Social Reform*, pp. 40-48.
23. *Ibid.*, pp. 49-54
24. Dharmapal, *Beautiful Tree, op. cit.*
25. Nurullah and Naiak, *A Student's History of Education in India, 1800-1949*, Bombay, 1949.
26. Y. Vaikuntham, *op. cit.*, p. 181.
27. *Ibid.*
28. Robert Nathan, *Progress of Education in India, 1897-98 to 1901-02*, Calcutta, 1908, p. 136
29. G.O. Law (Education) 239, 14 Feb. 1923, p. 16.
30. Calculated from the *Annual Reports of Public Instruction in the Madras Presidency* for the years shown.
31. *Report on Public Instruction in the Madras Presidency* for the year 1922-23, p. 31.
32. Cited in G.O. education, 24, 29 Jan. 1937, p. 29.
33. For an account of Adi-Andhra Mahasabha, see Satyanarayana, *"Dalit Identity and Consciousness in Colonial Andhra"*, 1917-47 (mimeographed).
34. Ramakrishna, *op. cit.*, p. 186.

35. *Ibid.*
36. An account of the conferences of the Adi-Andhra Mahasabha is provided in various issues of *Krishna Patrika*. See, for instance, *KP*, Feb. 23, 1929.
37. This paragraph is based on the information contained in *KP*, June 23, 1934; *KP*, Oct. 1934; *KP*, Aug. 4, 1934; *KP*, April. 6, 1935; *KP*, May 25, 1935.
38. *Census Report*, Madras, 1931, Vol. 1. 344.
39. G.O. Law (Education), 493, 3, March, 1930.
40. Vaikuntham, Y., (Education), *op. cit.*, p. 75.
41. G.O. Law (Education), 153, 25 Jan., 1929.
42. Vaikuntham, Y., (Education), *op. cit.*, p. 186.
43. G.O. Law (Education), 153, 25 Jan., 1929. p. 3.
44. G.O. Law (Education), 87, 16 Jan., 1923.
45. G.O. Law (Education), 205, 11 Feb., 1924.
46. G.O. Education and Public Health (Education), 599, 18 March, 1937.
47. G.O. Law (Education), 1825, 24 Nov. 1924, G.O. Law (Education), 1717, 8 Nov. 1924; and G.O. Law (Education), 320, 13 Feb. 1939.
48. See G.O. Law (Education), 1870, 6 Sep. 1929 and G.O. 1375, 5 Sep. 1929.
49. G.O. Law (Education), 87, 16 Jan. 1923.
50. G.O. Law (Education), 1406, 17 Nov. 1922.
51. *KP*, 15 Aug. 1936.
52. *Ibid.*
53. See A. Satyanarayana, 'Dalit Protest Literature in Telugu: A Historical Perspective', in *Economic and Political Weekly*, Vol. XXX, No. 3, Jan. 1995, pp. 171-75.

4

Dalit Protest Literature in Telugu: A Historical Perspective

The objective of this chapter is to discuss the historical context of the emergence of a literary genre which reflected the growing identity, awareness and consciousness of the dalits during the colonial period. Although there was no literary genre distinctively known as 'dalit literature' during the pre-independence period in Andhra, an examination of the literary works of certain dalit intellectuals indicates that the oppression, agony and anger of the dalit masses is reflected in their writings. An attempt is made in this chapter to analyse the nature of literary representation of dalit problems and the emerging consciousness in the writings of selected dalit scholars. It focuses on the treatment of caste oppression, untouchability and dalit sensibility in the writings of dalit intellectuals.

In recent years the socio-cultural and political assertion of the oppressed masses belonging to the lower sections—the dalits has been accompanied by a distinct literary genre called dalit literature. It noted that:

> "the distinctiveness of dalit literature lies in its authentic unity of dalit language and content. In it the disillusionment and disgust of young dalits, often accompanied by a desire of revenge, come alive. It revives the memory of the pain and suffering of past generations. It confronts centuries of hypocrisy, deceit and violence sustained in the name of tradition."[1]

In Andhra Pradesh, the Karamchedu episode[2] marks a turning point in the growth of the dalit movement. A series of upper caste attacks on dalits in different parts of the state resulted in the formation of various dalit organisations which are presently channeling the assertion and political articulation of the dalit masses. A wide variety of political formations, cultural organisations and ideologies (ranging from liberal bourgeois to radical Marxist) represent the growing consciousness of the dalits in the state.

Broadly speaking, since the 1970s an increasing number of poets and writers drawn from the dalit communities of the states like Maharashtra, Karnataka and Andhra Pradesh have been producing literary works such as poems, short stories, novels and dramas representing the themes of caste oppression, untouchability, poverty, repression and revolution. The writings of dalit scholars also contain powerful denunciations of and fierce attacks on the caste system and on brahmanical Hinduism. It has been pointed out that the dalit *Sahitya* is considered to be a unique genre of modern Indian literature, for now untouchables themselves using the traditionally-denied weapon of literacy, are exposing the conditions under which they have lived, as well as directly rebelling (*'vidroha'*) against the Hindu institution which has assured their perpetual subordination to the 'Varna' order.[3] As far as Andhra Pradesh is concerned, it can be said that both the radical left movement and the Dalit Maha Sabhas have thrown up a new generation of dalit scholars, intellectuals and philosophers whose writings sharply reflect the changing perceptions and consciousness of dalit masses. In their writings, the dalit question is posed in terms of the annihilation of the caste system and the emergence of a casteless egalitarian society.

Historical Antecedents

However, the emergence of dalit literature in recent times is not without its historical antecedents. In fact, since the medieval period, the Telugu-speaking region of the Deccan witnessed the development of the Bhakti movement, which led to the emergence of a literary tradition among the non-brahmin scholars Vemana, Potuluri Veerabrahmam and who propounded anti-caste movements and denounced the caste system, social inequality and oppression.

The saint-poets emphasised in unequivocal terms the inequalities and injustices suffered by the lower and untouchable castes due to the varna order. The medieval bhakti tradition, therefore, first raised certain themes and issues regarding the life sufferings of those at the bottom of the caste hierarchy. By and large, the themes of the bhakti tradition reappear in the dalit literary tradition both during and after independence, even though the perspectives of the two traditions is different.

In Telugu literature the problems of untouchability and the poverty and misery of dalits were represented by nationalist and liberal scholars drawn from the upper castes.[4] In particular, the literature which was generated during the time of social reform movements contained various problems confronted by different segments of society. Social reformers such as Gurajada Appa Rao and Veereshalingam broadened the base and scope of literature as well as transformed the traditional character of Telugu literature "into a modern tool of communication".[5] In contrast to the conservative elitist literary tradition, modern writers such as Appa Rao and Gidugu Ramamurthy favoured and popularised the use of spoken language in literary creation. Though Gurajada and Veereshalingam are acclaimed as the "founders of new epoch in modern Telugu literature" their writings focused mainly on themes and problems such as bride price and widow remarriage, related to women of upper castes, mainly brahmins. Neither *Kanyasulkam* (Bride Price) nor *Raja Sekhara Charitam*, written by Appa Rao and Veereshalingam respectively, addressed the fundamental problem of caste oppression and the alienation of dalit masses from the mainstream society. This does not mean that their contribution to social reform is negligible, yet, strangely, problems central to the varna system escaped their attention. While they sought to reform certain evils of the Hindu social system, they failed to grapple with the ideological and institutional framework of brahmanical Hinduism. Their reading of classical texts and scriptures was only aimed at reforming some aspects of Hindu society, not to question and negate the varna system itself.

Thus the social reformers of modern Andhra did not inherit and continue the medieval bhakti tradition; it was discontinued. This discontinuation was possible perhaps because of the fact that unlike the bhakti saint-poets, the social reformers compromised the existing social order. Also, given their social background and intellectual and cultural tradition, they could not profess anti-feudal and anti-colonial/caste ideology and consciousness. Unlike the saint-poets they did not revolt against all kinds of social evils. They were selective in their philosophical and ideological standpoint. In this sense, the modern social reformers failed to generate and build a popular cultural and ideological movement against the caste system.

Nevertheless, the nationalist literature generated since the time of the Vandemataram Movement reflected the problem of the dalit masses, albeit to a limited extent. It was put to both social and political use. The Gandhian movement inspired a number of scholars who argued that national liberation would herald a new epoch in which discrimination and oppression of all sorts would be abolished. In order to build a united and coherent anti-colonial movement, they exhorted the people, through their writings, to eradicate social evils and unite. In this context, novels such as Unnava Laxminarayana's *Malapalli* (1922, 'Harijan Hamlet') and Ranga's *Harijana Nayakudu* (1933) are socially significant literary works. Both of them depicted the problem of untouchability and the misery of dalits, but they suggested that with certain changes and modifications, the existing caste system could be maintained. The solution to the dalit problem is offered within the existing framework of the caste system. In a sense, it was not a truly realistic representation of the dalit question. Therefore, in the writings of non-dalit scholars the problems of untouchability and caste discrimination were not reflected as serious and fundamental. They advocated minor reforms and adjustments, yet favoured continuation of the existing unequal social hierarchy. For them the dalit masses became an object of pity and sympathy. The nationalist intelligentsia, which was isolated and distanced from the dalit masses, failed to fully grasp and comprehend the oppression and discrimination faced by the dalit masses in their everyday life. Though they were inspired by the ideology of nationalism, they were insensitive to the socio-cultural and economic oppression of the dalit communities. The aspirations and emotional feelings of the dalit masses were not adequately taken cognisance of by the middle class intellectuals who were predominantly drawn from the upper castes. It was precisely for this reason that the Gandhian programme of 'Harijan upliftment' was a failure. A dalit poet ridiculed the commitment of pseudo-Gandhian upper caste activities towards the upliftment of untouchables. He wrote:

> You prove that you are the descendants of sages
> Outwardly you call us brothers
> You boast to have listened to the teachings of Gandhi
> Nobody follows (him), is not it injustice
> You forget the words of Mahatma Gandhi
> You burn with anger at the untouchables.[7]

Gandhi's constructive programme (of Harijan upliftment, temple entry, etc.) was popularised in Andhra with a view to integrate the dalit masses into the fold of the mainstream nationalist movement. However, his socio-political programme was never fully realised due to the alienation of the dalit communities for whom the nationalist appeal was meaningless insofar as it did not incorporate their sufferings, emotions and aspirations. Thus a dalit poet opined, 'Equality is Swaraj.'

However, if the nationalist literature of the 1920s only partially reflected the dalit question, the progressive literary tradition of the 1940s was no better; undoubtedly the progressive writers who were guided by the philosophy and ideology of Marxism[8] propounded the rise of a classless society. The Marxist literary and cultural movement became a powerful social force. But the basic flaw in this literary tradition was that it did not adequately take note of the different kinds of non-class exploitation such as caste, gender, ethnic group, and religion, which existed in society. Class struggle and class oppression were seen as universal laws. As Ambedkar pointed out, Marxist scholars in India failed to adequately understand and comprehend the caste-specific character of Indian society.[9] Though the progressive writers guided by a socialist perspective pleaded for socio-economic justice, their writings did not adequately reflect caste oppression and discrimination. Attacks on the caste system, abolition of caste oppression, social equality and self-respect of the dalit masses were not the themes that characterized their writings. Barring a few, a majority of the progressive writers were drawn from the upper 'savarna' castes. Thus like their predecessors (i.e., the nationalist intelligentsia of the 1920s) the progressive writers tended to address the problems confronted by the middle classes and advocated piecemeal social reform.[10] It has been noted by a literary critic that the progressive writers association was dominated by middle class intellectuals mostly drawn from the non dalit upper castes. He wrote, 'the progressive literature did not go beneath the middle class readers.'[11] Another scholar remarked:

> "... the literary activities of the PWA which were...confined primarily to middle class intellectuals, and also, to some extent, to the literate and marginally to a few people from lower middle and middle and poor peasants and working class sections. By and large, the major sections of lower order were left out of its impact."[12] It was so because, "all those drawn into the PWA were not a part of the Communist Party cadre. Some of them were fellow travellers and some were not even that."[13]

It is no wonder that then many scholars and intellectuals from dalit backgrounds were not a part of this progressive literary tradition. At the political level as well the Communist Party failed to integrate the vast majority of the dalit masses into the larger struggle for liberation.

An examination of the nature of social participation in the freedom struggle in Andhra indicates that there was no considerable participation of the dalit masses. This was mainly due to the fact that economically and educationally advanced upper caste groups dominated the Congress. Social inequality, caste discrimination, illiteracy, poverty, etc. kept the dalit communities away from the mainstream nationalist struggle, at least until the 1930s. The ideology of nationalism did not inspire them as they were subjected to severe socio-cultural discrimination and oppression by the same upper caste forces which championed and led the anti-colonial national movement. The upper caste leadership also failed to evolve a programme and perspective of socio-cultural emancipation for the dalits. Hence they distanced themselves from the liberation struggle. Also, the Gandhian programme and technique did not completely succeed in integrating them into the fold of the freedom struggle. The aspirations and emotional feelings of the dalit masses did not become an integral part of the nationalist ideology and programme. The nationalist literary and cultural tradition denied a legitimate place and role to them. Thus the political and socio-cultural assertion of the dalit masses developed independently and outside the organizational framework of the Congress party.

In Andhra, the struggle for the emancipation of dalits from the clutches of upper caste domination and for the achievement of social equality was launched by the Adi-Andhra Mahasabha. Its first conference was held at Bejawada on November 4-6, 1917, under the presidentship of Bhagya Reddi Varma. It was the beginning of dalit self-mobilisation for self-respect and social equality. A series of Adi-Andhra conferences were held between 1917 and 1938 in different parts of Andhra, which helped in the mobilisation of the dalit masses in their struggle for social justice.[14] The educated and enlightened sections within the dalit communities provided the direction, programme and leadership for the movement. Persons such as Bhagya Reddi Varma, Sundru Venkaiah, Kusuma Dharmanna, Vemula Kurmaiah, *et al.* provided the leadership for the dalit movement. The basic thrust of the movement was to critique the ideology of brahmanical Hinduism and counter the socio-cultural hegemony of the upper castes. It also sought to organize the dalit masses for achieving socio-economic and political equality. The main item in the agenda of the movement was the abolition of untouchability, caste oppression and discrimination. The counte-cultural movement and ideology propagated by dalit intellectuals contained a critique and negation of brahmanical Hinduism and undermend of the cultural tradition of caste Hindus. These aspects were well represented in the literary and cultural traditions of dalits in the 1930s and 1940s. The literary, cultural and ideological articulation of dalit identity and sensibility was projected by the first generation of dalit intellectuals. They were the products of western education, which was made available to them by Christian missionaries and the Brahma Samaj. During the first quarter of twentieth century, the spread of education (though limited) among dalit communities was made possible due to the prolonged activities of missionaries in coastal Andhra. Therefore, the Krishna, Godavari and Guntur districts witnessed the active movement of the Adi-Andhra Mahasabha. The dalit literary and cultural tradition was also established in Coastal Andhra. In the following section a random survey of the writings of dalit scholars is undertaken, with special reference to the literary works of Gurram Jashuva, Boyi Bheemanna, Kusuma Dharmanna, and also Bhagya Reddi Varma.

In an effort to create solidarity and identity among the dalit masses, Bhagya Reddi Varma asserted that the so-called untouchables were never a part and parcel of caste Hindu(Aryan) society.[15] He criticized the Aryan gods such as Rama who perpetrated injustices and atrocities on Shudras and dalits. He went on to suggest a break from Hindu tradition and religion as the primary necessity for putting an end to the plight of dalit communities as well as to maintain their separate identity. He stressed that dalits were the original inhabitants of the land ('sons of the soil') and called themselves the [6]Adi-Andhras'. This term was coined and consciously put to use to denote the unity of dalits. He opposed and rejected the derogatory term 'panchamas' used by the upper castes. Maha Kavi Gurram Jashuva questioned the creation of the panchama varna. He also questioned the wisdom of the upper caste Hindus in treating the dalit masses as panchamas/outcastes.[16] His poem reads:

> We heard that for the old Brahma
> Born Four Sons
> The wretched lower than the animal
> Who is this Fifth Caste person!
> Savithri! (Mother).

The Adi-Andhra Mahasabha demanded that the government designate the dalits as Adi-Andhras, and this was conceded. Similarly Bhoi Bheemanna coined another term MaMas which indicated the two main sub-castes within the dalits (Ma = Mala; Ma = Madiga). This term was deliberately used by him to foster the concept of unity among the dalit communities.[17] Jashuva was critical of sub-caste rivalry among dalit communities. He felt that ignorance was the main reason for this.

In addition to these terms the dalit writers also traced the common ancestry of dalit communities. They claimed that they are the children of 'Matangi Kanya' and the descendants of Arundhati. In his drama *Ragavashistham*, Bheemanna offered a critique of the brahmanical interpretation of the origin and status of dalits. It is intended to reject the brahmanical reading of certain Hindu classical texts. It is also a negation of the brahmanical view, which attributes the lowest and meanest birth to the untouchable castes. The marital relationship between Arundhati (the Matangi girl) and Vasishta (the Brahmin sage) is interpreted by Bheemanna to claim the highest social status for the dalits. The message conveyed through this drama is that the dalits are not the outcastes and that they have a legitimate claim for the higher social status and prestige/privilege enjoyed by the caste Hindus. Jala Ranga Swamy, in a long poem titled "who are the untouchables" criticized the upper caste Hindus for caste discrimination and asserted the rights of dalits to social equality. He reasoned that the so-called panchamas were the original people ('anaryas') of the Telugu country. The Aryan invaders defeated the anarya rulers and subjugated them. Further, the Aryan conquerors imposed their rule and culture on the anaryas. The latter were oppressed, discriminated against and relegated to slavery (outcaste). The poem reads:

> Some occupations were created and assigned to us
> We were named as serfs
> Caste discrimination was introduced, we were suppressed
> We were troubled with slavery/serfdom
> Occupational differences were imposed, we were alienated.[18]

While denouncing the Aryan conquest, which led to the enslavement of the dalits, the poet (Ranga Swamy) proclaimed the glory of their (anaryas) past by claiming the great sages and pious/chaste women of the ancient times. The poem reads as follows:

> The great Warriors of Puranas were our people
> Vashistha, Valmiki etc. belonged to our dynasty

Vedavyasa, Parasara were our people
Hanuman, Sugreeva were our brothers…
Did not the great mothers of Heros born amongst us
Did not they observe chastity
Is not Arundhathi, the daughter of our caste
Sabari, Matangi were our women…
A caste in which such great people were born being alienated
We were made lowly people, excommunicated[19]

Bhoi Bheemanna pleaded for social equality. He wrote:

Around the neck of the powerful Indian Nation
Caste, religion are the hangman's ropes…
Destroy the guile of caste and religion
Eradicate the human inequalities.[20]

The most forceful attack on upper caste Hindus, who are said to be responsible for the perpetuation of caste discrimination and excommunication of the dalit masses, was launched by Kusuma Dharmanna. He was a bitter critic of brahmanical Hinduism. In his long poem, 'we do not want the rule of black landlords,' he portrayed the miserable and pathetic living conditions of the dalit masses. He wrote:

(We have) only small huts outside the village
We do not have big houses
Air, light do not trifle
(We have) no delicious food, curry
To wear (we have) no Saree, Loin cloth
(We have) no tail, ornaments
(We have) no land to plough, eat food
(You have) no sympathy on our poverty.[21]

The claim for social equality was widely propagated by the Adi-Andhra Mahasabha through its resolutions and demands for the use of public wells, educational institutions, temples, etc, by the dalits. The aspirations of the dalit masses for social equality was negated and vehemently opposed by the arrogant upper castes, and dalits were subjected to physical attacks and reprisals. In the Andhra countryside a number of violent incidents occurred in the

1930s and 1940s when the dalit communities persisted in their struggle for equality and self-respect. A few instances will suffice to make this point clear. In Gajularega village (Vishakhapatnam district) a newly married dalit couple were taken in a procession on horseback through the main streets of the village; in Manglagunta (Chittoor district), dalits walked in the streets wearing footwear; in Eluru (west Godavari), dalits took out a religious procession on a festival day through the same street which was used by the upper castes; a dalit disciple worshipped the goddess Aluvelu Manga (wife of Lord Venkateshwara) in Tirupati for which a case was foisted against him.[22] These acts by the dalit masses enraged the upper castes in the respective villages and resulted in physical attacks on them. Such assaults from the caste Hindus helped in strengthening the feeling of their distinct identity. Thus caste oppression and discrimination became the central themes in the writings of dalit scholars. In particular, Kusuma Dharmanna in his writings and speeches (inaugural address to the Dalit Mahasabha Conference, Vizianagaram, 1936) exposed the false, hypocritical and cunning nature of Hinduism and ridiculed the brahmanical double-standards. He freely quoted verses from the works of the medieval saint-poets/scholars such as Vemana and Veerabhrahmam to denounce the unequal and inhuman Hindu social order.[23] He appealed to the dalit masses to unite and fight for socialism. He felt that it was through the achievement of social equality alone that the dalit masses could hope for a decent living and self-respect. By socialism ('Samyavadam') he meant,

> "a society where there will be no distinctions based on caste, religion, rich and poor; a society in which there will be no place for discrimination and internal rivalry."

The urge for dignified living, self-respect and social equality is powerfully presented in the works of Jashuva and Bheemanna. Jashuva, a great creative poet and a literary genius of the modern times, was humiliated and subjected to intense mental agony by the inhuman caste system as well as by arrogant and casteist scholars. He was treated as a literary outcaste by the scholarly world which was dominated by the upper castes, mainly the Brahmins.

His creative genius, merit and literary talent were not recognized and encouraged because of his low birth and dalit background. But he was not a coward. He resisted and exposed the cruelty of caste oppression through his pen. He said, " Life taught me many lessons. I have two teachers (Gurus)—poverty and Caste/ Religious discrimination. If one taught me patience, the other one increased my power to resist, but did not convert me as a slave. I intend to pierce through caste distinction, and poverty and prove that I am a human being. I wield a sword. My sword is my poverty. It has no hatred against the society as such. But hatred on its policy."[24] In the poetry of Jashuva the anger, agony, disgust, misery and the daily bitter experiences of the dalit masses/communities are most authentically and realistically represented. His famous poetical works, *'The Bat'*, *'The Orphan'*, etc. indirectly mirror the bitter experiences and stark realities of his personal life. It is noted that 'The Bat' graphically reflects his growing resistance, consciousness and longing for better human values. In this text he posed a number of questions to Hindu society, religion and culture which is responsible for the perpetration of untouchability. 'The Bat' is the first poetical work in which a dalit is the hero. The poet speaks through him. It depicts the miserable life and sufferings of the dalit masses.

> When his (Dalit's) hands do not work
> The green fields hesitate to yield crops
> His sweat, provides food for the world
> But he himself has no food.[25]

The material condition of the dalit masses who worked as agricultural labourers is revealed in such poems. He ridiculed the Brahmins who treat the dalits as untouchables but use the food-grains produced by them as offerings to the gods in the temples; when they (the dalits) do not produce food the gods will go hungry.

> By swallowing the blood of the wretched (dalit)
> Lives the iron ankleted Mother
> Upon smelling his air hisses with vengeance
> The four-hood Hindu Cobra.

This poem is a reflection of how the poisonous snake called Hinduism perpetuates oppression of dalits by savarnas.

Jashuva wrote his bitter and moving poetry at a time when the dalit masses were launching struggles for self-respect, independently and outside the framework of both the Congress and left parties. Boyi Bheemanna captured the intensity and essence of the struggles of the dalits for socio-economic and political justice and reflected them in his two plays, *Paleru* ('Annual Servant') and *Cooli Raju* ('The Labour King').

Paleru depicts the village life of coastal Andhra, which was characterized by socio-economic stratification in which the agricultural labourers were drawn basically from the dalit communities, while the landlords belonged to the upper castes. The dalits were economically and educationally the most backward community. Government efforts and Gandhian programmes played no significant role in their upliftment. Social evils like untouchability and caste discrimination continued to be practiced. Moreover, caste ideology denied them any access to knowledge and education. The hero of the play, Venkanna, a dalit 'Paleru', works for the same landlord who employed his forefathers. He is a victim of hereditary bonded labour practiced by the upper caste landlords in the name of custom and tradition. The little paleru, on seeing the upper caste children of his age going to school, is also inclined to study. In spite of rigid customary sanctions the hero, with the help of an upper caste school teacher, was encouraged to go to school and study. But his landlord cannot tolerate such an idea. He does not even like the paleru singing songs in the fields. However, with the help of the school teacher and an upper caste girl, the paleru decides to escape from the village and to go to Rajamundry (a nearby town) and join the school run by the Brahmo Samaj. One day when the landlord comes to know about the intentions of the paleru, he scolds his father. The dialogue is instructive of the attitudes of the upper castes towards the efforts of the dalit masses to educate themselves and acquire knowledge:

> Kuberaiah (landlord): O, son of a he buffalo!
> Did anybody go to school in your family?
> Pullaiah (Dalit): Yes sir, Ah Ah is it? No sir no.

K: Is not it a sin for you to read (and write)?

P: Big sin lord. Very big sin indeed. Neither during the time of my grandfather, nor my father, myself, nor even my son Yenkadu...

K: Stop. It is alright until your time. With your son Yenkadu the tradition of your family is destroyed.

P: No my lord. I swear, I pledge my life. My son is not like that.

K : You son of a donkey. Why does a son of a slave need education?

P: To whom my lord? Even if you cut my stomach, there is no word in it.

K: Oh! Your Yenkadu.

P: Oh my goodness.

K: He will be of no use.

P: O my God! (beats chest).

K: He is not doing any work. He always sings and reads books. Stop him from doing agricultural labour. Educate and make him a collector. Get lost.

P : We are your slaves my lord. Save us my lord. I will kick that son of a donkey. I will bury him. What stops you my lord? You should have broken his bones.

K : Well. I did something. If you can teach him good manners and behaviour keep him here or else look for some other way. As you are dependent on me since your childhood I am just thinking. OK you can go.

The Father goes home and beats his son. Later the boy runs away from the village, pursues his studies and secures a BA degree. After that he becomes a Deputy Collector. He also marries the upper caste girl, his childhood friend.

The central theme of his play is an urge for social equality and the acquisition of knowledge and education by the dalit masses for a decent living as well as for a respectable place in society. In it there is a suggestion that through education and inter-caste marriage social mobility is possible. The author opined that the problems of dalits is not only that of class. In Indian society the dalits, unlike other castes, have no opportunity to lead a respectable life. Hence dalits should be educated and should obtain good official positions. This play also represents the educational and professional needs of dalits, for education was seen to be a social and political power. The play is imaginary no doubt, but it is a guide to many real life experiences of the dalit masses. It was staged in many villages of coastal Andhra. As a literary creation it became the basis for social change/mobility. The author remarked that many young dalits, inspired by the play, left their traditional occupation and took to education. The popularity of this play is indicated by the fact that in 1953, Bheemanna (the author) was facilitated in Ponnur village, Guntur district, on the occasion of its hundredth performance.

In this chapter we have presented an analysis of the beginning of a literary genre which can broadly be called dalit literature.[26] Although most of the scholars whose writings are examined in this article did not exclusively write about and/or for the dalit masses, yet being products of dalit communities they represented the problems of the masses and their emerging consciousness in their works more sympathetically and realistically than the non-dalit scholars who preceded them. There seems to be a fundamental difference between the savarna scholars who projected the dalit problem in their writings and the representation by the dalit scholars. The non-dalit (upper caste) scholars were distanced and stood aloof from the dalit masses. They were also unfamiliar with dalit emotions, aspirations and living conditions. If at all there was any solidarity, affinity and link between these scholars and the dalit names it was purely emotional. Such an emotion was guided by an ideology of nationalism and Marxism, about which the large majority of the dalit masses were ignorant. In contrast, the dalit intelligentsia had good knowledge of and insight into the life experience of the masses about whose problems they wrote; their thoughts and feelings were fused with those of the masses. The subject matter for their works was provided by the everyday life experience and existential problems of the dalit masses. These writers, who found inexhaustible raw material in the society and community in which they and the masses were born, shaped it into a realistic literary representation. The main characteristic feature of dalit literature was its contemporaneity and realistic presentation. The savarna scholars who depicted dalit problems in their writings were guided neither by the philosophical and ideological tradition of the bhakti saint-poets nor by the liberation ideology and philosophy of Phule and Ambedkar. The dalit scholars critiqued the brahmanical social order and Hindu ideology based on the philosophy and ideology of both the bhakti saint-poets as well as Phule and Ambedkar. In this sense it can be said that the dalit intellectuals of the pre-independence period were the forerunners to the contemporary dalit literary and cultural movements in the state.

REFERENCES

[An earlier version of this paper was presented at a seminar on 'Caste and Power in India', organized by Satyashodhak: Centre for Social Research, Hyderabad, at Kakatiya University, Warangal, March 12-14, 1994.]

1. J.K. Lele and R. Singh, *Language and Literature of Dalits and Sants: Some Missed Opportunities, op. cit.*
2. Karamchedu is a prosperous village in Guntur district. It is dominated socio-economically and politically, by the Kammas, a dominant peasant caste, "In 1985 July 17 unable to bear the assertion and self-respect of the dalits, the kammas armed with spears and crowbars and all sorts of weapons killed six persons, raped nine women and wounded as many." K. Padma Rao, *Social and Philosophical Movements in India*, Ponnur, 1990, p. 12.
3. J.B. Gokhale-Turner, "Bhakti or Vidroha" in *Journal of Asian and African Studies*, Vol. XV, Nos. 1-2, 1980, p. 29.
4. Before the Gandhian era the living conditions and problems of untouchable communities were depicted in novels such as *Helavati* (1913) and *Matrumandiram* (1919). See S.V. Satyanarayana, "Dalita Sahityam: Charitraka Nepathyam" in *Abhyudaya*, January-March 1993, p. 93.
5. V. Ramakrishna, "Literary and Theatre Movements in Colonial Andhra: Struggle for Left Ideological Legitimacy", *Social Scientist*, Vol. 21, Nos. 1-2, 1993, p. 71.
6. For a critical analysis of social reform movements in Andhra see K. Venkaiah, *Prajaswamika Parishkaram*, Guntur, nd, pp. 16-43.
7. Jala Rangaswamy, *Who are the Untouchables*, Rajamundry, 1930, p. 9.
8. See Ramakrishna, *op. cit.*, pp. 73-77.

9. B. R. Ambedkar, *Collected Works*, Vol. 3, Bombay, 1990.
10. See K. V. Ramana Reddy's Telugu articles edited by Ch. Prasad, *Adhunikaandhra Sahithya Charitra*, Vijayawada, 1992, pp. 154-55.
11. *Ibid*. p. 150.
12. Ramakrishna, *op. cit*., p. 78.
13. *Ibid*, p. 76.
14. See Gail Omvedt, *Dalits and the Democratic Revolution*, New Delhi, 1994.
15. D. Ramulu Nayak, M.V. "*Bhagya Reddi Varma, Life and Mission*", unpublished M. Phil. dissertation, Dept. of History, Osmania University, Hyderabad, 1992.
16. Cited in C. Narayana Reddy, "*Sameekshanam*", Hyderabad, 1981, p. 27.
17. See the autobiographical account of Bheemanna, *Haimavathi Paleru Nunchi Padmasri Varaku*, (Telugu) Hyderabad, 1978.
18. Rangaswamy, *op. cit*., pp. 3-4.
19. *Ibid*., pp. 4-5.
20. Cited in Satyanarayana, *Telugu Udyama Geetaalu*, Hyderabad, 1991, p. 429.
21. *Ibid*., p. 116.
22. K. Dharmanna, "Samyavadanni Sahinchani Hinduism", reproduced in *NALUPU*, November 16-December 15, 1992, and January 1, 1993.
23. *Ibid*.
24. Cited in N. Gopi, "*Jashuva Pratighatana Chaitanyam*" (mimeo).
25. *Ibid*.
26. See Satyanarayana, *op. cit*., pp. 44-62; K. Prasad, *Dalita Sahityam*, Vijayawada, 1993; K. Padma Rao, *Mahakavi Jashuva Samajika Tatwamu*, Ponnuru, 1992.

5

Dalit Identity and Consciousness in Colonial Andhra, 1917-1947

In the existing historical literature on modern Andhra, the emergence of a Dalit consciousness and of a distinct Dalit sensibility did not receive adequate attention.[1] What the Dalits thought about their condition, in their own terms, has not been properly analysed by scholars. The fact that Dalits have the intellectual ability to creatively and analytically reflect on their conditions, in their own language, both historically and sociologically, has been missed out. Most scholars tend to characterise Dalits as a social force that is passive and mute, lacking any initiative and self-assertion. Thus, the efforts of Dalits to represent "themselves to themselves and to others" in their own terms need explanation and elucidation. Furthermore, the emergence of well informed Dalit thinkers and commentators makes possible the analysis of the way in which Dalits symbolise their experience of oppressive subjugation, and moreover, how they struggle to create new socio-cultural identities and ideological bases for autonomous reflection and self-action. Anger is thus configured in these representations in terms of self-awareness, consciousness and imagination of empowering identities. It must be stressed that the literary representation of Dalit resentment and anger towards upper caste dominance has been a historical phenomenon. The emergence of a distinct Dalit poetry, literary tradition and the creation of "texts of resistance"[2] and "protest literature"[3] not only reflectes changing consciousness, but also symbolises the intensification of the Dalit quest for dignity and social justice.

The main purpose of this chapter is to examine the sociohistorical context and articulation of Dalit self-perception and consciousness under colonialism. Central to this is an analysis of the nature and character of *Dalit intellectual ferment* and alternative ideological formulation. During the colonial period the Dalit self-identity was constructed and articulated in terms of a critique of Brahminical Hinduism, caste ideology and philosophy. Thus denunciation of the existing caste system and untouchability were a recurring themes in Dalit scholarly writings, poems, short stories, essays and plays. In this paper, an attempt is made to analyse some of the writings of Dalit scholars like Kusuma Dharmanna, Nakka Chinnavenkaiah and Jala Rangaswamy. Further, it seeks to explain the historical roots of the Dalit *protest* in colonial Andhra between 1917-47 and to demonstrate how it sought to undermine and challenge the prevailing social order. An attempt is also made to describe some aspects of the growth of Dalit mobilisation through an analysis of the rise and growth of the Adi-Andhra movement during the pre-independence period.

Articulation of the Self and the Other

It can be said that the assertion of the Dalit identity is rooted in colonial Andhra, which, since the beginning of the twentieth century, had been undergoing both socio-economic transformations as well as socio-political turmoil. The completion of major irrigation systems and the growth of commercial agriculture resulted in increasingly stratified agrarian societies in the rural Andhra districts.[4] Having been placed at the bottom of society's caste centred hierarchy, Dalits, in masses, were the chief victims of exploitation and oppression at the hands of upper caste landlords and the rich peasant class. Caste restrictions and obligations condemned them to a toilsome, undignified and degrading means of livelihood. The traditional occupation of the Malas was to work as agricultural labourers for caste Hindu land-owning communities. Thus they became the "backbone of the agricultural labour force" in colonial Andhra. Similarly the caste-defined traditional occupation of the Madigas was leather work and making footwear. But most of them worked as agricultural labourers. Moreover, the social distribution of landed property closely corresponded to the caste hierarchy, wherein the Brahmin and Sat-Shudra communities like the Reddy, Kamma, Kapu, Velama etc. had considerable access to land and other economic resources, while the Dalits were compelled to work mostly as field labourers. An examination of the census data available on caste and occupation indicates that the Mala and Madiga communities constituted the bulk of the agricultural labour force and worked as farm servants, *palerus* and casual workers. Very few of them possessed land.[5] The involvement of the entire family, i.e., men, women and children was a unique feature of Dalit communities. Unlike other lower Shudra castes, the overwhelming participation of Dalit women in agriculture and other related occupations is very conspicuous. Gail Omvedt has observed that, "Data indicates low work participation of women among the Brahmin castes... contrastingly, among the peasant Jatis it is quite high.. while it is highest of all among the Dalits."[6] Hence, the main source of livelihood for the Dalit households was productive and manual labour.

The dependence of Dalit communities on upper caste landholders, and the exploitative relationship between them, was articulated in numerous poems and short stories by Dalit scholars. In a powerful poem, "Maakoddie Nalla Doratanam" (We Do not Want This Black Landlordism), Kusuma Dharmanna 'a born poet, a gifted speaker, an able leader'[7] and a 'Kavi Veera'[8] depicted the miserable condition of Dalits, thus:[9]

> We don't want this black landlordism, O God, "We don't want"
> If we don't have dignity in the society "We don't want"
> As Palerus for the whole twelve months
> We live with hunger
> Our Wives should work as Coolies, Children must tend cattle
> Even if we all toil together, we have no clothes to wear, nothing to eat.,
> "We don't want"
> Our debts would not be cleared off, O God
> Mercilessly they make us slaves
> If we cultivate lands and provide milk they (caste Hindus) sit and enjoy
> They go on increasing our debts
> They beat us and drag us to courts
> O God, they destroy our livelihood, "We don't want"
> Though we are husbandmen, they abuse us

By taking the names of our mothers and wives
They kick us, squeeze our blood and flesh
Compel us to plough the lands, But O God
They hate the Malas and Madigas, "We don't want."

In another long poem, Harijan Shatakam wrote about the suffering of Dalit agricultural labourers.[10]

In Sunshine, Rain and Cold
Why would the (Dalit) labourer serve the Ryot?
What is the reward/result?
The Ryot would feed him with worthless stuff
He (the Ryot) would increase his (labourer's) debt
Crush him and drag him into the street
You (the Dalit labourer) plough like a Bull
Bring happiness and pleasure to the Ryot
Yet Doesn't he hate and wound you?

In this poem, the poet describes how the toiling Dalit masses produce wealth by their hard labour, and how caste Hindu rich peasants perpetuate violence on them. The sorrow and anger of Dalit labourers is creatively presented in this poem. It also depicts the multiple dimensions of exploitation of Dalit masses by the rich peasantry. The conflict between the rich peasant and the agricultural labourer is brilliantly and powerfully portrayed in Kusum Dharmanna's poem. The significant aspect of this poem is "the true representation of unfolding contemporary social reality"[11] under colonial conditions. Further, the poet calls for the unification of the labouring masses who were divided and whose caste had fallen to the ground. He also exhorts them to proclaim their self-respect, carry on the social revolution, and take revenge by resorting to strikes. He felt that Dalit masses would be able to eradicate their poverty, acquire wealth, respectability and rights only by waging a relentless struggle and if necessary sacrificing their lives.

The representation of human degradation, exploitation, poverty, and miserable economic conditions was meant to suggest and inculcate a sense of homogeneity among the Dalits, and emphasise the need for organised collective activity. The unity of the community was stressed in order to mobilise them under the exclusive organisation/association of Dalits themselves. Perhaps, it was also meant to remind fellow caste men to challenge and reject their slavery to the dominant upper caste exploiters. In one speech, Dharmanna questions the assumption that Dalit communities should be condemned for their entire lives to exist as coolies and slaves. He exhorts them to assert their individuality and confidently offirm that, "Yes I am a human being. I have self-respect. I do want leisure and pleasure in life."[12] He also argues for self-help and denounces dependence on others. Further, he calls for the self-upliftment of the entire community.

The idea of oneness among Dalits was also propagated by tracing their common ancestry and social roots. Bhagya Reddi Verma, the foremost leader and intellectual of the Adi-Andhra Mahasabha, rejected caste Hindu constructions of their own selves as Panchamas and Chandalas. He coined the new name of Adi-Andhra, and enunciated the theory of being sons of the soil and the original inhabitants. He also denounced the low status attributed to the Adi-Andhras and asserted their equality with others. The Adi-Andhra identity was justified by accepting the great Rishis and Goddesses of ancient India like Valmiki, Vashishta, Vyasa, Parasara, Mantanga, Arundhati, Sabari as ancestors. Similar views were echoed by many other Dalit poets like Jala Ranga Swamy.[13] As Bharat Patankar and Gail Omvedt have elsewhere pointed out central to the thinking of Dalit intellectuals in different parts of colonial India "was the Adi theme, a definition of themselves as the original inhabitants of the country, the claim that their own inherent traditions were those of equality and unity, and the total rejection of caste (chaturvarnya, varnashrama dharma) as the imposition of the conquering Aryans who used this to subjugate and divide the natives. Very often, this went with a rejection of Hinduism as the religion of the invaders and the main support of caste society."[14] In his Presidential Address to the first Adi-Andhra Conference, Bhagya Reddi Verma remarked,

> "We are not Dogs or Crows. Just as a Brahmin's mother gives birth to him, our mothers also give birth to us. Did their mothers feed them with milk and our mothers feed us with Blood? No. Not at

> all. We are also human beings like them, but not animals. God has given us all the abilities just as he had given the Brahmins. We have the same soul as that of the Brahmins."[15]

Kusuma Dharmanna ridiculed and denounced caste Hindus for the inhuman and irrational practice of untouchability :[16]

> They consider us inferior to Dogs and Foxes
> Sit beside a Leprosy patient
> Domesticate Dogs and Monkeys with affection
> Love Cats and Birds
> Don't trouble Pigs
> Allow Crows to touch water
> But abuse us and don't allow us to approach them.

He also sarcastically remarked that because caste Hindus worship Dogs as Shiva, Monkeys as Hanuman, Pig as Varaha, they treat the poor Dalit human beings as being inferior to these animals. The consciousness that Hindus worship animals and condemn human beings is similar to that of Phule's expression in his famous book *Gulam Giri*. Expressions such as "we are not animals" reveals the agony, anger and hatred of Dalits against the arrogant upper castes." By claiming the Adi-Andhra identity, they sought to disown their low status in society. Attempts were also made to obtain a new group identity through a change in nomenclature and by concerted action, to get this officially recognised. A study on the Scheduled Castes of Andhra noted that,

> "Till the 1921 census, the Malas and Madigas were the only two castes to be listed as "Depressed Classes" in the Telugu speaking areas of [the] Madras Presidency. But, by 1931, the list included a number of castes... Most of these castes claiming impressive titles such as Matangi, Arundhathi, and Godari, were none other than the offshoots of the Malas and Madigas. By claiming these titles they were seeking to disown their low status."[17]

The Adi identity was also stressed by citing legends from Hindu mythology.[18]

The assertion of self-respect was an equally important aspect of the growing Dalit consciousness during the colonial period. Dalit intellectuals questioned the legitimacy of caste Hindu rationalisation of untouchability. They refused to acknowledge the Hindu philosophical justification of ascriptive social order and inequality.[19] Thus, Kusuma Dharmanna rejected the notion that untouchability was attributed to the Dalits because they did not follow the *Varnashrama Dharma.*

He wrote:

> You have been excommunicated
> Because you have left the Varna Dharma
> Say the Caste Hindus, but
> Brahmins have left the study of Vedas
> Kshatriyas have forgotten their caste profession
> Shudras have stopped cultivation
> Father, then "where is the Varnashrama Dharma in this?

The poet blames caste Hindus for excommunicating the Dalits and the perpetuation of untouchability. He continued:[20]

> As a result of Age old caste Hindu enmity
> We are distanced from the village
> We are not great in any sense to the village Munsiff (patel)
> Karnam (Accountant), we are a stinking lot
> Kammas and Kapus do not mix with us, O God
> We have become a stinking lot for the whole people.

In another poem Dharmanna calls upon fellow Dalits to burn and destroy the devil of untouchability and uphold their self-respect. Another notable Dalit poet, Nakka Chinnavenkaiah, in his poem "*Antudoshamu*" ("Sin of untouchability")[21], appealed to the upper castes to end the practice of untouchability and asserted that real freedom would come only after it was abolished. Further, he said that temple entry and the use of common wells would promote unity and interaction among the whole community and lead to social equality and harmony. Jala Rangaswamy in his two long poems, "*Antaranivarevaru*"[22] ("Who are the untouchables"?) and "Mala Shuddi"[23] ("Cleanlines of Malas?") vividly described the social deprivation of the Dalits and demanded social equality with others. He disputes the Brahminical interpretation of the reasons for the low and untouchable status of Dalit communities. He does this by reinterpreting some of the Hindu Texts and asking the caste

Hindu to re-read them. In their poems, the "Dalit triumvirate" viz., Kusuma Dharmanna, Nakka China Venkaiah, and Jala Rangaswamy, constructed a distinct ideology of the annihilation of caste and social equality, which was quite contrary to the Gandhian nationalist ideology. They wrote these poems in the 1930s at a time when the Gandhian mass movements were at their peak, yet their poetry did not reflect and represent the political aspirations of the upper caste nationalist intelligentsia. For Dalit intellectuals, real freedom and liberation meant the end of untouchability, excommunication and social discrimination. They demanded social equality, self- respect, and dignity as an integral part of independence (Swarjyam/Swantatryam).

The emergence of the Dalit movement and Dalit literary texts was related to the specific socio-political upheaval in colonial Andhra which was characterised by the growing social reform (Brahma Samaj, Arya Samaj, etc.) and non-Brahmin movements, under the leadership of upper caste Hindus. Likewise, the constitutional reforms, viz., the Montague Chelmsford Reforms also gave an impetus to the self-organisation and political mobilisation of the Dalits in their demand for a share in colonial representative institutions. The rise and growth of the Adi-Andhra movement since 1917 was influenced to a significant extent by the earlier social reform movements, for a number of leaders of the Adi-Andhra Mahasabha were associated with them. Bhagyareddi Varma is a case in point. Moreover, some of the Brahmins of the Brahmo Samaj in Coastal Andhra were instrumental in imparting a sense of 'self and the other' awareness among the Dalits by imparting modern education to them. Many schools and hostels exclusively meant for the untouchable communities were established by leaders of the Brahma Samaj. In fact, many of the first generation Dalit intellectuals and leaders were the products of such educational institutions.[24] It has been said that, "The Brahmins were instrumental in grooming several of the educated Harijan leaders outside the Christian fold...by the 1920s when Gandhiji took up their cause at the national level, there was widespread awareness of their conditions among the untouchables in Andhra, and several untouchable leaders had already come to the fore...What Brahmoism, however, succeeded in doing was to impart a social consciousness which nevertheless fostered a sense of identity among the untouchables."[25]

However, an examination of the historical process of the evolution of Dalit consciousness and a shared identity reveals a significant break with the early reform movements, both in terms of ideology and in terms of organisation. In a sense, the growth of the Adi-Andhra Mahasabha represented the widening of the principles of the broader non/anti-Brahmin movement and its social radicalism in colonial Andhra, for it mounted a serious attack on the notion of caste hierarchy and sought to create popular unity based on rationalism and humanism. The Adi-Andhra movement also signified the new found solidarity among the lower castes; it articulated their determination to escape the ascriptive and hereditary fixation of occupation, and formalised their struggle to appropriate emerging new forms of the power structure. The ideology of liberation formulated by Dalit intellectuals in colonial Andhra was aimed at the destruction of fundamental social inequalities in the social order, such as caste hierarcy, discrimination, and untouchability. Thus, unlike the social/caste reform movements among the Sat-Shudra upper castes such as the Kamma and Reddi Mahajana Sabhas, which were essentially "adjustive" in nature and aimed at effecting minimal changes, the Dalit transformative movement sought to challenge established patterns of dominance and resistance in social relationships, as well as the existing value system. These critiques surface cogently in the works of Dalit poets, who are thus able to represent the aspirations of the political mobilisation effected by the Adi-Andhra Mahasabha.

Dalit Mobilisation

The major themes focused on by the Adi-Andhra movement between 1917-47 were primarily related to the socio-economic upliftment of the Dalit communities, as well to the issues of land, education, employment, and representation in decision-making bodies. The Dalit movement in colonial Andhra can be broadly divided into two phases: the first phase lasting from 1917-1932, and the second one from 1932-1947.[26] Although at the initial stages positive response and sympathy was forthcoming from certain liberal upper caste individuals, the first phase essentially represented the self-mobilisation of Dalits outside the organisational/ideological framework of the Congress. The second phase was characterised by interactions between the Dalit and nationalist/left [Note: the nationalist left movement, or the nationalist and left movement?] movements. It also marked an earnest desire on the part of Dalit communities to exhibit their consciousness of their rights, condemning untouchability, discrimination and demanding political and other rights. In various conferences of the Adi-Andhra Mahasabha, several resolutions were passed with the following demands: free education, the sanction of scholarships to meet expenses such as books, food, and clothing, to start hostels for boys and girls, to withdraw recognition and stop government funds to educational institutions which do not admit Dalit children, to provide employment to Dalit youth, to establish vocational institutions and cottage industries for the benefit of the Dalit communities, to punish caste Hindus if they prohibited Dalits from drawing water from public wells and tanks, or prevented their entry into places such as temples, choultries, and hotels, to nominate Dalits and reserve adequate seats for them so as to ensure proper representation in all statutory bodies from the village panchayat boards to the legislative councils, to grant government waste lands, and patta and laka lands on lease with minimum/free rental, to establish labour and credit co-operative societies, and finally to reserve a certain percentage of jobs in all government services.[27] The Mahasabha also urged Dalits to give up drinking and abolish intra-community/ sub-caste divisions, and stressed the importance of unity within the community. Between 1917-37 nearly 15 conferences were held in different parts of the Andhra districts voiling the grievances of the Dalits. Besides the provincial conferences, local level (district, taluq and city) conferences were also organised. The geographical spread of these various conferences suggests that the Mahasabha had been able to draw rural masses into its fold. It also attracted a significant following from the educated sections of the community, such as teachers, clerks, and low-paid employees. In fact most of the local level conferences (particularly in the coastal districts) were initiated and organised by them. The leadership of the Mahasabha was mainly drawn from the educated and reasonably well-off sections of the community, viz., the Malas and the Mala Dasaries.[28]

A content analysis of the resolutions passed by the Adi-Andhra Mahasabha indicates that the Dalits were essentially resentful of the monopoly of socio-economic resources by the upper castes, primarily the Brahmins, and that they demanded access to the economic and educational fields as well as a reasonable share in the institutions of power. These demands, it may be said, were also in accordance with the demands of the broader non-brahmin movement of the 1920s. It is pertinent to note that the Justice Party government of Madras responded favourably to some of the demands of the Adi-Andhra Mahasabha with regard to education, employment and political representation.

As a measure of providing social justice to the down trodden dalits, the Justice Party ministry with the backing of the colonial State initiated certain concrete measures like providing free elementary education to their children in the local board schools as well as establishing separate schools for them through the newly created Labour Department. The land question raised by the Mahasabha was also addressed by the Ministry in terms of assigning government wastelands and lankas to Dalit rural poor peasants and labourers. In order to provide social justice to the downtrodden Dalits, the Justice Party ministry, with the backing of the colonial State, initiated certain concrete measures such as the provision of free elementary education to their children in the local board schools, and the establishment of separate schools for them through the newly created Labour Department. The ministry also addressed the land question raised by the Mahasabha by making available government wastelands and *lankas* to rural poor Dalit peasants and labourers. However limited the efforts of the Justice Party Ministry might have been, they provided a sense of relief to the Dalits.

As far as the question of political representation of Dalit communities was concerned, the Madras Government sought to ensure the participation of Dalits in the decision-making bodies by nominating some leaders of the Adi-Andhra Mahasabha like Sundru Venkaiah, and Naralasetti Devendrudu.[29] A close affinity was sought between the non-Brahmin and Dalit movements in the context of containing Brahmanical supremacy. But given their lack of organisational coordination and programmatic unity, the non-Brahmin leadership of the Justice Party failed to build a cohesive movement with the active support of the Dalits.[30] Some of the Andhra zamindars belonging to the party had a personal connection with the Adi-Andhra leadership.[31] The Adi-Andhra movement in the 1920s was, however, isolated from mainstream political organisations like the Justice Party and the Congress, which were led by caste Hindus. The autonomous character of Dalit mobilisation and organisation is also indicated by the fact that neither the regional (Andhra movement) nor national (Non-cooperation) movements had attracted any significant following from among the Dalit communities, although some of the upper caste nationalist spokesmen had exerted an influence over the Adi-Andhra Mahasabha.[32] Even there, the interaction between Dalit and other mainstream movements was minimal. The integration of the Adi-Andhra movement into them may be characterised as insignificant. For instance, the participation of the Dalit masses in the nationalist movement in Andhra districts was negligible if not absent as a majority of them were either indifferent and or opposed to it precisely because these movements, led by the upper caste, did not adequately reflect the aspirations of the vast majority of Dalits. At least, this was the perception of the Dalit intellectuals as reflected in their writings. Similarly, leaders of the Mahasabha also refused to be dragged and actively involved in political/nationalist controversies irrelevant to the Dalit masses.[33] Yet an element of co-option of some Dalit leaders into the major political parties was noticeable. The caste Hindu leadership of those parties attempted to provide some sort of representation to Dalits by nomination of their leaders to newly created institutions of power in a subordinate position.

Nevertheless, the launching of the Gandhian "Harijan upliftment programme" in the 1930s was a significant event which led to the development of close relations between Dalits and the Congress. The founding of a branch of the All India Harijan Sevak Sangh in 1932 at Vijayawada facilitated the participation of the local Congress leaders in the welfare activities of Dalits in colonial Andhra. The Andhra Rashtriya Harijan Sevak Sangh had established branches in all the Telugu speaking districts of the erstwhile Madras Presidency and had obtained financial assistance from the Central organisation.[34]

The caste Hindu dominated Sevak Sangh carried out programmes such as the cleaning of Dalit localities, establishing schools and separate hostels for Dalit students, digging of drinking water wells for Dalit communities, facilitating temple entry for Dalits, and providing financial aid to poor Dalit families. Gandhi's visit to some parts of Andhra also gave a moral boost for the activities of the Sangh. Donations were also collected during his tours and utilised for "Harijan upliftment." An activist of the Dalit movement wrote, "During Gandhi's tour, lakhs of rupees were collected from the people in the name of Harijan Biksha (Fund) and he (Gandhi) earmarked the funds to each district from the collections for the purpose of providing for the needs of the boarders admitted into hostels managed by the provincial and district Harijan Sevak Sangh branches."[35] The main thrust of Gandhi's visit to Andhra in 1933 was to campaign against the evil practice of untouchability and secure temple entry for the "Harijans." On 17th December, 1933 he personally led them into two temples in Siddhantam Village, Gudivada taluq, Krishna district.[36] On this occasion he said, " I am happy to throw open these two temples for the Harijans. The people who are responsible for this act of mine are pious. God is the same for the pious and the sinner. How do we know whether Harijans or Savarnas are sinners?... Treat Harijan as Brothers. Harijans should be clean. Do not eat dead animals. Don't drink alcohol. May God protect you."[37]

The so-called "Harijan Upliftment Programme" was carried out in various parts of Andhra districts. Volunteers of the Harijan Sevak Sangh who had visited many villages, attempted to convince caste Hindus to permit Harijans to use public wells and enter the temples.

Numerous symbolic gestures of tolerance, fraternity, and brotherhood were made by the pro-Congress Savarnas in a couple of places. News of such acts as the entry of Dalits into specific Hindu temples, the drawing of water by Dalits from walls and tanks, inter dining between caste Hindus and Dalits were also reported in the local Press.[38] However, the Gandhian programme appeared to be more symbolic than real. It could not inspire many savarna Hindus "to change their hearts" and sincerely work for social equality. His teachings regarding tolerance and brotherhood seem to have been short-lived. The upper caste leadership of the Sangh clearly failed to persuade most of their brethren to follow Gandhian ideals in letter and spirit. In implementing the ideals of Gandhi, the Congress activists faced many practical problems at the grass roots level. They found that many orthodox caste Hindus in the village were strongly opposed to the entry of Dalits into temples and the grant of access to wells. A local official of the revenue department at Bhimavaram, West Godavari district felt that several members of the "depressed classes" were suspicious about the avowed intentions of the caste Hindu leaders and hence preferred to remain aloof."[39] Commenting on the participation of Dalits in a Satyanarayana Vratam, (religious worship which is usually performed only by caste Hindus) at Tenali, Guntur district, the Revenue Divisional Officer remarked, "The occurrence…is unusual but beyond that solidarity incident in which caste people mingled with the depressed classes in the worship, I find public opinion suspicious and reticent in such matters as temple entry, common worship, common wells inter-dining and the like. They dislike these intensely and they are totally against the grain."[40] A local level Dalit association in Krishna district noted, "Gandhi has the interests of the depressed classes at heart. But all high caste Hindus are not Ghandhijees" and rhetorically questioned as to why Gandhi did not undertake a vow against caste Hindus stating, "If the Caste Hindus do not throw open the temples, wells, streets, etc., and treat the depressed classes as their equals and come to a common understanding with them in a specified time I am determined to fast to death."[41] The district Labour officer of East Godavari mentioned that though a few Dalits had visited some temples in

Rajahmundry town and performed Bhajans in front of them, the gates were kept closed and admission denied to them.[42] The Anjaneyaswami temple where they were allowed to perform their Bhajans was a very insignificant one, maintained by a non-Brahmin and open on all sides to any person who passed it on the road. At the same time, the gates of the other important temples in the town remained closed on the suspicion that Dalits would force their entry into them. The District Magistrate of Krishna reported, "On 26th September, 1932-33 caste Hindus of Bandar instigated some Adi-Andhras to enter a temple. The temple Archakas locked the doors against them. Similarly unsuccessful attempts were made by some Congressmen at Bezawada...to get Adi-Andhras to enter temples.[43] There were also instances of purification ceremonies being held in those temples which were thrown open to Dalits. Therefore, it was most improbable that the orthodox trustees of many temples would consent to open them to Dalits. In many parts of Andhra there was a strong feeling against any such concession being granted to them. It was legitimate then, that the Dalits were angry and extremely suspicious about the bonafides of caste Hindu social reformers.

The most conscious activists of the Adi-Andhra Mahasabha were quite alert and quickly pointed out the fallacies and inadequacies of the Gandhian nationalist programme for Dalit liberation. Some of the militant sections of the Mahasabha were very pessimistic about the exhortations of Gandhi and his disciples regarding untouchability, discrimination and temple entry. Even the prominent leaders of the Sangh confessed to the inadequacies and gaps in the actualisationof Gandhian idealism. Some of the glaring inconsistencies were highlighted and exposed in the press by literate Dalits. For instance, a Dalit from Krishna district criticised Nageshwar Rao Pantulu, a Brahmin politician, a Congress leader and President of the provincial Harijan Sevak Sangh for not allowing Dalits to enter his own temple in his native village. He asked him either to immediately throw open the temple for Dalits or make his stand public through the press. It was indeed an embarrassing and clear rebuff to the senior nationalist leader.[44] Another instance of religious/social discrimination against Dalits in Ellore town was also reported by a member of the Adi-Andhra community.[45] A prominent upper caste social reformer, Mother Gangaraju, who voted in favour of the Temple Entry Bill in the Madras Legislative Council, had on the basis of rumours petitioned the local police to prevent the attempted forcible entry of Dalits into Hindu Temple on the day of the Ekadasi festival as well as to protect "Hindu society and Dharma." Consequently the Sub-Magistrate passed orders directing the Adi-Andhra to complete their religious celebrations and leave the main streets by 9 a.m. Further, they were also directed not to interfere and cause inconvenience to the caste Hindu processions. In effect, this was meant to ban Dalits from the main streets, confining them to their localities during the festival celebrations in the town.

This incident confirmed for the Dalits their distrust of the sincerity of the hypocrite caste Hindu reformers. In yet another instance, some Dalits of Machilipatnam town reported that they were prevented from listening to the Harikatha along with the caste Hindus. When they protested against it, an upper caste person became violent and aggressive.[46] In the same town, the most glaring incident of discrimination involving a premier educational institution was narrated by a Dalit activist.[47] The caste Hindu school committee members had declined appointment of a Dalit graduate in their school on grounds of his caste, despite the fact some of them were pro-Congress freedom fighters and had participated in the activities of the Harijan Sevak Sangh. In a village in Anantapur district, *sanatanists* refused to allow Dalits to draw water from public tanks and threatened social boycott or excommunication if they persisted. This incident was shown in a Telugu film "Malapilla,"[48] which depicted the condition of Dalits in colonial Andhra. Kusuma Dharmanna also narrated several instances of social discrimination against the Dalits in different parts of Andhra.[49] The emergence of Dalit Journalism in the 1930s further played a significant role in highlighting upper caste atrocities on Dalits and in creating awareness among the Dalit masses. It may be stressed that journals like *Jayabheri* and *Navajeevana*[50] edited by Dalit scholars successfully moulded Dalit consciousness and articulation. The journalistic reporting made it clear that the implementation of the Gandhian programme by the obstinate upper caste leaders was slow, reluctant and halfhearted.

Incorporation of Dalits into the Congress fold through the Harijan Sevak Sangh did not bring about any noticeable change in the inter-caste relations. Harassment and victimisation of the Dalits persisted despite Gandhian appeals to caste Hindus. Moreover, the upper caste nationalist double talk about "Harijan Welfare" was exposed by the activists of the Adi-Andhra Mahasabha who pointed out the discrepancies and inconsistencies in the activities of the Congress leaders. Dalit intellectuals posed certain penetrating questions to caste Hindu nationalists regarding the abolition of discrimination and untouchability.

Bhagya Reddi Varma remarked that the foremost demand of the Dalit masses was the abolition of untouchability and the acquisition of social respectability. He felt that once the Dalits acquired reasonable material comforts they would certainly participate in the political sphere. His question is, how can a person with an empty stomach understand politics?[51] Although Dalit leadership did not desire postponement of political freedom till social equality was achieved, they tended to doubt the sincerity of the upper caste nationalists in establishing an egalitarian society. They maintained that it would be improper to demand/achieve independence without first abolishing untouchability. Further, most of them asserted that unless social equality is achieved, freedom would be meaningless and visualised freedom with dignity, honour and social justice. A Dalit poet asked, 'whether these (caste Hindu) social cowards who fear to mix with us, will become heroes of national liberation?, He wrote:[52]

> In the name of freedom they fight with the Government
> Demand independence but don't give us freedom
> Don't allow us into their temples
> Don't permit us to stay in choultries
> Prevent us from drawing water from wells
> They say no rights to Malas
> If we are denied rights
> How will you achieve freedom?

To conclude, the early decades of the present century witnessed the emergence of the Dalit movement as an organised, assertive and conscious factor in the socio-political development of colonial Andhra. Despite certain limitations, such as the lack of strength, the lack of a dominant/hegemonic voice due to its heterogeneous composition and concerns, and its dependence on caste Hindu political organisations, it maintained its own identity and remained the sole representative of the Dalit masses. Nevertheless, the founding of the Adi-Andhra movement which predated the Gandhian programme of "Harijan Upliftment" was a pronounced self-act of the Dalit masses and their organic intellectuals, and sought to articulate their suffering and misery within the context of the growing mass nationalism and the anti-colonial struggle. Although the upper caste nationalist intelligentsia sympathised with the Dalit masses in terms of suggesting certain ameliorative measures, the emancipatory ideology was formulated and articulated by the Dalits themselves, independent of the nationalist discourse. The Dalit intellectual articulation succeeded to a very large extent in exposing the inadequacies, limitations and gaps in the Gandhian paradigm of Dalit liberation.[53] It also forcefully contested the hegemonic nationalist ideology propounded by the upper caste intelligentsia. In a sense, the Dalit question in Andhra during the colonial period had posed certain fundamental issues to the nationalist ideology, and its elite ideologes had compelled them to come to terms with the emerging social reality. The growing movement of Dalits for self-respect, social justice and an egalitarian social order necessitated a serious reflection on and resolution of the problems of caste and nation. In other words, the Dalit question was an important presence in the nationalist agenda of liberation during the pre-1947 period.

REFERENCES

In this chapter, the term Dalit refers to the erstwhile untouchable communities of Malas, Madigas and 57 other castes in Modern Andhra. During the Colonial period they were also known as Panchamas, Depressed Classes, Harijans, etc. The Malas and Madigas constituted more than three fourths of the untouchables in colonial Andhra. *Census of India*, 1931, Madras, Vol. XIV, Pt. I

An abridged version of this paper was presented at the Indian History Congress, (Modern Indian section) 58th session, held at Bangalore on 14-16 November, 1997.

1. M. Venkatarangaiah, (ed.), *The Freedom Struggle in Andhra Pradesh*, Vol. III & IV, Hyderabad, 1969. B. Kesavanarayana, *Social and Political Factors in Andhra, 1990-1956*, Vijayawada, 1976.
2. M.B. Schwartz, "Indian Untouchable Texts of Resistance: Symbolic Domination and Historical Knowledge" in H.L. Seneviratne, (ed.), *Identity, Consciousness and the Past*, Delhi, 1997, p. 177.
3. A. Satyanarayana, "Dalit Protest Literature in Telugu" in *Economic and Political Weekly*, Vol. XXX, No. 3, 1995, pp. 171-75.
4. See A. Satyanarayana, *Andhra Peasants under British Rule 1900-1940*, Delhi, 1991, Chapter 2, G.N. Rao and D. Rajashekar, "Irrigation and Agrariyan Expansion in Andhra-A log-term Overview" (Mimeo).
5. *Census Report*, 1921 and 1931, Madras, Part I.
6. G. Omvedt, *Dalit and the Democratic Revolution*, Delhi, 1994, p. 18.
7. J.B. Raju, "The Champions of the Downtrodden in Andhra Pradesh" in *Andhra Pradesh State Harijan Mahasabha-Special Souvenir*, Hyderabad, 1976.
8. *Krishna Patrika*, June 29, 1935: The title of Kavi Veera was bestowed by the 8th Harijana Mahasabha held at Rajamundry.
9. Ashok Kumar, Ed., *Dalita Geetalu* (Telugu), Hyderabad, 1993, pp. 68-68B, Translation is my own.
10. Cited in K. Muthyam's review article in *Varta* (Telugu Daily), June 21, 1997. (Translation is mine).
11. *Ibid.*
12. *Krishna Patrika*, March 14, 1936, p. 9. It has been said that this song was most popular among the Dalit masses and it inculcated a new consciousness among them. It is compared to Gitanjali of Tagore. Pamu Ramamurthy, *Harijanodyamam* (Telugu), Kakinada, No date, p. 67.
13. *Antaranivarevaru*? (Telugu) Rajahmundry, 1930, pp. 3-4. I am grateful to Prof. Ranganadhachary, Dept. of Telugu, Hyderabad Central University, for this reference.
14. Bharat Patankar and Gail Omvedt, "The Dalit Liberation Movement in Colonioal India" in *Economic and Political Weekly*, Vol. XIV, No. 748, p. 417, 1979.
15. *Krishna Patrika*, November 10, 1917. K.S. Singh writes, "According to a Telugu legend, Lord Siva's two watchmen connived with each other and killed the divine cow, Kamadhenu. They were found

guilty and were cursed by the divine characters to be born as menial servants. Thus, those two watchmen, Mala and Madiga, and their descendents have become two menial castes." *Scheduled Castes*, Hyderabad, 1995, p. 872 and also see Edger Thurston and K. Rangachari, *Castes and Tribes of Southern India*, Vol. IV, New Delhi, 1993, pp. 292-324, and 329-387.

16. Ashok Kumar (Ed)., *Dalits*...p. 68B.
17. Uma Ramaswamy, "Self-Identity among Scheduled Castes: A Study of Andhra" in *EPW*, Vol. 9, No. 47, p. 1963. See Chinna Rao, Yagati, *Dalits Struggle for Identity: Andhra and Hyderabad*, New Delhi, 2003.
18. Thurston and Rangachari, *Castes and Tribes of Southern India*, Chapters 3 and 9.
19. Ashok Kumar, Ed., *Dalits*... p. 68A (Translation is my own).
20. *Ibid*., p. 68E (Translation is mine).
21. *Ibid*., p. 66.
22. J. Rangaswamy, *Malashuddhi* (Telugu), Rajahmundry, 1930.
23. *Ibid*.
24. V. Ramakrishna, *Social Reform in Andhra*, Delhi, 1983, p. 186.
25. Uma Ramaswamy, "Self-Identity", *op. cit*., p. 1961.
26. For details see G. Omvedt, *Dalits*, Chapters 3 and 9.
27. See *Krishna Patrika*, June 15, 1926; Jan. 8, 1927; Feb. 18, 1928; Feb. 23, 1929; Nov. 16, 1929; Aug. 13, 1932, Nov. 18, 1933, June 29, 1935; Jan. 9, 1937.
28. Majority of the leaders of Adi-Andhra Mahasabha like K. Dharmanna, V. Kurmaiah, B. S. Murthy, etc. belonged to the Mala community – a Dalit sub-caste Mala Dasaris/Dasus are the priests to the Vaishnavaite Malas.
29. *Krishna Patrika*, Jan. 8, 1927. Also see M.B. Gautam, "The Untouchables Movement in Andhra Pradesh" in *A.P. State Harijana Conference Special Souvenir*, p. 71.
30. E. Irschik, *Politics and Social Conflict in South India*, Berkeley, 1969.
31. Some of the Pro-Justice Party Local Zamindars like the Raja of Pithapuram, Gollapalli Zamindar, Zamindar of Mirzapuram etc. commanded respect from the organisations of Dalit Movement. Some of them also presided over Adi-Andhra conference, see *Krishna Patrika*, Oct. 31, 1936.
32. For instance, K. Nageswar Rao Pantulu, A. Kaleswara Rao, etc. had closed personal connections with the leaders of Adi-Andhra Movement.

33. A. Kaleswara Rao, *Najeevitakatha-Navyandramu* (Telugu), Vijayawada, 1959, pp. 237-242.
34. *Krishna Patrika*, Oct. 27, 1934, May 25, 1936 and Nov. 11, 1933. As many as 41 night and 1936, 11 July 11-day schools were started for Dalits in the 12 Andhra districts and amount of Rs. 8,637 was spent. Also see Sept. 30, 1938 on Dalit education by the provincial organisation in 1935-36.
35. M.B. Gautam, "*The Untouchables*", p. 72.
36. *Krishna Patrika*, Dec. 23, 1933. Also see Dec. 3, 1933.
37. *Krishna Patrika*, Dec. 23, 1933.
38. *Krishna Patrika*, Oct. 29, 1932, Dec. 3, 1932, Feb. 18, 1933, Dec. 9 & 23, 1933.
39. Cited in M. Venkatarangaiah, *The Freedom*, Vol. IV, p. 537.
40. *Ibid.*, p. 541.
41. *Ibid.*, pp. 544-45.
42. *Ibid.*, pp. 549, 553.
43. *Ibid.*, p. 557.
44. *Krishna Patrika*, Dec. 30, 1935.
45. *Krishna Patrika*, Jan. 1, 1928.
46. *Krishna Patrika*, Sep. 27, 1924.
47. *Krishna Patrika*, Aug. 15, 1936.
48. *Krishna Patrika*, May 4, 1938.
49. *Nalupu*, Nov. 16-Dec. 15, 1992. I owe this reference to Dr. K. Ilaiah, Dept. of Political Science, Osmania University.
50. *Jayabheri* was brought from Rajahmundry under the editorship of Kusuma Dharmanna; while *Navajeevana* was started under the editorship of B.S. Murthy since 1939 from Madras.
51. *Krishna Patrika*, Nov. 10, 1917.
52. Ashok Kumar, *Dalita...*, p. 68
53. *Navajeevana* reported many incidents of upper caste violence on Dalits and lapses in the nationalist programme of Harijan Welfare, see 18-5-1947, 8-6-1947, 26-10-1947.

6

"Against Social Imperialism": Ideology and Consciousness of Dalit-Bahujans in Colonial Andhra, 1842-1947*

An attempt has been made in this chapter to analyse the process of the emergence of ideology and consciousness among the dalit-bahujan communities of Andhra in the colonial context. It also outlines the history of the dalit-bahujan intellectual tradition and describes the growth of lower caste protest movements in the late nineteenth and early twentieth century. It examines the role of various agencies, forces and factors in fostering socio-political upheaval and shaping the awareness of dalit-bahujans in modern Andhra. The contribution of religious ideology (Christianity) and identity movements (Justice Party and Adi-Andhra Mahasabha) is also stressed in this chapter.

This chapter is divided into the following: the Introduction, containing a statement of the problem under investigation. The second section is devoted to historiographical review. Socio-economic profiles of selected dalit-bahujan communities are presented in the third section. The fourth section examines the evolution of dalit awareness. Bahujan articulation is dealt with in the fifth section.

A word about the title: the term "Social Imperialism" was coined by veteran scholar of modern India, K.M. Panikkar, in a small treatise titled, *Caste and Democracy*. This pithy phrase aptly describes the nature of Brahmanical supremacy in India. Dalit means broken/ oppressed. It has been widely used by militant dalit activist groups, the *Dalit Panthers* in Maharashtra a few decades ago. It refers to those belonging to the bottom and lowest segment of Indian society. In the context of Andhra Pradesh, these communities are referred to as Malas, Madigas, Depressed Classes, Outcastes, Untouchables, Panchamas, Adi-Andhras, Harijans, Scheduled Castes etc. Some British officials called them "the underworld" of Indian society. But in recent years, particularly since the 1980s the term Dalit is increasingly becoming popular among activist groups and intellectuals. The dalit activists rejected the term 'Harijan' as patronising and humiliating. The term Bahujan is also gaining currency among social activists and scholars associated with broader social and civil rights movements. It is consciously used to project a common shared experience of oppression and discrimination among non-dalit groups, generally known as the lower Sudra castes and the most backward castes. Hence, in order to emphasise the commonness of experiences, I refer to these groups in terms of an inclusive category, of Bahujans, to indicate the emergence of a feeling/identity of 'caste-in-itself.' Of course, it does not mean that there are no internal differentiation and variations. But in the context of pre-independence experiences, it is possible to use this term to denote unity rather than diversity. As we shall see later, in terms of articulation of views, visions, experiences and perceptions there was a lot of commonality among these communities. The term also connotes a shared suffering and oppression as well as an urge for self-reliance, dignity and equality among the lower castes of modern Andhra society. Lower and down trodden castes is synonymous with dalit-bahujans. Throughout this essay dalit-bahujans and lower castes (disprivileged) is used interchangeably.[1] By definition, dalit-bahujans excludes the upper castes viz., Dwijas and Sat-sudras (see Table 1). Although Tribal and lower class (poor) Muslims are a part of dalit-bahujans; they are not included in this chapter.

I

There has been a consensus among professional historians that a comprehensive history of the development of social, economic and political thought/ideas in various regions of Indias need to be written. The dominant nationalist historiography maintained that the rise of political consciousness during the colonial period was due to the activities of elite-led associations and political parties, like the Indian National Congress. This perspective is based on the assumption that the dominant nationalist ideology articulated by the upper caste-class truly mirrored the will of the people of India. The identification and equation of the rise of socio-political consciousness with the emergence of the pan-Indian organisations seeks to legitimise and justify the movement launched by the Congress party in national-political terms and tends to exclude and undermine other forms and processes.[2] Nineteenth century India in general, and south India in particular, witnessed diverse forms of socio-political awakening and mobilisations characterised by unevenness a cross different segments of the population, more so among the lower castes/communities. Recent debates generated by subaltern historiography,[3] in particular, drew the attention of scholars to undertake and explore the diversity, multiplicity and complexity of ideas, intellectual traditions, cultures etc. at the micro-regional level. In general, there has been an excessive emphasis on the growth of hegemonic nationalist ideas and ideology articulated by the upper class/caste, western- educated intelligentsia.

> "Much of what we consider to be political consciousness in India originated in areas where there were concentrations of institutions and individuals which provided the facilities and direction for the creation of a modern educated elite."[4]

This kind of analysis presents only a partial picture of the guiding forces behind the nationalist upsurge in colonial India. Macro level discourses on Indian nationalism—"the all-consuming passion in public life"—lack sensitivity to the diversity of ideas or thought processes. The grand, mega-narrative of the nationalist movement and its agenda tended to highlight the vision of "the leaders" who were supposed to have shaped the destiny of the Nation and accorded sanctity to their thought. Any contrary or divergent ideas and ideologies, visions, perceptions, and aspirations by sections below the upper caste-based middle class intelligentsia have been termed as parochial, narrow, sectarian, communal, casteist and hence non/anti-national. It has been assumed that in the making of the nation, nationalism articulated by the nationalist leaders alone was pre-eminent. There is also inadequate discussion in the existing historical literature on the visions and perspectives of the non-elite, local, vernacular-based intellectuals and spokesmen. It has been suggested that,

> "in part this relative neglect has arisen from the very magnetism of the nationalist movement itself, of the personalities that led it, and of the cause that they championed with such fervour."[5]

Further, it was assumed that the national movement was the only response under colonial conditions. The fact that there were multiple and varied reactions and responses to it has been missed. How different segments of Indian society, both across time and space, have understood, interpreted and articulated the ideology of nationalism and the visions of the nation is not adequately explored thus far. There is also an urgent need to focus on the context, local traditions and articulations by the organic intellectuals of the disprivileged sections of Indian society. Subaltern historians have pointed out that in the course of the anti-colonial movement, long before the political nationalist ideas were articulated by the elites, illiterate masses had projected their own vision of a future society, however hazy and vague that might have been. But the mainstream historians paid little attention to the initiatives taken by the non-dominant groups, which often had a profound effect on the growth of nationalist consciousness and socio-political movements as well as in shaping the nationalist agenda.[6] Given the advances made by subaltern historiography, it has become necessary to pay more attention to non-governmental, non-English sources and literature in rewriting the social history of modern India, especially at the regional level. In order to capture the divergent views and ideas expressed by subaltern groups, we have to document and analyse popular political, social and ideological activities over a period of time. The fact that pan-Indian nationalist ideology did not sufficiently influence the lower orders of society, at least till about the first quarter of the twentieth century, needs elucidation and explanation. The dominant nationalist historiography which paid less attention to the organisations, institutions and ideologies which arose from among the lower castes could not explain why, for instance, in parts of south and western India had dalit-bahujan communities not taken part in the early nationalist political and/or social reform movements. They, in fact, became anti-Brahmin, actively opposed to and openly denouncing the upper caste leadership. They tended to discount "Brahmin nationalism" and expressed doubts about the validity of their movement and at times disagreed with their programme, since it was unconcerned with their quotidian lives. The articulate groups among the lower castes began to ask questions like, whose nation was it going to be and what kind of a nation was sought to be built. In a sense, the ideal upper caste nationalism was at variance with popular nationalism, as articulated by the disprivileged groups.

In the light of above observations, it is imperative on the part of historians to review and reassess the established notions of nationalist social reconstruction in relation to the views and ideas of the non-hegemonic social groups. The context, meaning and essence of lower caste articulations, pertaining to the establishment of modern national society based on egalitarian principles of equality, liberty and freedom need to be analysed. Since historical discipline is no longer a mere chronological record of wars, kings, great men etc. and as its horizon/realm has been considerably expanded in terms of new social history, history from below, people's history etc., it should be possible to unearth the hidden dimensions at the regional level. In order to illustrate an aspect of the hitherto unexplored areas of modern Andhra history, I may point out that the contribution of Christian missionaries to the growth of lower caste consciousness, ideology, social movements etc., has not been adequately documented and analysed by historians. Also the social consequences of Christian missionaries' activities did not receive adequate attention. Moreover, the existing historical scholarship is almost silent about the alternative visions, ideas and perceptions that took shape during the course of the nationalist movement. A detailed history of dalit-bahujan ideology and intellectual traditions is yet to be written. It is hoped that a region-specific approach would yield "a rich harvest of regional social histories with a wealth of detail and subtle nuances of meaning of context and relationships." I am also of the opinion that our understanding of modern Andhra history would be incomplete, partial and distorted unless and until we make a concerted and systematic attempt to record, document and analyse the experiences and activities of the disprivileged sections of our society. I believe, that practitioners of historical discipline have to write the history of "history-less" masses, which have so far been marginalised both within society and intellectual discourse. They are the victims of the conspiracy of silence of the dominant scholarship in social sciences. Since history is also an agency of empowerment of the weak and down-trodden in forming their identities and consciousness, social scientists have a role to play in reconstructing their historical experience, visions and contribution to social progress. In recent years, "history-conscious social scientists and sociologically-minded historians" have been taking a fresh look at modern Indian history and reinterpreting it. Hence, it is pertinent to raise some issues so as to initiate new agendas for regional historical research.

II

Historiographical Comments

Any new writing and/or new interpretation of history is only possible after a careful survey of the existing trends in modern Andhra historiography. Indeed, earlier generation of historians did initiate a study of the socio-political movements. The nationalist historians depicted the nationalist movement in terms of stages, episodes and the contribution of leaders. They gave prominence to the activities of the Indian National Congress and down played the role of non-Congress organisations and movements, their ideologies, programmes etc. in the freedom struggle.[7] They also tended to project an idealistic version of nationalist discourse and mobilisation and missed the popular dimensions.

The Cambridge historians, Washbrook[8] and Baker[9] presented a contrary view to the nationalist paradigm/perspective. Though they rightly critiqued the eulogistic depictions of nationalism and the nationalist movement, yet they debunked the ideology of nationalism itself. They also exaggerated and highlighted the selfish formations of cliques, factionalist networks, patron-client relations etc. but failed to take cognizance of the impact of nationalist ideology on different segments of south Indian society and their mobilisational strategies. Both of them equally ignored the socio-cultural and political movements unconnected with the factionalist and patron-client mobilisations. They projected the lower caste followers of elite leaders as passive and instrumentalist. Hence, their studies lacked focus concerning the rise and growth of lower caste ideas, movements and their significance.

Scholars like Ramakrishna[10] and others have departed from a purely political history perspective and examined the socio-cultural aspects of modern Andhra. These studies are a welcome addition to the growing literature on the social history of modern Andhra. Recent works on social history focus on caste associations and highlight the growth of consciousness and ideology among the dominant non-Brahmin castes. But most of them are governed by the "sanskritisation" model and thus project a partial view of the emergence of consciousness among different social groups, particularly the lower castes. While they emphasise the ritual dimension of articulation of certain communities, they focuss insufficiently on the secular social protest angle. Thus Ramakrishna writes:

> "The 'lower castes'...were seeking to imitate the so-called higher castes and adopt their ways of life in rituals and ceremonies.... In their quest for a superior position in society, they also wanted to 'sanskritize' some of their ways of life."[11]

In his article on Non-Brahmin movement in colonial Andhra, Chinnaya Suri[12] analyses the multi-dimensionality of emerging social protest, but he too deals inadequately with dalit-bahujan articulations and vision. His emphasis is more on the Sudra upper castes like Kammas. Velcheru Narayana Rao's[13] essay on modern Andhra intellectuals, does not mention even a single scholar, pandit/jnani belonging to the dalit communities. While analysing the role of intellectuals in social change, he is surprisingly silent on the non-elite organic intellectuals of the lower castes. Naturally, all the intellectuals he cites belong to the higher castes, the majority of whom were Brahmins. It is intriguing to note that, being a noted scholar of literature, Narayana Rao has forgotten to name any of the dalit scholars like Gurram Joshua, Kusuma Dharmanna, Bhoi Bheemanna etc. He has not taken into account the ideas of dalit-bahujan intellectuals. As a matter of fact, none of the above scholars adequately focuss on the nature of dalit movements and their role in the evolution of ideas and intellectual traditions in colonial Andhra.

My approach in this essay is different from the above cited works, in the sense that I argue in favour of going beyond the sanskritisation paradigm and analyse the non-ritual, democratic and egalitarian dimensions of lower caste consciousness, ideology and mobilisation. Recent studies by Hanlon,[14] Aloysius,[15] Bandyopadhyay[16] etc., have contributed many insights into the study of the social history of the lower castes. "Demand for higher position or adoption of the so-called pure ritual symbols or 'Sanskritization' need not be taken as expression of narrow social ambitions or mere emulation of the upper castes. For these also meant a protest against inferior social position and associated disabilities, as well as appropriation of certain symbols that had so long been the exclusive privileges of a few at the top. And the demand for a share in the economic resources and political power was indeed a challenge to the existing system of their distribution."[17] Negating the sanskritisation model, Aloysius observes that the lower caste movements were:

> "challenges to ritual exclusivism, in order to overcome civil and religious disabilities by crossing the pollution line and doing away with differentiation and distancing religious and secular symbols. These processes are basically social protests and challenges to ascriptive hierarchy.... Their attempts at sanskritization, education, claim for employment at par with the other castes and their stake to be represented in various public forums were indications of the passing away of the old order."[18]

He also commented that historians in general have completely ignored the social reform movements of the lower castes and have written reform history without any reference to the enormous efforts made by the lower orders outside the narrow circle of the upper castes. It is also equally applicable to the writings on social history of modern Andhra Pradesh thus far.

> 'Velcheru Narayan Rao also noted the imbalance of social history perspective, owing to the cultural dominance of brahmins, their models had too often been taken to be the only models of culture in the country. Veeresalingam's work on widow remarriage was aimed to help mainly brahmin women and not women of all castes. Veeresalingam had never considered the various customs and problems related to the status of women in non-brahmin castes. Nevertheless, the general impression remained that he was a social reformer, while in reality he had only been a brahmin reformer.... Similarly, Gurajada Appa Rao depicted Brahmin problems. The village scenes in *Kanyasulkam* were limited to Brahmins families.... The viewpoint was that of Brahmins. This misperception, which was not corrected, led to exaggerated importance of the Brahmin reformers and diminished the role played by the non-Brahmin reformers."[19] (I would include the dalits).

As I will show later, the dalit-bahujan communities in colonial Andhra aspired for secularisation, humanisation and liberalisation of civil society as much as the elite nationalists. Their conception of nationalism is inclusive of socio-economic and political justice. A Sudra intellectual opined:

> "The exclusion of most of the castes from sharing in the political life of the country has left little room for the growth of feeling of common interest and public spirit. The caste system, which is born of the most abject spiritual slavery, has resulted in political slavery.... The spirit of caste is inimical not only to the growth of national unity but also to the emancipation of the individual.... Priest-ridden, karma-obsessed, maya-enslaved mentality is the source of all the miseries under which the Hindus are groaning.... Spiritual slavery, fatalism and superstition have smoothered all power of self-reliance and all sense of freedom."[20]

Although the lower castes disputed their degrading status and re-interpreted some of the Hindu texts, they were not aspiring to become Brahmins, but were consciously contesting/negating the Brahmanical interpretation. They comprehensively denounced the caste system and desired to dismantle it. Their urge for ritual equality was very much rooted in their secular conception of modern society and nation. They visualised a nation and civil society free of inequality and social oppression. They intended to emerge as free and equal citizens of the civic/political community of the emerging nation. A spokesman of the Justice Party wrote:

> "...The idea of a nation involves the oneness of culture and implies the binding together of a similar portion of mankind by other than mere political ties. Nationality does not depend upon but transcends political allegiance, religious belief and economic interest. Nationality is a form of consciousness of kind, which binds men together irrespective of their political allegiance, religious beliefs and economic interests....When caste and status delimit life, men are driven to be either fools or hypocrites. No democracy can be built on restrictions, which hinder individual liberty and free association. No democracy can grow in a social environment in which the distinction of inferiors and superiors forms an essential and permanent idea."[21]

Recent studies by scholars like Chinna Rao,[22] Chinnaiah[23] and Thirumali[24] etc. have shown that dalit organic intellectuals had articulated concepts of equality, freedom, social justice and so on, in a very comprehensive manner. In writing about the ideas and movements of illiterate lower castes, historians may and do encounter the problem of sources and relevant information. How to record and interpret their voices is, of course, problematic. It may be difficult if we only or mostly confine ourselves to English language sources. But alternate vernacular sources are available in plenty through the writings of lower caste intellectuals, poems, novels such as drama, contemporary press reports, autobiographical and biographical accounts, activities of caste associations, caste histories etc., and throw ample light on their ideological formation. Even government sources like the Census, Gazetteers, Commission/ Committee reports and so on contain hidden data, which needs to be "de-coded." As far as colonial Andhra is concerned, a lot of Christian missionary sources are available, which are yet to be used by scholars. I wish to make a modest attempt at providing certain insights, based on my current ongoing research.[25] In the following sections, I shall try to document the process of the evolution of dalit-bahujan ideology, consciousness, its nature, context and character.

III

Dalit-Bahujans: Socio-Economic Profile

A peculiar feature of the caste system in modern Andhra Pradesh has been that it does not correspond to the pure *Varna* categories. Unlike in the Gangetic-valley region, for instance, there are no pure *varnas* of *Kshatriyas* and *Vaisyas*. Another peculiarity is the extraordinarily high position of the Brahmins in the socio-economic hierarchy. Scholars who have studied the south Indian caste system pointed out that it could be divided into three broad social groups, viz., the privileged (Brahmins), the underprivileged (Non-Brahmins) and the unprivileged (Untouchables). In this chapter, I categorise them as the Dwija castes, the Sat-Sudra upper castes and the Dalit-Bahujan communities. I am aware that this is an arbitrary classification, because within each category there is a certain amount of internal differentiation. But it is found useful for the purpose of a broad understanding of the social system that prevailed in colonial Andhra and the kind of articulation providing among different castes/communities. In spite of social differentiation within the dalit-bahujans, there was a vast amount of similarity and commonality, at least during the period under study, in terms of material conditions, beliefs and aspirations. On the basis of information contained in the District Gazetteers, Census, Ethnological reports/surveys etc. it is possible to reconstruct the broad socio-economic conditions of the lower castes in modern Andhra.[26] During the colonial period, the social structure was intertwined and closely corresponded to the structure of landholding, socio-economic privilege and power. The ritualistically superior castes, like the Brahmins, also held significant economic resources in terms of landholding, access to modern education and public employment. The British colonial rulers formally abolished the prevailing caste-specific and caste-defined positions over land and other resources, systematised the landholding patterns, and introduced formal legal/juridical relationships; yet caste hierarchies continued to exist and overlap with the hierarchies of economy and power. However, socio-economic transformation under colonialism did result in the formation of new classes, which were formally separated from the traditional caste system. Thus there was a clear-cut convergence between caste and class, as far as the lower castes were concerned. The data presented in the tables will show that, by and large, caste-class categories converged and were interlinked.

Dalits

In terms of the geographical spread, only two communities, the highest (*Brahmin*) and the lowest (*Mala and Madiga*) were representative. They could be considered as all-Andhra castes. However, within the dalit groups there was also a regional dimension. The *Malas* were in a majority in coastal Andhra districts; of all the *Mala* population 75 per cent of them lived there, whereas most of the *Madigas* lived in the Rayalaseema region (60 per cent of them inhabited there). As the Census figures show, the *Madigas* who were traditional leather workers, were gradually transformed into manual labourers. Around 17 per cent of them were dependent on their traditional occupation in 1921, and 68 per cent of them worked as agricultural/field labourers. The *Malas* worked mainly as agricultural labourers. It has been estimated that less than 10 per cent of dalit communities owned agricultural land. Hence, their main source of livelihood was manual labour. Being at the bottom of the social hierarchy and burdened by tradition, they performed all sorts of 'impure' and odd jobs. On the subject of their productive capacities a colonial official remarked: "They are by no means unworthy as citizens. Many of them are industrious as menials, artisans and agricultural labourers and carry out all the necessary, if unpleasant, chores of life. They scavenge in a country that knows no sewers, they flay animals, they remove carrion, they carry the dead and perform all the menial duties of life… the outcaste's services to the community are not negligible. Where there are railway and canal works, there they are to be found working at piece work, where young and old, male and female, work with baskets of earth on their heads, like ants on the antheap."[27] The self-perception of dalits themselves is articulated thus: "There is no other class which labours so hard towards production in this country as the *Panchamas*. Though poor, there is no doubt that they are intelligent."[28]

Table 1
Caste System in Colonial Andhra

		% to total population of Andhra District of Madras Presidency
A.	*Dwijas* (Forward Castes Brahmin/Komati/Raju etc)	6.87
B.	Non-Brahmins:	
	Sat-Sudras (Kamma/Balija/Velama/Reddy etc.) Reddy caste was not mentioned in Census Reports. But it is assumed that the Kapus of Rayalaseema and Nellore districts were Reddies	16.04
C.	***Bahujans*** (Lower Sudra Communities)	15.78
	i. Agricultural Castes (Kapu/Telaga/Kalinga/Gavara etc.)	
	ii. Vocational/occupational castes (Gauda/Golla/Yadav/Kuruma/Uppara/Odde etc.)	10.01
	iii. Services Castes (Chakali/Mangali/Kummari etc.)	4.13
	iv. Artisan Castes (Kamsali/Panchanam/Padmasale etc.)	3.85
	v. Fishing and Hunting Castes (Boya/Bestha/Mutrachi/Palli/Jalari)	4.12
	vi. Nomadic/Semi-nomadic Castes (Lambada/Sugali/Yanadi/ Yerukala etc.)	1.81
	vii. Miscellaneous,Begging and Dependent Castes	4.61
	viii. Christians	1.88
D.	*Dalits* (Madiga, Mala etc.)	13.18

Source: *Census of India*, 1921, Madras, Vol. XIII, Part-II, Tables IX and XIII.

The access to education and employment was quite negligible for dalits. Though certain Sudra communities achieved some socio-economic mobility, it was denied to the dalits as a whole, as can be seen from the data. No social or political organisation really championed their cause till about the middle of the nineteenth century. It was only the Christian missionaries who provided them solace, comfort and self-respect.

Service Castes

The majority of the washermen community (*Chakali*) performed their traditional occupation. As per the 1921 census 80 per cent of

Table 2
Caste and Education, 1901
(Selected Castes)

S.No.	*Name of the Caste*	*% of literacy*
1.	Balija	6.20
2.	Boya	0.44
3.	Brahmin	35.44
4.	Chetti	15.39
5.	Devanga	03.21
6.	Dhobi/Chakali	00.29
7.	Gamalla	00.98
8.	Golla	00.54
9.	Kalinga	02.45
10.	Kamma	02.49
11.	Kamsali	08.31
12.	Kapu	01.93
13.	Komati	28.91
14.	Madiga	00.12
15.	Mala	00.29
16.	Mangali	01.83
17.	Mutracha	00.95
18.	Oddie	00.22
19.	Sale	02.53
20.	Telaga	03.83
21.	Velama	01.28
22.	Christians	10.93

Source: Madras Census Report, 1901, Vol. X, Table IX.

the actual workers depended on it. In the villages they also acted as torch and palanquin bearers in marriages and temple ceremonies. Besides washing, they had also to carry out all kinds of menial services. The literacy rate among them was less than one per cent (1921). Being a low caste, they were also subjected to discrimination and humiliation. Their caste association *Rajaka Sangham* complained about many instances of oppression by upper/dominant castes. The *Mangalis (Naibrahmins)*, besides being hair

Table 3
Caste and Employment, 1921 (Selected Castes)

S. No.	Name of the Caste	Total workers	Number of persons employed in Govt. Service, Law and Professions	% of total workers
1	2	3	4	5
1.	Balija	5.03 lakhs	13,383	2.65
2.	Boya	2.15 lakhs	1,499	0.69
3.	Brahmin	1.74 lakhs	14,102	8.09
4.	Golla	4.63 lakhs	1,472	0.31
5.	Gauda/Settibalija	0.86 lakhs	1,230	1.42
6.	Kamma	4.27 lakhs	1,048	0.24
7.	Kamsali/Viswabrahmin	1.01 lakhs	503	0.49
8.	Kapu	10.80 lakhs	2,815	0.25
9.	Madiga	3.88 lakhs	3,398	0.87
10.	Mala	7.74 lakhs	5,494	0.70
11.	Mangali	0.82 lakhs	4.766	5.78
12.	Sale	1.36 lakhs	496	0.36
13.	Telaga	2.36 lakhs	4,133	1.75
14.	Tsakala	2.51 lakhs	744	0.29

Source: *Madras Census Report*, 1921.

cutters were also village musicians and doctors. The Census data of 1921 recorded 364 Males and 306 Females as practitioners of 'Medicine.' During the pre-independence period the barbers acted as village surgeons and their women worked as midwives/nurses (*dayas*). However, due to the advancement of modern medicine and hospitals their traditional occupations of '*vaidya*' and midwifery received a setback. Hence, the census data recorded the declining position of their occupation over a period of time. They used to have small plots of land and worked as cultivators, tenants, labourers etc. Nearly 50 per cent of *Mangalis* were dependent on agriculture (1921). Comparatively speaking their educational and employment profiles were better. Yet, a majority of them were in miserable socio-economic conditions. The *Kummaras* were also known as *Salivahanas.* They played a very important role in rural society in earlier days. Every household used to have earthenware and pots for cooking and storing water. However, the use of aluminum vessels on a large scale since the beginning of the twentieth century saverely affected their occupation. The manufacture of machine tiles and the use of concrete cement had also deprived the *Kummaras* of their source of income. Hence they took to agriculture. Though the community was not considered unclean, they were discriminated against and did not have social interact socially with the upper castes.

Artisan Castes

There were a number of weaving castes known by various names such as *Sale, Padmasale, Devanga, and Jandra.* Due to competition from textile mills their occupation was greatly affected and gradually their position had become unremunerative and uneconomical. The available data clearly indicates the deteriorating position of weavers during the first quarter of the last century. In 1911, 63.61 per cent of them were dependent on their traditional occupation but by 1921 it had reduced to 48.85 per cent. While only 7.36 per cent of them were dependent on agriculture in 1911, in 1921, 36.52 per cent of their total population lived on it. An interesting aspect of the weavers' families was that a number of their women worked as agricultural labourers in order to augment the household resources. As is clear from the tables presented above, they were educationally backward and their employment chances were meagre. The *Viswabrahmins/Panchanamvars* were known for their professional genius and extraordinary skills of their trade. Like the weavers, they were also affected by the forces of modernisation and de-industrialisation since the late nineteenth century. Their professions suffered due to the lack of patronage of old aristocrats, nobility and the wealthy. The Census data shows that the percentage of *Kamsalis* dependent on their traditional occupation was declining over time: from 78.70 in 1911 to 69.68 in 1921. Consequently, they had taken up other professions like cultivation, petty trade, and manual labour. Their women folk were forced to work as agricultural labourers to maintain the family. However, their educational/literacy levels were reasonably good. After the Brahmins and *Komatis*, they were the most literate people in colonial Andhra. However, their employment opportunities were quite poor. Due to their familiarity with classical scriptures, the *viswabrahmins* quite often disputed the Brahmanical ideology and started asserting equality with Brahmins. Their caste associations played a significant role in the awakening of these communities. Among the Backward castes of colonial Andhra they were the earliest to challenge the Brahmanical supremacy and to articulate notions of social and ritual equality.

Vocational/Occupational Castes

Among the vocational castes there were many subdivisions/sects, yet they pursued identical professions. The *Gollas/Yadavas* were the sheep/goat rearers and milk vendors. It was basically a pastoral community, which was gradually transformed into settled agriculturists in the upland areas of north coastal Andhra and the Rayalaseema regions. Thus apart from their hereditary occupation, *Gollas* had also acquired land and were engaged in cultivation. Besides tending sheep/goats, the *Kurumas* (a sub-caste of *Gollas*) also weave cumblies. The cumbly weaving declined in course of time due to competition from textiles mills. Since the income they got from their traditional occupation was declining, they were compelled to give it up and resort to cattle-rearing, coolie work as porters, *hamalies*, cart men etc. The Census data of 1921 shows that in the first quarter of the twentieth century more than 75 per cent of these communities pursued agriculture, while only about 12 per cent of them were engaged in their traditional occupation. Though the occupation of shepherds was not unclean, it was not considered as dignified by the higher castes. There is a popular Telugu saying, which reads: "*Enthamanchi Gollavanikaina Yapakayantha Verri untundi.*" The community was generally treated with scant respect as they were ignorant and illiterate. Their educational and employment accomplishments were very deplorable; in 1921 less than two per cent were literate among the

Gollas. The toddy tapping communities of *Gaundlas* and *Settibalijas,* were also forced to take up other occupations like cooli work and field labour. Some among them were engaged in agriculture as small peasants/tenants, while, others migrated to other places in search of employment. Most of the *Settibalijas* of coastal Andhra went to Burma for livelihood since the late 19th century; in the fields of education and employment their achievements were low. In general, they command no social respect due to their low-level occupation.

Fishing/Hunting Castes

They were known by different names, but can be divided into two categories. *Pallis, Jalaris, Vodabalijas, Agnikulakshatriyas,* mainly inhabited in the seashore villages and slums or in isolated areas of seaside towns. They basically catch sea fish and lead a miserable life. On the other hand, the *Bestas, Mutrachas, Boyas* etc. were mainly fresh water fishermen in the interior areas. Tanks, channels, streams, wells and so on are their major sources of fishing. However, as the census data indicates, the fishermen communities were gradually pushed out of their traditional occupation and involved in all sorts of jobs like cultivation, agricultural labour and other miscellaneous pursuits. Less than two per cent of them pursued their traditional calling in 1921. The *Mutrachi* community was largely a fishing, hunting, cultivating and labouring group of Dravidian descent. During the pre-colonial period they were engaged as foot soldiers and militia by the local potentates. Subsequently, they lost their hereditary occupation and were engaged as cultivators, petty traders, grain-dealers, cart-drivers, palanquin bearers, watchmen etc. Their women worked as domestic servants and agricultural labourers. The *Boyas/Valmikis* are considered to be the best hunters and are experts in collecting honeycombs from the crevices of overhanging rocks. As per census data a vast majority of them were agriculturists and were employed as constables, peons, watchmen, talaris, etc. The Boyas were economically very poor and lived in huts/thatched houses. Due to their inferior profession they were treated with disrespect in the society. Thus on the whole, the fishing/hunting castes occupied a very low position in the caste hierarchy. The nature of their occupation, dwelling houses and the surroundings all contributed to their low and degrading status. The middle-men/brokers often exploited them. They were educationally very backward. Thus their caste organization, the *Agnikula Kshatriya Sangham* demanded various measures for their socio-economic betterment: A colonial official wrote about the Bestas of Nellore district thus: "They are becoming literate and more responsive to positive/good influences. In fact, they show signs of developing into a civilized caste. However, it is the unemployment problem that is keeping most of them poor and the general lot of the ordinary Bestha is rather pitiable. The Besthas occupy a low scale in the social status."[29]

Semi-Nomadic Castes

Odderas/Upparas were a community of tank diggers, well sinkers, road makers and earthmovers. Their traditional occupation is earthwork, stone cutting, construction of houses and roads, masonry, and coolie/labour work. The major source of employment for them was the Public Works Department and the construction and maintenance of railways/roads. They were normally engaged in groups and move from place to place in search of employment. Some were also engaged in agriculture. Both men and women worked as agricultural labourers. The ethnological evidence suggests that they were originally salt-workers and the name U*ppara* is derived from the Telugu word *Uppu* (salt). During the colonial period, when private manufacture and selling of salt was forbidden they were forced to take to earthwork, tile burning and daily labour. Most of them lived in temporary thatched shelters close to the work places. Since members of the whole family were employed in work, the children had no opportunity to attend schools. As a result, the whole community was educationally backward. Just about 1.50 per cent of them were literate in 1921.

Cultivating Castes

The *Kapu/Telaga* communities were mainly land-based and depended on agriculture as their main source of livelihood. Most of the *Turpukapus, Gavaras, Kalingas* in the districts of Ganjam and Vizagapatam were small peasant landholders and worked as agricultural labourers and coolies. Though these communities constituted about 16 per cent of the total population of Andhra districts during the first quarter of the twentieth century their socio-economic conditions were deplorable. The *Turpukapus/Kalingas* were subjected to the exploitation of landlords/zamindars. A vast majority of them remained as poor peasants and tenants. Their womenfolk were also employed as agricultural labourers. They did not benefit substantially from the changing agrarian relations under the impact of colonial rule such as monetisation, commercialisation and commodity production. However, the *Kapus/Telagas* of the delta districts of East and West Godavari, Kistna and Guntur were relatively better off due to fertile soils and assured irrigation.

It is clear from the above description that Andhra society during the colonial period was so hierarchically structured that majority communities, the dalit-bahujans, were deprived access to all sorts of resources. In the foregoing pages, I have outlined the socio-economic conditions of selected dalit-bahujan castes in order to link it with their socio-political articulation. In fact, changes in material conditions and growing awareness among them largely determined their responses to the emerging situations.

IV

Religion as Emancipatory Ideology: Christianity and Dalit Awakening

Struggles against the ideology of Brahmanical supremacy and ascriptive hierarchy in Andhra Desa date back to the late medieval period, which witnessed significant social fluidity/mobility among the sudra castes, especially weavers and other artisans.[30] These communities resisted Brahmanical precedence and dominance over certain ritual practices and sought equality. The Bhakti movement espoused their perceptions and visions. It often assumed a militant character and led to the emergence of Veera Saiva and Veera Vaishnava cults that denounced the caste system and untouchability. "A spirit of sympathy for the lower castes and classes of Hindu society has been a distinguishing feature of Vaisnavism." In Andhra Desa, two great social reformers viz., Potuluri Veerabrahamam and Vemana spearheaded the fight against caste oppression and Brahmanical dominance. Both of them hailed from non-Brahmin castes. They vehemently attacked the caste system and social evils. They also propagated their views and ideas through simple verses and used "two weapons of satire and irony to attack social inequalities." Their sayings, verses, and poetry combined with sweet humour and sarcasm were intelligible to the common masses. So much so, that the *tatwalu* of Potuluri and verses of Vemana became an integral part of the folklore of Andhra Desa.[31] These saint-philosophers of the pre-colonial era propounded humanism, social equality and fraternity. Issues raised by the Bhakti saints have re-appeared during the mid-19th century, though there was no continuity of themes. Nevertheless, social reformers of the early nineteenth century, particularly the Christian missionaries have appropriated the Bhakti traditions, to some extent, to attack Brahmanical Hinduism and the caste system as well as to shape dalit consciousness. They were also aware of the nature of pre-colonial protest movements like the *Vaisnava* cults and hence some of the ideas of the Bhakti tradition were embedded in the preaching of the missionaries.

Scholars have studied about the ritual and legal battles launched by *Vaisyas, Viswabrahmins* etc., against Brahmins in the 19th century, but nothing much is known regarding dalit and other lower caste protests.[32] As I pointed out above, in the existing literature very little information is available pertaining to the process of socio-cultural awakening, thinking and ideological formation among the dalit-bahujan communities. Mention has been made to the role of social reform movements like Brahma Samaj, Arya Samaj and leaders like Veereshalingam Pantulu, Raghupati Venkataratnam Naidu, yet less attention is paid to the role of Christian missionaries in the awakening of lower castes in colonial Andhra.[33] The social and ethical dimensions of Christianity influenced many social reform leaders in India, including Veereshalingam.

Anjaneyulu wrote:

> "At no other time in the earlier history of Andhra so much real ground work done in the field of language and literature. This along with the message of the Christian gospel, brought by the foreign missionaries, with the accent on the ethical aspect, served to create a new intellectual atmosphere conducive to honest doubt and free discussion of the time honoured rituals and practices in the Hindu society. Here was indeed a challenge to an old culture from the new... Innate sense of justice, fair play and human dignity prevailed... The influence of Christianity cannot be ruled out as an important factor in shaping his views... The influence of the Bible is also evident in the evolution of Veereshalingam..."[34]

The famous dalit poet Gurram Jashuva was a product of the Christian missionaries. Therefore, it can be said that it was mainly owing to the work of Christian missionaries among the dalit-bahujan communities in colonial Andhra that they became aware of their unequal status and rights. Undoubtedly, the work of missionaries was the most significant, comprehensive and best organised effort among all the social reform associations in the nineteenth century. Humanitarianism was one of the important motives of missionaries in fighting caste oppression, besides religious propaganda. Contemporary sources mention that the missionaries were sensitive to and moved by the appalling and degrading conditions of the dalit-bahujans, their misery, squalor as well as by the practices of untouchability and exclusion. Hence, "the inner most chords of their tender hearts have been touched and their upright soul stirred to a just anger and to a firm determination to reform the social system responsible for it." In a sense, they became the pioneers of social service among the dalit communities, notably at a time when upper caste Hindus bestowed no thought and action on their welfare or uplift, but only "kicked and spurned" them like dogs. Indeed, it was the missionaries who treated them with compassion as human beings, taught them self-dignity and essential equality with other fellow beings. It has been noted that conversion had not only an individual act but also a long-drawn social process where families, communities, kith, kin, friends etc. joined as collectives. Thus it is necessary to take into consideration and understand the socio-economic context in which religious conversions had taken place. Conversion in terms of an ideology of social egalitarianism and liberation also needs to be contextualised. In the case of lower castes/communities in colonial Andhra, it was a definite means of escaping from social disabilities and hierarchically structured/ranked caste society and to seek improvement. It may be surmised that through conversion they sought to create for themselves a new social order, which would delegitimise the traditional notions of status and rank. To quote Manickam: "To the people from the Depressed Classes the benefit of Christianity appeared substantial enough to warrant a move to change their religion...this they did in large numbers by way of social protest."[35]

The earliest protestant Christian missionary activities among the Telugu-speaking communities in Madras Presidency took place in the second decade of the eighteenth century.[36] However, large scale conversion of the lower castes in the rural and urban areas of colonial Andhra had taken place mainly during the second half of the nineteenth and the first quarter of twentieth century. Several missionary organisations of various denominations like Roman Catholic and Protestant were involved in the localised, grassroots and simultaneous conversion movements, which were initiated and led by dalits. Although Christianity was popularised among many communities including the Brahmins and other higher castes, a vast majority of converts were drawn from the dalit bahujan communities/castes. Unlike the Roman Catholics, the Protestant missionaries were closely involved in the dalit mass movements of conversion. They also addressed the caste and dalit question more intensely and consistently. Hence, I will only concentrate on their attitudes and contribution towards dalit-bahujan emancipatory initiatives and movements. Recent studies by Oddie,[37] Forrester,[38] Webster[39] etc. have highlighted the Protestant missionaries' perceptions of caste and the catalystic role of Christianity in socio-cultural transformation. They have also shown that by the middle of the nineteenth century there was concern among the various

Protestant missionaries not only to condemn caste but also to eliminate it within the churches. The missionaries aimed at encouraging and strengthening the existing movements against caste oppression and discrimination. In many cases, they had taken initiative and supported issues relating to the welfare of dalit-bahujan communities. Thus the Christian missionaries saw themselves as "agents of social change." Available information from autobiographical, biographical and contemporary sources amply indicate that mass conversion movements in colonial Andhra were possible due to the sincere, dedicated and committed work on the part of the founders of the Christian missions such as the Hermannsburg Mission, London Mission Society, United Lutheran Church and Church Mission Society. The most prominent missionaries and founders of missions who propagated Christianity in colonial Andhra in the 19th century included : George and August Des Granges in Vizagapatam district ; Robert Noble, Masulipatam/ Kistna district; C.F. Heyer in Guntur district ; Vallet and Gronning, Rajahmundry/Godavari delta; Clough in Ongole/Nellore region; August Mylius in Nellore/South Andhra districts; Howell in the Rayalaseema region. The early British officials, like the Collector of Guntur, Henry Stokes, Collector of Kistna, John Goldingham, Nellore District Collector, Boswell, Chief Engineer Sir Arthur Cotton etc., also helped the missionaries.

It is interesting to note that many German missionaries were appointed by the Anglo-American church organisations to carry out work among the Telugus in the middle of the nineteenth century. For example, the founders of Guntur, Rajahmundry and Nellore missions were all Germans. They came all the way from many north German towns and villages to the Telugu country, learnt the language and were well-acquainted themselves with the local religious and, socio-cultural traditions. Many of them were fascinated by the sweetness of the language and the peculiarities of the social set up. The German missionaries were also keen observers of local customs and aspects of folk culture. They were familiar with the major Hindu philosophical and religious systems/ thought as well as the different sects and anti-Brahmanical protest movements. They cited many verses of Vemana and examined the pre-British mystic and yogic traditions. Regarding anti-caste verses of Vemana a German missionary quoted the following verse of Vemana in which he denounced untouchability. *"Es gibt keinen paria aus der welt, wer lught, der isti ein Paria, und wer zu jemand sagt: Du bist ein paria, ist selbst der grosste paria."*[40]

The first generation missionaries laid firm foundations to the new faith by their hard labour and tremendous sacrifice. Many of them fell victims to the climate and succumbed to death. Some of them were subjected to discrimination and humiliation by the upper castes. Yet they persisted with their spiritual preaching, particularly among the dalit communities. Their early efforts at converting the upper castes, like the experiments made in Nellore district by the Hermannsburg missionaries, failed. Thus a majority of the early converts were dalit bahujans. As there were no other social reform movements, it was Christianity, which sought to uplift them spiritually, morally, intellectually and materially in spite of all the hindrances by the higher castes. The Brahmin priests referred to the missionaries as "ambassadors of a false God." Nevertheless, the new religion was whole-heartedly received by the downtrodden masses, although the upper castes thought that it was a "disruptive force in the social make up of village life." From the narrative accounts of early missionaries, it is evident that there were numerous instances where the village headmen and local landed gentry intimidated and threatened the new converts and perpetrated atrocities on them. Especially, in the *Agraharam* villages ("Brahmin Paradises"), where the priests "ruled with iron hand" very little could be achieved.

However, it was found by the missionaries that comparatively dalit-bahujan castes in the Telugu region were more self-reliant and independent, hence took to the new faith, despite many obstacles. Therefore, in Andhra districts Christianity was known as the Mala and Madiga religion (*peddintolla matam*). In the Telugu area, "the Baptists became known as the Madiga religion, the Lutherans the Mala religion." It is important to note in this connection, that the Christian missionaries took full advantage of the pre-colonial anti-caste ideological traditions and movements such as the Raja-yoga, Potuluri, Yogi Narsaiah, Vaisnava and, other mystic traditions which were quite popular among the dalit-bahujan communities. Similarly, in the villages the lower castes were also used to the preaching of the wandering Gurus, the men whom the missionaries called the "heathen priests." Thus the pre-British religious traditions provided a cordial reception for them and the missionaries had the added novelty of being white, and were received with great curiosity and respect. Moreover, the common people had already heard messages similar to that of Christian teaching from the wandering gurus, "the men of genuine religious discernment" and hence "they found no difficulty in accepting a new incarnation of this man Jesus." The continuity from the old tradition could be seen. For instance, the first native Christian in Guntur—Stephen was the disciple of a native lower caste priest; so also was the first convert in Palnad, Malapati John. Likewise, many of the early Catechists and local preachers in the Hermannsburg mission had been the *Mala Dasaris*, who were well-trained speakers with a fairly good education and religious knowledge. Rajayogi Guru Yerraguntla Peraiah – the forerunner of the mass conversion movement in the Ongole region provided the classic example of the link between the old and the new religious traditions. Webster remarked: "Beginning in 1869 the number of baptisms began to increase markedly. The movement spread through the work of Peraiah and the other early converts… At the end of 1870 there were some 1103 Christians in 160 villages around Ongole, by the end of 1876 there were some 3000 and the mission field had greatly expanded."[41] So the Peraiah-led movement was "an avalanche, gathering up mass as it went along." Due to the influence of such lower caste preachers many of dalit-bahujan communities/people embraced Christianity. Dolbeer wrote: "It is quite apparent from the early history of the Lutheran missions that without these religious leaders the success of the work would have amounted to almost nothing. *They were the Key to opening the hearts of the common people in the villages.*"[42]

In the coastal Andhra countryside, in terms of material conditions there was not much difference between the dalits and other lower Sudra castes (bahujans). This fact accounted for a considerable portion of them accepting the new religion. Moreover, the spiritual and moral teachings of Christianity being anti-casteist and mainly targeted against Brahmanical supremacy, appealed to the lower castes, who were already familiar with such thinking. The bigotry and pride of the Brahmins was well observed by the Christian missionaries, who lived among the village communities. They also observed how the lower castes were subjected to the rapacious exactions and cruel oppression by the upper castes. In comparison to Hinduism, Christianity appeared to be a religion of compassion and sympathy, as distinctions of caste were of the very essence of the former and diametrically opposed to the spirit of the latter. Theoretically, and also in practice, Christianity provided equality. It also maintained that former caste distinctions should not be allowed to continue to the reproach and injury of those who had risen by virtue of their accomplishments and were worthy of their presently achieved elevated social position. In other words, Christianity sought to delegitimise the ascriptive social order. Christian thought differed from that of Hinduism with regard to the justification/legitimation of social hierarchies and the nature of social justice. While the basic principles of Brahmanical orthodox Hinduism like *karma*,—"as a man sows so shall he reap"—rebirth, *moksha* etc. justified the caste system, Christian religious thought unequivocally debunked, denounced and condemned it. Hanlon observed: "In protestant Christian theory, all men shared an original spiritual equality before God. Christianity deprecated human status derived from merely human social or religious hierarchies as compared to the merit of individual faith and virtue. This emphasis on individual merit and the concept of original human equality gave rise to a universally valid ethic for the construction of human societies, and formed their only ultimate source of legitimacy."[43] Further, "Missionary polemic laid a far greater emphasis on the idea of deliberate Brahmin conspiracy to enjoy social privileges with as little effort as possible." Whereas the high caste moderate social reformers tended to regard them (Brahmins) as "the victims of their own weakness and failed in their natural task of social leadership,"[44] the anti-Brahmin ideas articulated by the missionaries had a powerful influence on the thinking of the lower caste intellectuals in the nineteenth and twentieth centuries.

Some of the Protestant missionaries belonging to the American and Hermannsburg Missions in the nineteenth century considered caste as opposed to the very core of Christianity and consistently attacked it. Especially, the founders of Guntur and Nellore missions were the arch enemies of the spirit and practice of the caste system. August Mylius of Hermannsburg Mission in Nellore district, as a matter of principle and praxis took a harsher view of caste and did not allow caste distinctions to be observed among Christian converts, for he believed that "there can be no difference between the word of God and the spirit of God." He was a strict disciplinarian and did not hesitate to take extreme measures of punishment, if anybody violated the norms of Church. In one instance, when one of his fellow missionaries Dahl tended to befriend the upper castes and spend more time with them to the neglect of the lower castes, he succeeded in removing him from Nellore. Mylius also consciously encouraged inter-dining and inter-mixing among the church members and fostered ideas of social equality within the community. The other Anglo-American missionaries encountered problems of caste distinctions and inter-caste animosity, yet they handled it tactfully, with care and diligence. The missionaries not only took note of caste distinctions between the higher and lower sections, but also within the dalit communities like the Malas and Madigas. The peculiar traditional and cultural belief systems among them were handled with caution and sensitivity. However, often the Mala-Madiga animosity and conflict caused anxiety to many a missionary. But the larger community-consciousness was fostered in practice through the institutions of church and school, at least during the second half of the nineteenth century.

From the writings and observations of many Christian missionaries, who lived among the rural communities of the Telugu area for long periods of time ranging from 10-15 to 40 years, it is clear that Brahmanical supremacy was based on illiteracy, ignorance and superstition of the vast majority of lower castes. Some of the missionaries also vividly described everyday instances of caste discrimination and oppression. They felt that since these disprivileged communities were deprived/denied modern education and institutions with access to spiritual and secular knowledge they could not effectively challenge upper caste domination. Hence, the Christian missionaries established many educational institutions in villages and semi-urban areas, in which many of the boys and girls belonging to the lower castes were educated. Of course, the missionary educational institutions had a dual function: to make schools as agents of conversion and to impart Bible/Christian religion. Nevertheless, for the dalit-bahujans it was their best opportunity to gain access to western education and knowledge, which had been hitherto denied to them. Even if the Christian missionary schools were started as instruments of proselytisation they became cradles of learning for many generations of lower caste children who had been denied formal education for ages due to the Brahmanical maxim, "that the lower classes of the people shall not be permitted to learn to read" and "a literate Sudra is to be avoided like a drunken man or a mad bull." The missionaries recorded a number of first-hand, eyewitness and personal instances where the upper caste village headmen, and Brahmins together had prevented Christian teachers from starting a school, often threatening to drive them out of the village and, if they persisted, with punishment. Many a time, however, the missionaries came to the rescue of the lower castes and continued to provide education and train their children in spiritual and secular fields. All the mission schools had mixed caste students and often faced problems of adjustment and co-operation between pupils of lower and higher castes. Due to the quality education of missionary schools, the upper castes reconciled. In the beginning, these schools had played a significant role in moulding the ideas, behaviour and character of the educated dalit-bahujan communities. "As these people learned to read and write and as they realized that they had a champion in the person of the missionary, their attitude towards life and towards those who had always dominated their lives changed drastically."[45]

Therefore, for the lower caste persons the Christian missionary appeared to be a saviour, because in times of distress and necessity he was present to help them. Besides education, the missionaries also provided impartial relief to the worst affected lower caste population during famines, epidemics and other disasters. At times the individual missionaries became targets of attack and even poisoning by the upper castes, for their help and encouragement to the dalit-bahujan communities. The Hermannsburg missionaries in south Andhra districts, the Baptists in Ongole/Nellore region and the American Lutherans in the Guntur area did yeomen service to the distressed population during the famines. It is no wonder then that for the lower castes, Christianity appeared as the real hope and alternative dependable source of assistance in a context in which the upper caste Hindus were unconcerned with their well-being. Though there were some charitable measures undertaken by the local landlords and other philanthropists, they were not really accessible and beneficial to the dalit communities, since between "the Hindu community and the Pariahs there is little love lost.... Pariahas have no chance of rising above their present condition of extreme poverty and degradation." A contemporary Brahmin official of the Madras Government remarked thus: "the best thing that can happen to them, the Pariahs, is conversion either to Christianity or the Muhammedan religion."[46]

Naturally, the individual Christian missionary was rightly perceived by the lower castes as an incarnation of "*Narayanamurthy,*" because it was he who extended them material and moral help and supported them "bodily and spiritually" in times of need and distress. Of course, the material and financial help offered by the Christian organisations was a "big attraction" for the poor people. Thus, struggle against caste discrimination and efforts to eradicate untouchability have become an important part of missionary ideology and activities. It was mainly due to the endeavours of Christianity that the lower castes got the benefits of modern education and employment. The educational and socio-religious efforts of the missionaries also contributed immensely to a new awakening among the downtrodden castes and communities of Andhra society, which enabled them to gradually claim equality and self-respect. The findings of my study do not wholly support the thesis put forth by scholars like Nicholas Dirks,[47] who maintain that Christian missionaries were mere "agents of colonialism" and contributors to the "construction of modern, colonial caste discourse." By focusing on the missionaries as the earliest source of dalit consciousness and uplift, I do not want to sound either like a simple proponent of missionaries or to suggest that West was the only agency of transformation. However, the efforts of missionaries in the Andhra countryside did facilitate religious conversion and the formation of anti-caste and anti-Brahmin ideology among dalits. And also, what was significant about the missionarie's work was the fact that they incorporated certain aspects of indigenous (read Bhakti) tradition in their preaching, which shaped dalit consciousness in the nineteenth century. Therefore, religious ideology propounded by Christianity became acceptable to the dalit-bahujan communities. Since the Christian missionaries were the pioneers of western education/knowledge among the dalit-bahujan castes, they were responsible, to a large extent, for imparting an identity to them.

The Adi-Andhra Upsurge

In colonial Andhra, various social reform movements and ideologies also facilitated the assertion of dalit identity and self-respect during the first quarter of the twentieth century.[48] In addition to the Christian missionaries, a number of social reformers, liberal and progressive forces also denounced untouchability and caste discrimination. Indeed, generations of dalit educated youth and intellectuals were nurtured by many reform organisations such as the Brahma Samaj, Arya Samaj, and the Adi-Andhra Mahasabha, who fostered in them a sense of self-respect, dignity and individualism. Consequently, a host of dalit organic intellectuals through writings, speeches, and associations launched an attack on the Brahmanical ideology. They were quite instrumental, in intellectual and ideological terms, in critiquing, delegitimising and undermining the ascriptive social order and social inequality based on birth. In particular, the "Dalit triumvirate" viz., Kusuma Dharmanna (*Nalladoratanamu and Harijana Satakamu*), Jala Rangaswamy (*Antaranivarevaru and Malasuddi*), Nakka China Venkayya (*Harijana Keertanalu*) constructed and articulated a distinct ideology of the annihilation of caste and social inequality. It is also important to note that these writings appeared in the context of the politicisation of dalits in the 1930s (Gandhian programmes of Harijan Upliftment and the Gandhi-Ambedkar controversy). The distinct and autonomous dalit identity and assertion of the 1920s and 30s was rooted in the socio-political turmoil in colonial Andhra; *the Adi-Andhra Mahasabha, Constitutional Reforms, the Justice Party, Self Respect Movement, Harijan Sevak Sangh, Poona Pact etc.* A political commentator remarked in the early 1930's thus:

> "The mere possibility of political change has awakened the depressed classes from their age-long torpor, and their insistent demand that the institution of untouchability should disappear, has become one of the most live questions of modern India. Never has the Hindu community, in its history, been faced with so serious a crisis and what is most significant in this truly momentous movement is the all-but -universal support the reformers have received from the Hindu community. *That the choice lies between the caste system with its attendant social tyranny and political power on the one hand, and democratic institutions with the possibility of social progress and political power on the other, has been clearly grasped*...This is the reason why the fight for the equality of untouchables has become a tremendous struggle between the political forces of the country in alliance with all the impulses of social reform and educated thought on the one side, and religious orthodoxy, political reaction and social obscurantism ranged on the other."[49]

This was also a period which witnessed the emergence of a distinct dalit literary tradition and the creation of "texts of resistance" and "protest literature" reflecting the changing consciousness and ideology of the dalits' quest for social justice, visions of modern nation and freedom. An examination of the proceedings of the Adi-Andhra Mahasabha, journalistic writing of dalit intellectuals in the vernacular press (in *Navajeevana*, for instance), and other sources indicate that dalits resented the monopoly of socio-economic resources by upper castes and demanded access to education, employment, public places as well as a reasonable share in the institutions of administrative and political power. It was in the context of growing dalit assertion and movements under the auspices of Adi-Andhra Mahasabha through its local level branches that the dalit masses faced upper caste intimidation and atrocities. Dalit activists reported a series of such incidents. A few examples: in Kavita village when dalit pupils were admitted into a local board school, as punishment the upper castes burnt their houses and poured kerosene oil in their wells in Ponnamanda village; when dalits rode bicycles they were attacked; in Challuru village the celebrations of Kunti festival by dalits was resented; in Gazularegam a newly married dalit couple was not allowed to ride on horse. In all these instances, dalits had to bear upper caste fury and animosity. Interestingly, when such atrocities were perpetrated on dalits, the upper caste led socio-political organisations did not come to their rescue or express solidarity. These incidents also confirmed the distrusts of dalits regarding the sincerity and commitment of caste Hindu Gandhian reformers. Thus in his presidential address to the *Andhra Rashtra Pradhama Adi Jana Sampurna Swantantra Mahasabha* in 1936, at Vizianagaram, Kusuma Dharmanna bitterly attacked the hypocritical caste Hindu nationalist leadership of colonial Andhra. He cited many personal experiences of upper caste deception and hypocrisy. In the course of his speech he exposed the inadequacies, limitations, and gaps in the nationalist paradigm and discourse of dalit liberation and exhorted dalits to work for complete freedom (*Sampurna Swantram*). He believed that a caste divided society would not constitute a genuine and legitimate nation and those (viz., the privileged castes) who claimed to represent it were its real enemies, because they seeked to maintain the hierarchical divisions within society in order to exercise their domination. He felt that complete *swaraj* for the downtrodden castes meant not mere achievement of political freedom, but a freedom that improved their moral and material character and well-being. Since, he did not visualise much benefit in being within the Hindu religion, he suggested religious conversion as a means of social emancipation. The ideas of Dharmanna and other dalit scholars contested the prevailing hegemonic nationalist and social thought propagated by the upper caste ideologues and sought to articulate a different vision. A dalit spokesman wrote: "Independence (*swarajyam*) will be obtained by the collective efforts of all the people. It requires unity. In India it is lacking.... If untouchability were eradicated, there would be equality. It would facilitate unity among the people. With unity and united action freedom could be achieved."[50] (My own translation). Such alternative visions were formulated within the context of anti-colonial struggles. The dalit intellectual assertion and the autonomous mobilisation of dalit masses through their own associations and initiatives led them into direct engagement with the issues concerning their emancipation along with national liberation. Thus, dalit consciousness and ideology played a noticeable role in shaping the nationalist agenda of liberation during the pre-independence period.

V

Bahujan Articulation of the Self

At the turn of the twentieth century, Andhra society witnessed a sort of internal churning/turmoil because of a new awakening among many non-Brahmin communities and castes pertaining to their status. Even before the Justice Party agenda began to influence the minds of educated sections within the Sudra communities, concerned and sensitive individuals took the initiative to launch modernisation programmes for their respective caste groups.[51] In this section, I will highlight such initiatives as reported in the vernacular (Telugu) press to indicate the nature and context of the emerging consciousness and ideology among certain Sudra castes. In an article "*Sudra Jati Kokavinnapamu* (An appeal to the Sudras) Bashyamnaidu, a *Kapu/Telaga* from Bandar wrote:

> "It is known that all the communities discuss the issues concerning their welfare in the form of Sabhas. Our community does not have such an organisation. Hence it is imperative on our part that we should take interest in organising a conference to rectify our faults and work for upliftment. The important aspect at present is unity in our community. We can achieve many things with unity. The conference would enable us to think and discuss the ways and means of our educational and economic development as well as to eradicate social evils. Not many persons within our community are educated and employed. Fifty per cent of our people work as agricultural labourers and other low paid jobs.

Majority of them are poor and starving. To overcome all these disabilities we must educate ourselves. It is very important. If we were not educated our position would further deteriorate. Hence, start night schools in each village and town. Educate the women and organise Sabhas in the village, once in a fortnight or month and discuss issues concerning our welfare. If such conferences were held, we would achieve progress soon. Instead of wasting money and energies on litigation and court cases, it is better to utilise them for the establishments of schools, libraries etc. Educate our children and send them to foreign countries for obtaining better skills in agriculture, commerce and others. We have many historical instances where communities, which struggled hard and sacrificed attained name and fame. Work for the betterment of our fellow caste men and achieve laudable objectives. Do it at the earliest and contribute your might to it." (my own translation).[52]

This appeal to the community for working hard and achieving progress was received positively and many such responses were reported. Most of them agreed with the spirit and essence of the appeal and noted that the urge for association and collective efforts was growing. Consequently, a *Kapu/Telaga Sangham* came into existence.[53] This spontaneous and voluntary spirit was clearly visible in many of the caste associations that were formed in the first quarter of the twentieth century. However, the political dimension was added later. So the socio-cultural awakening preceded the politicisation of caste groups. Commenting on the First Telaga Mahasabha, the editorial of *Krishna Patrika* observed the following:

"The first Telaga Mahasabha held on 7th October (1923) in Bandar is an evidence of the fact that there is all round national awakening. Nearly 3000 Kapus from various villages, taluqas attended it. Delegates came from all the 13 taluqas of the district and even from small villages. They are not English educated. They are not politicians or political leaders. Only a few of such people attended it. Vast majority of them are true Kapus (*Acha Kapulu*), landholders, agriculturists and labourers. They are the sons of the soil, innocent and large-hearted people, who work in the green fields and tender cows.... Why so many village folks came in groups? The politicians and the educated Kapus might utilise their support for selfish ends.

> They might use them as instruments for obtaining higher positions.... These are negative features. But, behind all this there is a growing consciousness among them. It is apparent in their faces. It is a natural consciousness. That is caste... caste might be narrow, local but it is not an illusion (*kalpitam*). Just as family, individual, it is natural. The Telaga Mahasabha is the embodiment of caste consciousness (*prabodamu*) i.e., 'we are Telagas, we are Kapus'. This self-consciousness awakened the community... This self-pride brought so many of them together. The non-Brahmin movement might have been politically insignificant, but undoubtedly socially it was a great success. It awakened the hitherto backward communities, which were steeped in superstition/ignorance, and inculcated in them self-respect and self-confidence...No other movement achieved such an all round progress in such a small period... Its influence has come to stay. It penetrated deeply into all the non-Brahmin communities. In future, the educated Brahmin and non-Brahmin alike would have to pave the way for the common/rural masses. If it is observed with this perspective, the caste feeling, which is spreading in the Telugu districts, is a welcome development. Caste pride is a fact. It ignites the dormant forces. It enhances self-confidence and strengthens the community. It should not be stopped... Today every community/group is awakened...out of this conflict and turmoil peace would prevail. The Telaga Mahasabha has inaugurated a new Dawn."[54]

There has been a general feeling among the educated sections of the communities like *Kapu/Telaga, Viswabrahmin,*[55] *Gauda/Settbalija,*[56] *Palli/Agnikulakshatriya,*[57] *Chakali/Rajaka,*[58] *Padmasale*[59] that caste associations are not anti-national and/or that caste associations are negative expressions of nationalism/patriotism. They asserted that each caste has specific problems to confront; hence the associations have to address the peculiar aspects concerning them and then undertake caste reforms. It was also felt that when all of them united and worked for the upliftment of their respective caste groups, the national organisation would be strengthened. "Publicists" like Kurma Venkata Reddy, a leading Justice Party politician, articulated the need for self-assertion and association. While inaugurating the First Godavari Telaga Mahasabha in 1927 he said:

> "Each caste should work for its welfare and also co-operate with others for the overall social development. If every individual co-operates Nation would progress/develop. That is called nationalism/patriotism. Just as nationalism is appreciated, so also is caste fellowship. In Andhra Desa many castes.... have established their own associations and are working for their betterment. We are late in awakening and organising our caste association. We are cultivators. Agriculture is our main occupation. We produce social wealth. We have to improve agriculture and introduce new technology in order to modernise our profession. We have to use our voting rights. It is a valuable right. The governments are dependent on it. It can change ministries and governments. Government should be in the hands of the majority people. We should not allow the minority to exercise power. In this district, we are in the majority. So we should get our legitimate share proportionate to our population. We are like 'frogs in the well', power would not come to us. We should work hard... *kashte phale* (work is reward) is also applicable to administrative power...we should politicise our community and bring about political awareness. For this we all should unite and achieve success."[60]

In the awakening of the non-Brahmin communities both the socio-cultural and political dimensions were evident. The over all perceptions were identical. The lower Sudra castes like *Chakali, Palli, Gauda, Yadav, and Telaga* emphasised the need to modernise their professions and obtain modern education. They also resisted discrimination and humiliation. Thus the *Agnikula kshatriya Sangham* in Godavari district protested against the upper caste comments about their status. When the Brahmin dominated *Krishna Patrika* adversely commented about their caste as *"Neeti kakulu"* (water crows) many protests were registered by them. The editorial offered an apology and offered explanation saying that "each caste is free to change its nomenclature. In our view, nobody has any right to object [to] it. We wish the community success in their educational progress."[61] Similarly, the educated youth of the *Chakali* community in Kistna district protested against the highhanded behaviour of upper caste village headmen and demanded certain rights. It is also evident that the lower castes aspired to take up other respectable professions. All of them were unanimous in denouncing the monopoly of certain castes/communities in the fields of education, employment and power. In the context of the electoral politics of the 1920s and 30s each caste group was trying to exert pressure to obtain concessions and benefits for themselves. Acquisition of modern education, public employment and modernisation of professional skills were stressed mainly by the lower castes. Education was considered to be the panacea for social evils and socio-economic betterment. Many caste associations mobilised education endowment funds, established hostels and granted scholarships to the poorest needy students. The *Viswabrahmin Sabhas* deplored the irrelevance of liberal western education for their occupational/professional progress. They desired the development of vocational education as an appropriate tool for the socio-economic upliftment of the artisan communities. The toddy tappers (*Gamallas*) pleaded for an education that would provide knowledge regarding the production of industrial/commercial goods like jaggery and coir products. Similarly, the weavers aspired to upgrade their traditional skills with the help of modern techniques. In essence, all the lower caste spokesmen perceived that remedy for their plight/suffering lay in modern education, self-help and modernisation schemes. "Education, foreign travel, railways, refreshment rooms etc. have been bringing about reforms which even kings...can never dream of achieving,"[62] wrote the correspondent of a vernacular paper. Another reported: "Viswabrahmins desired that their sons should have higher education and government service, and devise means to obtain the education for their children to carry on their industries and the necessary industrial training."[63]

A Kapu/Telaga spokesperson wrote:-

> "Awaken Brothers. Develop education. Be educated. Education alone is strength (*pattugomma*) the riches and comforts are not permanent. The other educated castes are suppressing us. Since we are not educated there is no unity among us. O Rich people spare a small fraction of your wealth for the growth of education. Feel that the strength of community is your strength. When the fellow caste men are suffering with problems, you can't be indifferent...."[64]

The educated sections from among the lower Sudra castes made such sentiments and emotional appeals. In fact, it is not entirely correct to say that only the English/Western educated urban elite took the lead in caste reforms. The rural/rustic and vernacular educated lower level officials, petty traders, cultivators, the non-elite groups, were in the forefront of various social and cultural movements. It is also not true to say that it was only politisation of the caste that led to the formation of caste associations and other reform activities. In fact, much before the Justice Party and Self Respect movements made an impact, initiatives were taken by the educated (both English and vernacular) classes from among the Sudra castes. Even the semi-literate and uneducated rural people were brought into the fold of reform movements in the early decades of the twentieth century. However, the politicisation process initiated by the non-Brahmin movements in the context of constitutional reforms did hasten the process of reform zeal among the Sudra castes/communities in colonial Andhra.

It was against the background of growing aspirations and hopes for progress and socio-economic upliftment among the dalit-bahujan castes, that the Justice Party initiated and led socio-political protest against Brahmin domination which played an important role in moulding their consciousness in the 1920s and 30s. "The emergence and growth of the Non-Brahmin Movement did exercise a considerable impact on the Dalit movement. It brought together the Sudras and Anti-Sudras to challenge and resist the dominance of the Brahmins and higher castes. In the course of organising themselves against the upper castes, and in particular, the Brahmins, the non-Brahmin castes were able to develop greater solidarity, cohesion, and a new sense of identity, self-esteem, and assertiveness."[65] Political and intellectual assertion of the lower castes became more sharp and pronounced in a situation, in which the Brahmin community disproportionately held privileged positions in the spheres of education and employment. Hence, educated sections from among the lower Sudra castes felt that the Brahmins blocked their opportunities. Invariably, the non-Brahmin ideologues (including dalits) articulated notions of "equitable distribution of resources," "equality of opportunity," "equal rights and privileges," "proportional representation" and emphasised the democratisation of civil and political society. They were also unequivocal in rejecting the ascriptive ideology of caste and Brahminical supremacy. According to Laxmi Narasu, a leading intellectual of the non-Brahmin movement. "A polity of caste and privilege can never be consistent with social equality...only out of equal rights and privileges for all will emerge justice, dignity, human solidarity and unity."[66] Furthermore, "equality of opportunity meant that success should be determined by talent and energy and not by the accident of birth. The abolition of special privilege, the wider and more equal distribution of wealth, the extension of facilities for education...is some of the means of affording equality of opportunity."[67] The "gospel" of "self-determination" and "constitutional reform" brought-forth new social forces and political formations, which together mounted an attack on the exclusive positions of Brahmins. The anti-Brahmin consciousness and a broad non-Brahmin identity was conditioned and shaped by emotional and political expediencies. The non-Brahmin movement was perceived as "self-expression" of the majority. At the socio-cultural level, it was claimed that:

> "The justice movement is organized for the vindication of self-respect. The desire to reconstruct society on a more rational basis expressed itself in its varied activities. *Social Justice is the basic principle of its foundation. Social Justice is the main plank on which it first concentrated its efforts. The Principle of self-respect has caught the imagination of the people of rural areas.* The leaders of the movement realized that political power could not be permanent without the practical application of the principle of equal opportunities for all, including those who are termed non-political or depressed. The keynote of its work has been the service of the people hitherto despised as 'unpolitical masses."[68]

It is interesting to note that this statement of a Justice Party leader clearly echoes the opinions of the spokes-persons of various caste associations.

> "Owing to a combination of modern influences such as education, social and political reform, and irreligious propaganda, the Harijans are becoming more and more restless and discontented

with their social status and economic position and are here and there already in revolt, discarding the religion of their birth for others and none at all. Should that revolt become general and the Harijans fall away enmasse, the prestige of Hinduism will be damaged,"[69] remarked a social activist in 1936.

Prominent non-Brahmin intellectuals also visualised "a national society based on unity and fraternity, a new nation, of a new form of congruence between culture and power and a new way of relating the self with the other." To quote a Justice Party ideologue:

> "The dream of Indian nationalism will be realised fully with the passing away of caste from our land. Power cannot be safely vested in the people unless the mental habit, which sanctions and enforces the customary treatment of lower castes is changed. The emancipation of the people from suspicious communalism is the first milestone in the progress of responsible self-government of the country. National evolution will move on sound lines when all the component parts of the body politic are sound and strong enough to contribute their energy, experience, and intelligence, and when the organic connection and vitality of each link is healthy. With every unit of society growing strong and contented the whole society will be safe; otherwise national progress will be one-sided and irregular."[70]

The emerging consciousness of dalit-bahujan communities has been grounded on such ideological and intellectual articulations. The opposition of higher castes to the growing assertion of lower castes also helped cement broader non-Brahmin identity. The mainstream nationalist press and upper caste ideologues tended to denigrate non-Brahmin assertion. For instance the Brahmin-dominated *Andhra Patrika* commented: "the non-Brahmin movement is an artificial creation, that it has the support of only a small number of followers, and the bulk of the non-Brahmin community…stood aloof from it"[71]; "The attitude which the non-Brahmins of Madras are displaying against Brahmins is a self-destructive one and a national evil"[72]; "This community (non-Brahmins) being more influential in the matter of wealth, numerical strength etc. than the Brahmin community needs no separate representation".[73] Similarly, *Krishna Patrika* another Brahmin controlled newspaper noted: "This (caste representation) being once accepted, there will be no end to the consequent complications.... The suggestion of the Andhra Congress Committee that the non-Brahmin representation should be discussed by various bodies leads to the undesirable increase of mutual feuds".[74] Some papers also dismissed the idea of abolition of caste as 'specious arguments which are not in our interests," because "the caste system conduces to national advancement. The various castes in a nation are something like the numerous departments, which constitute the huge machinery of administration. The caste system is thus not a great evil after all."[75]. But on the contrary, the spokesmen of lower castes resisted discrimination and pleaded recognition of their just claims. They asserted that caste is "social imperialism,"[76] a "crippling disease" and described the Brahmins as a "privileged oligarchy." It has been argued that the attainment of liberty and justice has always been a negative process. Without rebelling against unjust social institutions and destroying age-old customs, "there can never be the free exercise of liberty and justice."

Available source materials such as press reports, resolutions of caste associations, autobiographical and biographical accounts amply make it clear that not all the castes and communities responded uniformly, but to the extent that certain caste groups became assertive, a broad pattern can be discerned in their thought process and ideological formation. Of course, the context, factors and actors which facilitated such an articulation and mobilisation also differed, for instance between the dalits and other lower Sudra castes (bahujans). But what were common to all of them were certain notions of social justice, egalitarianism and socio-economic mobility. There was a broad convergence of ideas among the lower caste articulations regarding the nature and content of democracy, freedom, nationalism, nation state etc. Likewise, the preponderance of the Brahmin caste and the ideological foundations of their supremacy became the most common areas of conflict and contestation between the upper and lower castes. The protest of dalit-bahujan communities against social and ritual dominance of the Brahmin community was also governed by their material conditions. They denounced the existing caste system and social arrangements not to uphold but to change and modify them. The so-called sanskritisation efforts of some of the non-Brahmin castes were surely aimed at it. By negating the Brahmanical monopoly of interpretation of the texts they were demanding the democratisation of priesthood and the right priesthood for others. It can also be interpreted as a protest against "Brahmanical exclusivity and sacerdotal monopoly." The dalit-bahujan movement might not have professed a "radical/revolutionary" over though of the existing system by violent means, yet their conscious efforts were directed at delegitimising and destabilising it; to what extent they succeeded is altogether a different question. But it was a fact that there was consistent demand to reduce the monopoly of certain social groups and equitable distribution of available opportunities/resources. It is in this unity of ideas/perceptions that one can visualise commonness in the social consciousness of dalit-bahujan castes in terms of the articulation of emancipatory ideology. Notwithstanding social, ritual and material differences, a majority of their spokesmen envisaged a future set-up based on the principles of egalitarianism and social justice. "Democratic principles visualise power and social authority rest not on individuals, families and group but the whole community...it denies the inequality of classes, castes and professions, the inequality based on birth and unalterable vocations. It asserts equality of rights, privileges, and opportunities,"[77] wrote K.M. Panikkar in 1933. He also denounced the caste system and propounded the theory of "3000 years of Brahmin domination."[78]

To conclude, the uniqueness of the socio-political assertion and consciousness of the dalit-bahujans in south India in the nineteenth -twentieth centuries lies in the fact that they attempted to undermine the ideological underpinnings of the Brahmanical social order and the tyranny of caste. A Sudra intellectual opined thus: "Caste organization crushes the individual under its dead weight and hinders progress by killing all consciousness of liberty...it is impossible to create a new people, united and cultured, without the abolition of caste and the uprootal of all religion whose life-blood is caste."[79] They also attempted to pave the way for a relatively more equal spread of secular power in modern society, by attacking the socio-cultural foundations of the old order. The movements led by them such as the Self-Respect Association, Justice Party, and the Adi-Andhra Mahasabha were based on notions of egalitarianism and a vision of the "homogenization of power within culture and society."

REFERENCES

* An earlier version of this paper has been presented in Andhra Pradesh History Congress, 27th Session, held at Tirupathi, on 4-5 January 2003 (Presidential Address, Modern Andhra) and also in the 65th Session of Indian History Congress, Presidential Address, Modern Section, Bareilley, December 28-30, 2004.

I am grateful to the Director of Francke Foundation, Halle, Germany for awarding me the Firtz-Thyssen Fellowship to do research on the contribution of German Christian Missionaries to Telugu culture. I am also thankful to Professor Rahul Peter Das, Institute of Indologie, Martin Luther University, Halle for his help and encouragement in getting the fellowship.

1. Professor Kancha Ilaiah is the foremost scholar who introduced dalit-bahujan as an analytical category in the social science research/writings; K. Ilaiah, *Why I am Not a Hindu*, Calcutta, 1994, Samya Publications, and "*Caste of Class or Caste Class: A Study of Dalit Bahujan Consciousness in Andhra Pradesh in 1980's*" (1995), *NMML* Paper, Delhi, (Memeo)
2. Tara Chand, *History of the Freedom Movement in India*, Vol. I, Delhi, 1976. Majumdar, R.C. *et al. An Advanced History of India*, Delhi, 1978.
3. Ranajit Guha (ed.) (1982-88), *Subaltern Studies*, Vol. I-VI, Delhi, Oxford University Press.
4. F. Eugene Irschick, *Political and Social Conflict in South India, The Non-Brahmin Movement and Tamil Separatism*, 1916-1929, Berkeley and Los Angeles, 1969, Press, p. 1.
5. Rosalind O' Hanlon, *Caste, Conflict and Ideology*, Cambridge, 1985.
6. Bipan Chandra, *et al. India's Struggle for Independence*, New Delhi, 1989. Sumit Sarkar, *Modern India* 1885-1947, Delhi, 1983.
7. Sarojni Regani, *Highlights of the Freedom Movement in Andhra Pradesh*, Hyderabad, 1972; M. Venkatarangaiah, *The Freedom Movement in Andhra Pradesh*, Hyderabad, 1974; B. Kesavanarayana,

Social and Political Factors in Modern Andhra, 1900-1956, Vijayawada, 1976.

8. David Washbrook, *The Emergence of Provincial Politics: The Madras Presidency, (1870-1920)*, New Delhi, 1976.
9. C.J. Baker, *The Politics of South India, (1920-37)*, New Delhi, 1976. Baker, C.J. & D.A. Washbrook (ed.), *South India: Political Institutions and Political Change, 1880-1940*, Delhi, 1975.
10. V. Ramakrishna, *Social Reform in Andhra*, New Delhi, 1983 and his article "*A Background to the Emergence of Caste Consciousness in Coastal Andhra Pradesh*" in S. Bandopadhay and Suranjan Das (ed.), *Caste and Communal Politics in South Asia*, Calcutta, 1993, Y. Vaikuntham, *Education and Social Change in South India: Andhra 1880-1920*, Madras, *1982*. Publications and his article "*Caste Associations and Social Dynamics in Andhra, 1900-25*", *DRS Project Report*, 2002 (Mimeo)
11. Ramakrishna, "*A Background*", pp. 101, 110.
12. Chinnaya Suri, "*Non-Brahmin Movement in Andhra*" Dr. Garigipati Rudrayya Chowdary "*Endowment Lecture-7*", Ramchandrapuram, 2000.
13. V. Narayana Rao, "*Intellectuals Role in the Process of Social Change*" in Yogendra K. Malik (ed.), *South Asian Intellectuals and Social Change*, Delhi, 1982, pp. 308, 16.
14. Rosalind O' Hanlon, *Caste, Conflict and Ideology, op. cit.*
15. G. Aloysius, *Nationalism Without a Nation in India*, Delhi, 1997.
16. S. Bandyopadhyay, "Caste, Class and Politics in Colonial Bengal: A Study of the Namasudra Movement of 1872-1937" in K.L. Sharma (ed.), *Caste and Class in India*, Jaipur, 1994, pp.19-53; Also see his book, *Caste, Politics and the Raj*, Calcutta, 1990.
17. Bandopadhyay, *Caste, Class*, p. 44.
18. G. Aloysius, *Nationalism*, pp. 79-101.
19. V. Narayana Rao, *Intellectuals*, pp. 16, 16.
20. P. Lakshmi Narasu, *A Study of Caste*, Madras, 1922, (Reprint), pp. 112-13.
21. *Ibid*. pp. 110-11.
22. Y. Chinna Rao, *Dalits' Struggle for Identity: Andhra and Hyderabad 1900-1950*, New Delhi, 2003. Also see his "Education and Identity Formation Among Dalits in Colonial Andhra" in S. Bhattacharya (ed.), *Education and the Disprivileged* New Delhi, 2002, and "Rise

and Growth of Dalit Movement in Andhra, 1906-1946", *Indian Social Science Review,* Vol. 5, No. 1 (2003).

23. J. Chinnaiah, "*Dalit Intellectual Discourse in Modern Andhra: A Study of Gurram Jashua (1895-1971)*", Unpublished M. Phil Dissertation Jawaharlal Nehru University, 1997.
24. I. Thirumali, *Against Dora and Nizam; People's Movement in Telangana,* 1939-1948, New Delhi, 2003.
25. I have been working on the theme of caste and class and published the following articles. Sector details (1) "Caste and Class in Rural Andhra: A Historical Perspective" in K.L. Sharma (ed.), *Caste and Class in India;* Jaipur, 1994 (2)"Dalit Protest Literature in Telugu: A Historical Perspective", *Economic and Political Weekly,* Vol. XXX, Jan, 1995; (3) "Dalit Identity and Consciousness in Colonial Andhra, 1904-1947", *Vikalp,* Vol. VI, No. 2, 1998; (4) "Growth of Education Among the Dalit-Bahujan Communities in Modern Andhra, 1893-1947" in S. Bhattacharya (ed.), *Education and the Disprivileged,* Delhi, 2002; (5) "Swarajyam/Swatramyam: Dalit Visions of Freedom in Modern Andhra" (to be published); "Upper Caste Violence Against Dalits in Andhra Pradesh, 1947-85" in Ch. Subba Rao and Francis (ed.), *Development of Weaker Sections,* Jaipur, 2000, pp. 193-205.
26. My survey of the socio-economic profiles is based on The District Gazetteers, Census Reports, 1891, 1931; E. Thurston, *Castes and Tribes of Southern India,* Madras, 1909, 7 Volumes; *Report of the Backward Classes Commission of A.P.,* 1970.
27. George Macmunn, "The Underworld of India" in *Great Britain and the East,* Vol. XLVIII, No. 1338, January 14-28, 1937, pp. 93, 133.
28. *Swadesamitram,* 1 July, 1913.
29. S.T. Moses, "The Besthas of Nellore" in *Journal of the Asiatic Society of Bengal,* N.S. Vol. XXVI, No. 1, 1930, p. 399.
30. Vijaya Ramaswamy, *Textiles and Weavers in Medieval South India,* Delhi, 1985; Soma Reddy, R. "Social Awakening among Certain Oppressed Communities in Andhra during the later Vijayanagara period", *South Indian History Congress Proceedings,* Quilon Session, January, 1988.
31. Brown, C. P., *Verses of Vemana,* Madras, 1911.
32. Chinnaya Suri, *Non-Brahmin,* pp. 14-15. G. Sudarshan Reddy, "*Caste Associations and Social Change in Andhra*", Unpublished M.Phil

Thesis, Department of History, Osmania University, Hyderabad, 1986.

33. V. Ramakrishna, *Social Reform*, pp. 134-189.
34. D. Anjaneyulu, *Kandukuri Veereshalingam*, Delhi, 1976, pp. 4, 37, 124.
35. S. Manikyam, "Mission's Approach to Caste" in Devasahayam, V. (ed.), *Dalits and Women*, Madras, 1992, p. 64.
36. My discussion of Christian Missionaries is based on the following works: E. Arno Lehmann, *It Began at Tranquebar*, Madras, 1958; J. Worrlein, *Dreizehn Jahre in Indien* (German), Hermannsburg, 1884 and *Vierzig Jahre in Indien* (German), Hermannsburg, 1913; F. Wishan, *Missionar in Telugu Lande in Indien* (German), Philadelphia, 1891; J. Richter, *Die Deutsche Mission in Sudindien* (German), Gutersloh, 1902; E.R. Clough, *While Sewing Sandals: Tales of a Telugu Pariah Tribe*, New York, 1899 (Reprint); Martin Luther Dolbeer, Jr., *A History of Lutheranism in the Andhra Desa, 1842-1920*, New York, 1959; , H. Grafe (ed.), *Evangalische Kirsche in Indien* (German), Erlangen, 1981.
37. These works include: G.A. Oddie (ed.), *Religious Conversion Movements in South Asia: Continuities and Change*, Curzon, 1997; *Religious Traditions in South Asia: Interaction and Change*, Surry, 1998; *Hindu and Christian in South-East India*, London, 1991; *Region in South Asia*, Delhi, 1991; *Social Protest in India*, Delhi, 1979; "Protestant Missions", "Caste and Social Change in India, 1850-1914" in *The Indian Economic and Social History Review*, Vol. IV, No. 3, 1969, pp. 259-91; "Christian Conversion in the Telugu Country, 1860-1900: A Case Study of One Protestant Movement in the Godavari Krishna Delta," *IESHR*, Vol. XII, No. 1, pp. 61-79.
38. D. Forrester, *Caste and Christianity: Attitudes and Policies on Caste of Anglo-Saxon Protestant Missions in India*, London, 1980.
39. J.C. B. Webster, *A History of the Dalit Christians in India*, Sanfrancisco, 1992.
40. Worrlein, J., *Vierzig*, p. 225.
41. J.C. B. Webster, *A History*, p. 41.
42. Dolbeer, *A History*, p. 102, [emphasis added].
43. Hanlon, *Caste*, p. 68.
44. *Ibid.*, p. 74.
45. Dolbeer, *A History*, p. 141.

46. Oddie, *Social Protest*, p. 145.
47. I am grateful to Mr. I. C. Wendt of USA for this reference and discussion on it.
48. Y. Chinna Rao, "Rise and Growth of Dalit Movement in Andhra, 1906-1946", *Indian Social Science Review,* Vol. 5, No. 1 (2003).
49. K.M. Panikkar, *Caste and Democracy*, London, 1933, pp. 38-39, [emphasis added].
50. See *Nalupu*, Nov. 15-Dec. 15, 1992 and Jan. 1-31, 1993.
51. This section is mainly based on the material continued in the Vernacular News Papers like *Krishna Patrika* (hereafter K.P.)15 and 21 June, 1921 and *Andhra Patrika* (hereafter after K.P.).
52. *KP*, 15 Feb., 1913; 8 June, 1929; 23 July, 1932; 13 Nov., 1937; and 15 July, 1939; 1 July, 1916; 24 May, 1924; 7 Nov., 1925; 12 June, 1926; 17 Dec. 1925.
53. For more information see *K.P.* 1 Mar. 22 Mar. 1913; 5-26 April 1913; 6 Sept. 1913; 13 Oct. 1913; 28 Nov. 1913; 5 Dec. 1914.
54. *KP*, 13 Oct. 1923 (Translations are mine).
55. *KP*, 27 Oct. 1911; 5-26 Jan. 1912; 4-11 Jan. 1913; 9 Jan. 1915; 29 Sept.1917; 9 July, 1921; 6 Feb. 1926; 6 Oct. 1928; 15 Sept. 1934; 2 May, 1938.
56. *KP*, 4-12 May, 1912; 12 April 1913; 7 June, 1918; 3 Dec. 1921; 14 June, 1924; 3 May, 1941; 6 Dec. 1924.
57. *KP*, May-15 June, 1918; Sept. 1918; 4 June, 1919; 22-29 Oct. 1921; 31 Dec. 1921; 8 Nov. 1924; 6 Dec. 1924; 20 Oct. 1928.
58. *KP*, 5 June, 1937; 19-23 Oct. 1937; 6 Nov. 1937; 25 Dec. 1937; 25 June, 1938.
59. *KP*, 4-25 Sept. 1915; 7 June, 1934.
60. *KP*, 17 Dec. 1927 (Translations are mi.e).
61. *KP*, 15 June, 1918.
62. *Sampad Abhyudaya*, 26 March 1920.
63. *KP*, 18 Sept. 1916.
64. *KP*, 24 May 1924 (Translations are mine).
65. Suresh, K, "The Dalit Movement in India" in Satyamurthy, T.V.(ed) (1996), *Region, Religion, Caste, Gender and Class in Contemporary India*, Vol. 3, New Delhi, pp. 364-65.
66. Laxmi Narasu, *A Study of Caste.*
67. *Ibid.*
68. A.P. Patro, "The Justice Movement in India" in *The Asiatic Review*,

Vol. XXVIII, No. 93, 1932, pp. 28-31, [emphasis added].

69. M. Arokiaswami, "The Bi..h of the Harijan Movement", in *The New Review*, Vol. IV, July-Dec. 1936, p. 183.
70. Patro, "*The Justice*", p. 28.
71. *Andhra Patrika* (here after *AP*), 25 Aug. 1919.
72. *AP* 27 Aug. 1919.
73. *AP* 19 February 1920.
74. *KP* 31 January 1920.
75. *Swadeshabhimani*, 23 November 1917.
76. Panikkar, K.M (1933) *Caste and Democracy*, London, p. 18.
77. *Ibid.*, p. 20.
78. *Ibid.*, p.18. "Throughout the whole system permeates the dogma of Brahmanic superiority. This is the foundation on which the whole edifice is created…the maintenance of institutions based on such obviously unjust principles, involved a conscious and deliberate policy, political, religious and educational, on the part of the Brahmins. In order to safeguard their interests, it was necessary for them to dominate councils of the State, to mould the religious development and control the educational machinery and literature of the community. This the Brahmins tried to do, and we know that they have been eminently successful from the fact that their predominance in Hindu social life continues unbroken even to the present time. For more than 3000 years the Brahmins have maintained…a complete sway over the masses of the Hindu population".
79. Laxminarasu, *Caste*, p. ii.

7

"*Swarajyam*/Swatantryam": Dalit Visions of Freedom

The main objective of this chapter is to analyse Dalit[1] perceptions of freedom, self-rule and socio-political emancipation under colonial conditions in modern Andhra. It seeks to interpret alternative visions pertaining to freedom articulated by Dalit organic intellectuals in their writings. The concept of the Nation and its constituents, as perceived by them, was fundamentally different from the dominant idea of the Nation. The totality of the Nation and the narrative of the freedom struggle was articulated by the upper caste elite nationalists. In the existing historical writings on modern Andhra, the emergence and articulation of a distinct Dalit self-perception, sensibility and ideology does not receive adequate attention. The historical relevance and significance of the Dalit question to the national movement and the relationship between nationalist and Dalit movements have not been acknowledged and analysed by mainstream historians. It appears that the marginalisation of Dalits in historical writings coincides with the marginalisation meted out to them in civil society. What the Dalit communities themselves, as members of civil society, thought about the meaning of the Nation and its essence and how they related to it is also not adequately analysed by scholars. The Dalit critique of the upper caste representation of the Nation and its ideology (nationalism) needs to be interrogated. Thus, in this paper an attempt is made to examine the socio-historical context and the articulation of Dalit perceptions of the Nation and freedom. The fact that, in the first three decades of the twentieth century, a well-informed Dalit thinkers and activists emerged indicates the ample scope there is to examine the ways in which Dalits perceived and interpreted certain concepts like that of the Nation, self-rule and freedom.

From the various writings of Dalit intellectuals it appears that real freedom for them meant freedom from caste oppression, elimination of untouchability and the end of social discrimination. They felt that social equality, self respect and dignity are an inalienable and integral part of independence i.e., *Swarajyam/ swantantram*. Though they did not privilege social equality over political freedom, they doubted the sincerity of the caste Hindu nationalists in establishing an egalitarian Nation-State. Dalit intellectuals asserted that unless social equality is achieved, freedom would be worthless. They visualised freedom with social dignity, honour and social justice. A Dalit poet angrily asks '[w]hether these (caste Hindu) social cowards who fear to mix with us, will become [the] heroes of independence[;] but don't give us freedom, don't allow us into their Temples, don't permit us to stay in choultries, prevent us from drawing water from wells. If we are denied rights, how will you achieve freedom[?]' Hence, he asserted *samanatwame* and *swantantram* (Equality & Freedom).

On the basis of writings and speeches of certain Dalit scholars and activists, (whom I prefer to describe as organic intellectuals), this chapter endeavours to locate authentic Dalit voices within Indian nationalists aspirations. Such aspirations are usually depicted as belonging almost exclusively and/or entirely to the upper caste elites. In the elitist discourse, nationalism only meant political opposition to foreign power. On the other hand, for the Dalit organic intellectual, it is dual struggle, both of an opposition to colonial power, as well as the fight against the caste system and untouchability. According to this view, the fight against colonialism and the caste system were essential for an integrated national freedom struggle. This view further contests fundamental elitis assumption: that the struggles launched under the aegis of Indian National Congress were not just anti-imperialist, democratic and secular, but also that the Nation was a given reality. In fact, there was a fundamental difference between the elitist and Dalitist perspective of what constitutes the Nation. What national oppression? How can it be overcome? The Dalit point of view asserted that a society divided by caste could not constitute a genuine and legitimate Nation and that those who claimed to represent it were indeed its antagonists, for they sought to maintain the hierarchical division within the Indian society in order to exercise their dominance over it. The upper caste nationalist's concern for Dalit amelioration was patronising and paternalistic. The national identity propounded by elitist Congress ideologues was not emanicipatory for Dalit masses. Dalit leadership argued that safeguards were necessary for the oppressed castes, for self-rule in a caste divided society. They needed and thus aspired for political power.

> "We feel that nobody can remove our grievances as well as we can, and we can't remove them unless we get political power in our own hands...without which we can't bring salvation to our people"[3], asserted Ambedkar.

There was a vast difference between the Dalit and elitist intellectual's perception with regard to the strategy of Dalit liberation; the former stressed the need for political power and empowerment of Dalit communities, while the latter envisaged and argued for reform and protection from above. The elite intelleactuals also claimed that the Indian National Congress stood for the welfare of the downtrodden classes and the represented them. But the Dalit intellectuals felt that the upper caste leaders of the Congress party, by championing the cause of nationalism, sought to maintain their monopoly of economic and social power that came with self-rule. *Swaraj* for Dalits did not simply mean the achievement of independence but rather, the achievement of freedom in a way that elevated their moral and material character and well-being. In the Gandhian discourse, *swaraj* and the abolition of untouchability were interlinked to such an extent that the one could not occur without the other. He constantly reminded fellow Hindus that, "being slave-holders themselves, they could not fight against their own slavery if they did not un-conditionally liberate the untouchables. He believed that caste Hindus should carry out the task of eradicating untouchability. It was for them, and not for the untouchables themselves, to atone for the custom that constituted the greatest blot on Hindustan."[4] Gandhi sought to represent the interests of Dalits by reforming Hindu society. Gandhi's notion of caste Hindus doing penance was aimed only at the removal of certain disabilities from the Hindu caste system. It did not promote or look forward to the eventual democratisation of civil society and sharing of political and administrative power by Dalits. In none of the nationalist pronouncements did they imagine an India where Dalits hold positions of power and authority. On the contrary, Dalits were expected to continue their various ancestral callings. But they were not expected or encouraged to occupy decision-making positions. Such an undertaking was the preserve of the upper caste elites. It is a well known fact that Gandhi firmly believed in the *varnavyavastha*, i.e. system of inherited occupations, according to which a person was duty-bound to do the job of his/her parents and forefathers. Accordingly, in an independent India the Dalits would fulfil their traditional roles. Gandhi's insistence on the retention and preservation of the varna order certainly hampered the radical restructuring of Hindu society effected through the abandonment of untouchability. As opposed to this Gandhian perspective, Dalits visualised a free nation in which they would emerge as citizens enjoying equal opportunities and rights. Moreover, they aspired to participate in the pursuit of *swaraj* which could not preserve the status-quo but heralded an egalitarian socio-economic order. Gandhi and other nationalist politicians were concerned solely with the issue of political independence from the British but relegated the Dalit question to the sidelines. However, politicisation of Dalits in the 1930's by Ambedkar's ideology and mobilization to their distinct and direct engagement with the issues concerning their emancipation along with national liberation. Yet in existing historical studies much prominence is given to the leading elite nationalist personalities, their activities and ideas, organisations and institutions, while the initiatives and perspectives of Dalit intellectuals and activists does not find an adequate place. In this article it is proposed to critically examine the nationalist/

neo-nationalist approaches and undertake an objective assessment of the role of Dalits in the national liberation struggle and their vision of freedom.

Dalits and Nationalism: Historiographical Approaches

The historiography of Indian nationalism is characterised by conflicting interpretations and opposing theoretical perspectives. Different schools of thought such as the imperialist, colonialist, nationalist, Marxist, etc. interpreted the Indian national movement, its essence and character from a wide variety of perspectives.[5] The imperialist die-hards and colonial rulers denied the existence of any nationalist ideology and a nationalist movement in India. They viewed the national struggle which developed since the late 19th century as not a people's movement but a product of the selfish needs and vested interests of the dominant elite groups who used it to serve their narrow sectarian and partisan needs. This school of thought virtually denies any active role to the different sections of Indian society. They were relegated to the background and were treated as passive and dumb creatures who had no perception of their needs or interests. The various tribal and peasant uprisings/ revolts were characterised as unwarranted deviations. Whereas, the nationalist-minded historians viewed the nationalist movement as a product of the popularisation and realisation of the idea/spirit of nationalism and freedom. They interpreted it as a movement of the people as a whole, a mass movement. Nevertheless, they had ignored and underplayed the internal contradictions of Indian society in terms of class, caste etc. They had also ignored the differing and often conflicting perspectives of the idea of the nation and nationalist ideology and strategy. Their characterisation of the nationalist movement as popular, class inclusive, open-ended etc., is certainly flawed, at least in the case of modern Andhra.

Like the interpretation nationalist movement at the all-India level, the nationalist movement in modern Andhra has also been interpreted by scholars in different ways. At present, the dominant trend is represented by the writings of nationalist, Marxist and Cambridge historians. Leading nationalist historians like Venkatarangaiah and Sarojini Regani tend to eulogise and glorify the freedom movement in terms of episodes and personalities. Regani wrote thus:

> "The history of freedom movement in India is a saga of great idealism and sacrifice on the part of her people. The people of A.P. also participated with great enthusiasm to make the noble dream of India's independence come true."[6]

She does not analyse how and why different sections of Andhra society wanted to sacrifice for the cause of freedom. What factors motivated them to participate in the freedom struggle? Why did certain communities and groups like the dalits did not actively participate in the various phases of the nationalist struggle? What kind of dream did they have regarding freedom? Whether the "noble dream" that the congress leaders represented that of all the masses, or partial? The analysis provided in her works is inadequate and blinkered. Another nationalist scholar wrote thus:

> "Mahatma Gandhi was the architect of India's freedom. His guidelines were meticulously followed by the Andhras and under him the freedom struggle became a mass movement...the other fact noticeable is that the freedom struggle in India is studded with episodes which at times wrung admiration from the people and leaders of the whole country."[7]

This sort of description missed out the multifarious nature of the freedom struggle. It took for granted that the people of Andhra as a whole shared the same vision of the nation and freedom. In the comprehensive history volumes written by Venkatarangaiah Dalits, their views, ideas, perceptions and movements did not find a place. He did not even mention the Adi-Andhra movements and the role of the downtrodden sections of Andhra society in the freedom struggle. His description is partial and heavily titled towards elite leadership and its activities. This elitist approach shared the prejudice that the making of the Indian nation and the development of nationalist consciousness and ideology at the regional level were exclusively and predominantly elite achievements. In nationalist historiography, these achievements are attributed to upper caste personalities (Konda Venkatappaiah, Gadicherla Harisarvotham Rao, Nyayapati Subba Rao, Ayyadevara

Kaleswar Rao, Pattabhi Sitaramaiah, Tanguturi Prakasam, etc.), elite institutions and organisations' (the District Associations, Andhra Mahasabha, Congress etc.) activities and ideas. No mention was made about the perceptions, aspirations and ideas of Dalit masses. As Ranajit Guha put it,

> "the general orientation of the elitist historiography is to represent Indian nationalism as primarily an idealist venture in which the indigenous elite led the people from subjugation to freedom. The history of Indian nationalism is thus written up as a sort of spiritual biography of the Indian elite."[8]

In contradistinction to the nationalist historiography, the Cambridge historians, like Baker and Washbrook treated Indian nationalist movement as "cloack for the struggle for power between the sections of the Indian elite, and between them and the foreign elite," thus effectively denying its existence and legitimacy as a movement of the Indian people for the overthrow of imperialism and for the establishment of an independent national state."[9] The so-called "Washbrook-Baker model"[10] of south Indian history lacks a frame- work to integrate the Dalit question into the nationalist movement. Their denigration of nationalism as "factionalism" did not take into account dalit perceptions and articulations. Although the works of these historians were considered to be "otherwise far more impressive" and a "substantial contribution to the empirical analysis of South Indian upper caste/class politics under British rule," they fail to pose certain important questions; much less do they provide analysis pertaining to Dalits, their consciousness and participation in nationalist politics as well as in the interactions between elite and Dalit politics.

Similarly the Marxist scholars[11] presented an account of the nationalist movement in terms of primary and secondary contradiction and class struggle, but did not take into consideration, non-class antagonisms and perspectives. In their otherwise coherent analysis, the caste and Dalit question was conspicuous by its absence. In spite of the fact that downtrodden communities like Dalits constituted a substantial group for the class based movements launched by the leftist organisations and parties, the inter-relationship between caste and class, political and social issues has been inadequately analysed. These studies also failed to provide a systematic historical investigation of the conflicting ideologies, programmes, strategies and mobilisation during the course of nationalist movement in Andhra. The undue emphasis laid on the class perspective hampered a holistic approach to the complexities of anti-imperialist struggles launched by different sections of Indian society. Also, the role of Dalit perspectives and their movements for socio-political emancipation did not find a place in the Marxist interpretations.

In this chapter our approach differs from the interpretations offered by the above scholars. We broadly follow what is now popularly known as the subaltern approach, which relates the attitudes, perceptions, ideologies, beliefs and activities of the downtrodden groups, like tribals and Dalits to the elite led movements. It also seeks to bring out the significance of the contribution made by these groups independently of the elites to the making and development of Indian nationalism in terms of their own ideologies and movements. Contrary to nationalist historiography which gives undue prominence to elite leadership in shaping the vision and goals of national liberation, this paper proposes to highlight the significance of the Dalit question during the freedom struggle in Andhra.

Dalit Articulation of Nation and Freedom

The elitist nationalists asserted that freedom from imperialism was the primary and basic issue for every Indian. But as far as the Dalits were concerned, far more fundamental and more immediately necessary was freedom from caste oppression. Thus, untouchability became a serious nationalist issue and also one of the strongest planks in the Congress agenda. In fact, of all the issues that came to the forefront during the Indian nationalist movement, untouchability and caste discrimination was an important one, particularly since the 1930s. The upper caste nationalists did speak against it. They viewed the centuries-old practice as a blemish and stain which tarnished the reputation and glory of India. It was considered as archaic and certainly not conducive to the cause of nationalism and democracy. The growing desire on the part of the politically conscious elite to abolish untouchability led to a situation where change was seen as imminent. Nationlist literature, both English and vernacular, were full of examples of Dalits' entry into temples, wells, inter-caste and communal dining as well as speeches and meetings for the sole purpose of increasing public awareness about the evils of the practice of untouchability. Even the nationalist-minded and pro-congress Dalits themselves believed that the eradication of untouchability was under way. Yet, in spite of their the expectations, the untouchability question and the empowerment of Dalits proved to be a much more complex problem than imagined. It was a significant issue in that it emerged as a national cause.

However, the problem with the elitist construction of untouchability in the nationalist narratives and discourses was that Dalits were invisible. They were considered to be voiceless, passive and objects of piety. Hence their representation was almost exclusively in the hands of the caste Hindu elites. For instance, Gandhi's reconstruction of Dalits as Harijans is clear proof of this. Dalit voices were mediated by the nationalist rhetoric. Dalits spoke through the lips of their self-appointed saviours. Dalits remained virtually silent in the public narrative about themselves, since more privileged social groups appropriated their voices in the interests of the nationalist agenda. However, there was Dalit articulation both written and spoken about untouchability and caste discrimination during the pre-independence period[11]. But these accounts of the historical and socio-political situation in the 1930s and 40s were ignored and co-opted by the cause of nationalism represented by the Congress party. The nationalist historiography of the Gandhian era also did not highlight the nature of Dalit articulation of nationalism and freedom.[12]

It must be said that the 1930s witnessed the emergence of India's Dalits as an important social force and the issue of untouchability was brought into the broader political arena of nationalism. As far as modern Andhra was concerned, an independent Dalit movement known as the Adi-Andhra Mahasabha had come into existence in 1917. The rise of autonomous articulation (outside the nationalist

Congress platform and organisation) of Dalit identity was rooted in the socio-economic transformation and the socio-political turmoil of colonial Andhra since the turn of the 20th century. In the 1920s and 30s enlightened Dalits rejected both the "Panchama" and "Harijan" identity and organised and mobilised themselves as Adi-Andhras. The new Adi-Andhra identity was intended to obliterate sub-sect (Mala, Madiga etc.) distinctions, rivalry and animosity. It was also believed that this new identity could reverse the stigma of centuries. Major issues focused and highlighted by the Dalit movement between 1917-47 were primarily related to their socio-economic upliftment and acquisition of land, education, employment, representation in decision-making bodies etc.[13] The Adi-Andhra movement of the 1930s manifested an earnest desire of Dalit masses to exhibit consciousness of rights, condemning untouchability, caste discrimination and demanding a share in political power through representation in local bodies from Panchayats to Legislatures. They were also resentful of the monopoly of socio-economic power and resources by the upper castes. In his long poem, *Antaranivarevāru* ('Who are the Untouchables') Jala Rangaswamy, a noted Dalit poet described the miserable socio-economic conditions of a large majority of Dalit communities and their oppression by caste Hindu landlords.[14] He denounced the practice of untouchability and caste discrimination against Dalits. He exposed the hypocricy of caste Hindu nationalists, who in the name of Gandhism, pretended to treat Dalits as Brothers but in reality did not follow his teachings. He also maintained that unless caste distinctions are destroyed and unity is achieved, freedom would certainly not be achieved. He said that Dalits and caste Hindus belonged to the same country (Nation) and are equally patriotic, hence they (Dalits) should be granted equal rights. He also mentioned that Dalits are capable of achieving *Swaraj* through sacrifice. He then asked, if seven crore Dalits are separated and excluded, where is the strength of the Hindu (Indian) Nation? He felt that unless all the Indian people are united, it is impossible to obtain freedom. Further, he opined that if Dalits are not united with others and their appeals are not heeded, *Swaraj* would not be achieved.

In another long poem *Malashuddi*[15] ('Cleanliness of Malas') Rangaswamy was quite blunt, assertive and exhorted fellow Dalits to awaken and demand their just rights. He wrote thus:

> O! Seven Crore People Unite
> Unite and demand (your) rights
> We are the foundation for Chaturvarnas
> Declare all are one, Demand Justice, fairness
> How long is this Slavery for Us
> When do we get the rights due to Us
> Unite and Demand rights
> In public places, public wells, public tanks
> In Trains, Boats, Thoroughfares
> In markets, temples (*mandirs*), public meetings
> Declare that we are fellow Human beings
> Hence listen to Us and uplift Us
> (My translation).

In the poem *Melukolupu*[16] ('Awakening') the pitiable life conditions of Dalit masses is realistically depicted. The poet gives a call to his brethren to overcome misery and destitution and become conscious of the future ahead of them. He writes:

> Go ahead of all other communities
> Don't sleep in darkness
> It is time to go forward
> Awake with courage and determination
> (My translation).

The writings of Rangaswamy reflected the changing socio-political situation of the 1930s. The self-mobilisation of Dalits under the banner of Adi-Andhra Mahasabha caused much politicisation and created a new consciousness among them. In his poem and essays Kusuma Dharmanna launched a bitter and scathing attack on the practice of untouchability and caste oppression. His two famous poems *Nalladoratanamu* ('Black Landlordism') and *Harijanashatakam* ('Poem of Harijans') written in the 1930s amply reflected the thinking and mood of Dalit intellectuals.[17] They were indeed responding to various issues raised in the context of Gandhi's Harijan Upliftment Programme and the Poona Pact. Through his poems Dharmanna posed penetrating questions to the caste Hindu Congress leaders regarding their theory and practice of *swaraj* and freedom. He wrote:

They say Swaraj, Organise meetings
Hail victory to Gandhi
O Lord! They Propound Hindu-Muslim Unity
Preach Popularisatin of Khaddar
Teach Patience is *Swaraj*
Organize Peace Corps.
But don't say what is our position on Earth
With kindness Gandhi wants to protect Us
He says no to untouchability
His disciples repeatedly utter Gandhi's name
They say "Let us achieve Swaraj"
But don't allow us to mix with them
They claim to be the true followers of Gandhi
Also claim that they did not forget his teachings
But burn with rage on Us, the Malas and Madigas

In their writings Dalit scholars also disputed Brahaminical interpretation of the reasons for their low and degrading status. They envisaged social equality as a precondition for freedom. Nakka Chinavenkayya asked the caste Hindu leaders, "How could you demand independence, without prohibiting untouchability?," and said "*Swaraj* could be achieved only when you stop untouchability." He described the attitudes of the upper castes towards Dalits thus:[18]

They forget that we are Human Beings
Treat Us worse than Dogs
Squeeze our Blood, Flesh and Bones
Enjoy the fruits of our Hard Labour
Do not tolerate if we wear shirts
Declare we only deserve a loin cloth
We feel happy to be educated
But you deny us education
Do not allow us join the Schools
If we lead a decent life
You become Jealous and Suppress Us

Therefore, he advised his fellow Dalits to demand their rights without fear. Literary representation of Dalit problems by Dalit intelligentsia indicates the strong feeling that they (Dalits) should represent themselves. Dalit spokesmen seem to have believed that caste Hindu scholars could not be trusted and that the nature of caste and social conflict, especially in the 1930s, was so great that not many caste Hindus could speak in defence of their interests and rights. Hence the independent Dalit writing and speach definitely represented the emergence of a new awareness and consciousness among the Dalit masses. The Dalit intellectuals like Kusuma Dharmanna and Jala Rangaswamy, being products of Dalit communities, reflected and represented the problems of Dalit masses and their changing consciousness in their writings more realistically and authoritatively than the non-Dalit scholars who preceded them. Moreover, these Dalit scholars have a lived experience, a knowledge of and a deep insight into the life experiences of the masses of whose problems they wrote and spoke. Especially the above poets, who found inexhaustible raw material in the society and communities in which they and the masses were born, shaped it into an authoritative representation. The significant feature of Dalit literature in the pre-independence period was its contemporaneity and realism. [19]The emancipatory ideology constructed and articulated by Dalit intellectuals in colonial Andhra was aimed at the destruction of caste hierarchy, end of caste discrimination and the abolition of untouchability. They visualised a nation of free and equal citizens. A Dalit activist pointed out that *swaraj* could only be obtained through collective mobilisation of the people of nation. People's unity is an essential ingredient of national struggle[17]. He wondered whether if India were to achieve *swaraj*, it would be for all people? Or only for non-Dalits? If it also includes Dalits why don't the caste Hindu nationalist leaders mobilise them? Why don't they abolish untouchability? He therefore, implied that without ending the disabilities of Dalits it would not be possible to bring about national unity, and without unity it would be impossible to achieve freedom and independence. Dalit spokesmen argued that unity of the Indian people is not possible without the abolition of untouchability. They disagreed with those who maintained that there is no relationship between untouchability and *swaraj*. They felt that the eradication of untouchability was an important prerequisite for social equality and unity. The only unity of the Indian masses would it possible to fight for freedom. Therefore, in their opinion, abolition of untouchability must precede independence.[20]

However, prevailing conditions in the 1930s and 40s *represented* increasing antagonism between Dalits and upper castes. Thus the Gandhian programme of Dalit liberation through his Harijan upliftment programme and Poona Pact did not make much sense to the vast majority of Dalit masses. The most articulate activists of the Adi-Andhra movement were very alert and pointed out the fallacies, inadequacies and contradictions of the nationalist project of Dalit liberation. A series of incidents of caste discrimination against Dalits in the 1930s exposed the hypocrisy of caste Hindu nationalists. A glaring instance of the persistence of discrimination was provided by the river and canal ferries of the Telugu coastal delta districts, where the freedom movement was more popular and spearheaded by the dominants upper castes. It has been reported that:

> "A member of the depressed classes might have to wait for hours before being taken over, as he and a Brahman would never be taken together and the Barhman always had priority. In the bigger boats plying on the two rivers and larger canals depressed classes however have to keep to a different end of the boat from Brahmans. In the cross-river ferries an influential Brahman would be taken over in preference to a crowd of depressed classes of prior arrival. In other cases either the Brahman or the depressed class person would hold back to avoid travelling with the other.... On the small canal ferries *(Ballakattu)* Brahman precedence is still the general rule, in certain municipalities depressed classes were denied the use of water taps reserved for higher castes, despite circumstances of proximity and convenience. The tale of minor disabilities and annoyances is long and the end not in sight."[21]

Through the growing struggle under the auspices of the Adi-Andhra movement, Dalits' claim for social equality and demands for access to public places gained considerable momentum. The assertion on the part of the Dalit masses led to physical attacks and reprisals on them by caste Hindus. Numerous instances of physical violence against Dalits in different parts of Andhra were reported in the local press during the 1930s and 40s. Growing demands of Dalits for socio-economic betterment were also resented by the upper caste landlords. The colonial government's ameliorative programmes for Dalits were intended to develop confidence, self-consciousness and self-respect among the Dalit communities. But such government activities in support of the Dalit poor met with some lip sympathy and great deal of practical opposition. The Labour Department of the Madras Government had to face a lot of opposition from rich landlords who led deputations to Government officials protesting against the programmes designed to benefit poor dalit peasants and agricultural labourers. There was also indignation and resentment at the special consideration shown to the Dalit communities in land assignment, house-sites and other measures. Indeed, bitter feeling against the rising of the oppressed under-dog was aroused in those who had kept them down. It was a definite indication of the true position in the rural areas where Dalit masses were not adequately protected. In most of the coastal Andhra districts Dalits constituted about 20 per cent of the total population and were the backbone of agricultural labour in the rice growing region. Despite their lowly status the Dalit communities played a large and important role in the economic life of the presidency. In one form or another they had been victims of landlords' oppression.

In order to overcome socio-economic disabilities and obtain empowerment Dalits demanded a reasonable share in political power through representation in the Legislative and local bodies. The Adi-Andhra Mahasabha in its 1929 conference at Gudivada resolved to request the Government to reserve 20 per cent (equal to their share in portal population) seats in the local boards, Municipalities and Legislative Assemblies.[22] During the controversy over the Poona Pact Dalit leaders in Andhra generally supported Ambedkar's demand for separate representation. A lot of discussion and debate was organised at different levels to resolve the contentious issue of the sharing of power in the context of constitutional reforms in the 1930's.[23] Although the local level caste Hindu congress leaders tried to convince the Dalit leaders to accept joint representation, it has been reported that the Dalit community was generally suspicious about the avowed intentions of the upper caste Congress leaders. Dalits could not have faith in the promises of the caste Hindu leaders since they were highly suspicious about their bonafides. Prominent Dalit leaders demanded proportional representation and reservations of seats in the legislatures. There was a general complaint by Dalits that caste Hindus have not admitted them to any new privileges. Moreover, the caste Hindu nationalists did not have any concrete agenda or programme to mitigate the sufferings of the Dalit masses.

Whenever Dalits demanded a reasonable share in power at the local level boards, Congress leaders evaded the issue. Although Congress leaders supported the election and nomination of some Dalit members to the local bodies, they never allowed them to hold important posts like the Chairman or President of the Board of Council. For instance, in 1932 when the issue of the Communal Award was being discussed, and Dalit activists pressed that Kusuma Dharmanna, a pro-Congress leader of the Adi-Andhra Mahasabha, who has been elected as a member of the Rajahmundry Taluk Board be elected as President of the Board and thus encourage the Adi-Andhras, the idea was resented by the congress leadership. A prominent Brahmin Congress leader of the East Godavari district explained at great length that the best interests of the community at large would be considered by all the (caste-Hindu) members concerned at the time of the election of the President and the claims pressed by the Adi-Andhra community would receive due consideration at that time. But he said *no promise or guarantee could be given.*[24] Similarly a number of other Dalit members of local boards were not encouraged to hold important positions in the local bodies, while the rich dominant caste leaders monopolised political power at the local level as Chairmen and President of Taluq and District Boards. Likewise, a number of other Dalit members of local boards were not encourged to hold important positions in the local bodies. The Dalits had to be subordinated to the leadership and dominance of caste Hindus. At the grassroots Dalits sincerely felt that they needed some sort of safeguards against undue influence on the part of the caste Hindus.

In the course of the Harijan upliftment programme and campaign in favour of the Poona Pact in colonial Andhra, there were the usual pious resolutions about the removal of untouchability, free entry into temples, access to wells, tanks, abolition of separate electorates etc. The Congress party leaders had endeavoured to create a positive impression that they were in favour of the removal of untouchability and temple entry. The Congress leadership thought that untouchability could remain as their prerogative and hence the Dalits were kept in the background. Dalits were also expected to allow Congress politicians to fight for them. If the dalit masses insisted on engaging in the struggle without the leadership of Congress, which was really what many Dalit groups had been doing in the 1920s and 30s, the Congress claim to represent Dalits would be compromised, along with its status as the only nationalist organisation representing all the people. Congress leaders had never wanted to allow the influence and authority of Congress party to decline.

Hence, in many places caste Hindu congress leaders had visited the Adi-Andhra houses in Dalit localities, preached universal brotherhood, and taken water from the Dalits in token of their sincerity. However, from the orthodox Hindus, particularly in the villages there was opposition to temple entry. Whenever Gandhi's disciples proposed to throw open the temples to the Adi-Andhras it was met with strong opposition.[25] The discrimination against Dalits was quite rampant in various fields -public wells, water tanks, river boats, ferries, temples, local bodies, etc. Even when dalits sought to acquire modern education as a means of mobility it was resented by the dominant caste Hindus. In fact, the Adi-Andhra movement and Dalit intellectuals desired to eliminate humiliation and discrimination by acquiring knowledge from western education. The emancipatory role of modern education was understood by Dalit activists and scholars. Through it they wanted to achieve social equality, status and dignity. In the various Dalit conferences, resolutions were passed urging the government to introduce free education for children of Dalit communities.

However, various reports of the officers of the Education Department of Madras Government mentioned the existence of deep-rooted caste prejudices, which were strong in the rural areas. It was considered to be one of the most important reasons for the slow progress of admission of Dalit pupils into the common co-education schools. There was widespread discrimination against Dalit students in the local board schools. It was reported that during the academic year of 1935-36, in the entire Madras Presidency Dalit students were admitted into only 55.8% of schools under public management. This meant that nearly half of the common schools were out of their reach. This discrepancy was largely attributed to the apathy of the local bodies and to caste oppression.[26]

The above description clearly indicates serious lapses in the nationalist agenda enunciated by the Congress party and the disjunction between precept and practice of the nationalist leadership. The emergence of Dalit articulation and an assertive Dalit movement exposed the lacunae in the Gandhian nationalist programme of Dalit liberation. The Dalit intellectuals effectively contested the hegemonic nationalist ideology constructed and propounded by the upper caste elites. The nationalist vision and concept of freedom as articulated by caste Hindu nationalists was certainly at variance with the views expressed by Dalit spokesmen. The nation visualised by the dominant Congress leadership appears to be partial and sectarian, for it did not include a programme and strategy of inclusion and unity for all sections of the Indian society. Dalits felt excluded in different fields like public wells, tanks, schools, and representation in local bodies. Moreover, issues central to Dalit emancipation such as untouchability and caste discrimination did not become an integral part of the nationalist programme, strategy and mobilisation. The upper caste nationalist intelligentsia privileged the ideal of *Swaraj* to such an absolute degree that all other issues concerning Dalits were pushed into the back seat. Thus Dalits to a very large extent didn't encourage the pursuit of a *Swaraj* which would preserve their status. Also the ideology of nationalism envisaged by the Congress did not incorporate Dalit aspirations and perspectives. As we have shown above, the Gandhian programme of Harijan upliftment failed miserably because of the obstinate upper caste leadership, which was reluctant and half-hearted in implementing it. The various instances of discrimination reported in the press and official reports exposed the double talk and hypocrisy of the Congress leadership. Moreover, the Gandhian notion of *Swaraj* appeared to be "delightfully vague", as he said "it is as much for the prince as the peasant, as much for the rich land owner as for the landless tiller of the soil."[27] But the Dalit concept of *Swaraj* was clear and frank. As we mentioned earlier, for Dalits *Swaraj* meant social equality, self-respect and dignity. Further real freedom and liberation meant the end of untouchability, excommunication and social discrimination. Dalit poets propounded an emancipatory ideology in terms of the totality of the nation in which the unity between Dalits and caste Hindus was envisaged and stressed.[28] They also articulated a notion of independent and free nation constituted by an equitable, egalitarian and democratic society and equal citizens.

The evidence presented in the foregoing pages also indicates that Dalit masses, by and large, were disillusioned with the Congress politics and were hence distanced from the nationalist movement. It was so precisely because Dalits were suspicious about the real intentions of caste Hindu congress leadership. With regard to two important issues, i.e., the end of discrimination and the sharing of political power, upper caste nationalists and Dalits held diametrically opposed view points. The fact that Dalits had not actively and enthusiastically participated in the freedom movement in modern Andhra is confirmed by recent sociological analysis and studies. "The Congress influence has always been directed to caste Hindus.... And it was this reason which provoked them to take part in the movement. The Depressed Classes and the Indian Christians have never been particularly interested in the Congress ... The social groups who actively participated in it were layers among the professional classes, affluent and middle class peasants, merchants and students with lawyers providing much of the leadership. It was a movement in the main of caste Hindus. The castes which played a prominent role in it were Brahmins, Komatis (Vaishyas) Kammas, Reddies, Rajus, Telagas and *Velamas*. Among the opponents of the movement were the lower castes like washermen and barbers, the depressed classes."[29] It has also been mentioned that the vast majority of Dalits had been apathetic towards the freedom movement. Their apathy can be explained in terms of the nationalist movement's inability to evolve an ideology, programme and strategy to incorporate their visions of the nation and freedom.

REFERENCES

1. The term Dalit has become popular only in recent times. In this paper it refers to the Malas, Madigas and other untouchable communities of Andhra, who are known by various names such as depressed classes, Panchamas, Adi-Andhras, Harijans, Scheduled Castes, Excluded Castes, Exterior castes, etc. The process of Dalit identity is discussed by Y. Chinna Rao, "Change in Nomenclature: A Historical Note" in A Pinto (Ed)., *Dalits: Assertion for Identity,* New Delhi, 1999, pp. 84-95. Also see Chinna Rao Yagati, *Dalit Studies: A Bibliographical Handbook,* New Delhi, 2003, Introduction.
2. The phrase/concept of organic intellectual is used by Gramsci. See, A. Gramsci, *Prison Note Books,* London, 1974.
3. Cited in G. Omvedt, *Dalits and Democratic Revolution,* Delhi, 1994, p. 168.
4. Quoted in T. Hubel, *Whose India: of the Independence Struggle in British and Indian Fiction and History,* London, 1996, pp. 151-53.
5. For a critical review of Indian Historiography, see B. Chandra, *et. al., India's Struggle for Independence,* Delhi, 1989, pp. 16-23.
6. S. Regani, *Highlights of the Freedom Movement in Andhra Pradesh,* Hyderabad, 1972, p. VII.
7. M. Venkatarangaiah (ed.), *The Freedom Struggle in Andhra Pradesh,*Vol. III, Hyderabad, 1974, p. VII. Also see other works by B. Kesavanarayana, *Social and Political Factors in Modern Andhra.*
8. R. Guha, *Subaltern Studies,* Vol. I, Delhi, 1994, p. 2.
9. See C.J. Baker, *Politics of South India, 1920-37,* Delhi, 1976 and D.A. Washbrook, *The Emergence of Provincial Politics: The Madras Presidency, 1870-1920,* Delhi, 1977; Baker and Wash brook, (ed.), *South Indian Political Institutions and Political Change,* Delhi, 1975; For critique of the historiographical approach of Cambridge Historians see B. Chandra, *et. al, India's Struggle for Independence,* p. 20 S. Gopal's Book Review of Baker and Washbrook Works in *Indian Economic and Social History Review,* Vol. XIV, No. 3, July, Sep.

1977, p. 405.

10. Y. Chinna Rao, "Some Aspects of Historiography of Nationalist Movement in Andhra 1920-40," *Osmania Journal of Historical Research*, Vol. 6, No. 5 (1990-1992), p. 67.
11. Y.V. Krishna Rao *et. al. Andhra Pradesh Communist Udyama Charitra* (Telugu), Hyderabad, 1983.
12. For details, see Hubel, *Whose India*, pp. 147-60.
13. See A. Satyanarayana, "Dalit Identity and Consciousness in Colonial Andhra, 1914-47", in *Vikalp*, Vol. VI, No. 2, 1998, pp. 41-56.
14. J. Thirumala Rao and K.P. Ashok Kumar, (ed.), *Dalitageetalu* (Dalit Poetry), Hyderabad, 1993, pp. 33-43.
15. *Ibid.*, pp. 45-53.
16. *Ibid.*, pp. 44-45.
17. *Ibid.*, pp. 55-58.
18. *Ibid.*, pp. 58-60.
19. See A. Satyanarayana, "Dalit Protest Literature in Telugu: A Historical Perspective" in *Economic and Political Weekly*, Vol. XXX, No. 3, January 1, 1995, p. 175. Also see Chinna Rao Yagati, *Dalits Struggle for Identity* (2003), Chapter on Dalit Protest Literature.
20. *Krishna Patrika* (5 June, 1921; 9 June, 1921; 27 Sep. 1924).
21. M.W.M. Yeatts, *Census of India*, Madras, Vol. XIV, Pt.I, Madras, 1932, p. 344.
22. See *Krishna Patrika*, 29 Feb. 1929.
23. M. Venkatarangaiah, *The Freedom Struggle*...pp. 535-58.
24. *Krishna Patrika, ibid.*, p. 553.
25. *Ibid.*, p. 536.
26. "*Growth of Education among the Dalit-Bahujan Communities in Colonial* Andhra, 1893-1947" in S. Bhattacharya (Ed.) *Education and the Disprivileged*, New Delhi, 2002, pp. 50-84.
27. Cited in G. Aloysius, *Nationalism without a Nation in India*, Delhi, 1997, p. 180.
28. J. Thirumala Rao and K.P. Ashok Kumar, (Ed.), *Dalitageetalu*, p. 68.
29. M. Venkatarangaiah, "Sociology of the Freedom Movement in Andhra: An Official View", *Itihasa*, Vol. I, No. 1, Jan.-July, 1973, pp. 174-75.

8

Religion of the Poor: Dalits and Christianity in Colonial Andhra

The role of Christian missionaries in religious conversion and socio-cultural change, as well as in the development of educational, health and self-improvement schemes in modern India, has been acknowledged by many historical studies.[1] Recent studies on the growth of Christianity in modern India focused on the interconnections between conversion movements, social reform and social change. Christian missionaries were considered to be the great institution builders, since they pioneered works relating to social reform, language/literature/philology, and the socio-economic development of weaker sections. Hence, Christianity has been described as the "religion of the poor." In fact, education and social upliftment have become synonymous with Christianity in India. During the latter half of the nineteenth century the impact of Christian proselytisation and evangelisation was felt throughout the country. Thus Christians have become an integral part of the diverse population of India. It was also during this period that movements of mass conversions took place in South India, including the Telugu country. The Christian missionaries had been perceived as the protagonists and patrons of the poor. The image of the missionaries as persons committed to justice and equality, prepared to espouse/champion the cause of the oppressed as well as to act as advocates of the underprivileged caught the imagination of the downtrodden masses and facilitated mass conversions of lower castes into Christianity in the Telugu districts of erstwhile Madras Presidency (south India), German and other Protestant missionaries were instrumental in organising various programmes of socio-economic advancement for the benefit of the lower castes and communities.[2]

In recent years, historians of modern south India are becoming more and more aware of the role and contribution of Christian missionaries in the development of language, literature and culture. A considerable number of studies on south Indian Christianity have been published in the last few decades,[3] analysing the complexities of Christian mass movements which interacted with local societies and also the effects of conversion. However, the impact of the German missionary enterprise is neglected, despite the fact that some important studies are available.[4] Moreover, within south Indian studies Telugu Christianity hasn't been sufficiently studied. Only few studies went consciously beyond the framework of the usual denominational histories and hardly any deeper research has been done so far on the role of German missionaries in Andhra Desa.[5] Among the German missions that worked in modern Andhra the Hermannsburg Mission is the most important one, but so far no attempt has been made to study its role and contribution in the development of Telugu language, literature and culture. Hence, an attempt will be made in this paper to highlight the significant contribution of German missionaries, like Benjamin Schultze, August Mylius and others, in the spread of education and social consciousness and socio-cultural advancement of lower castes/ communities. It seeks to examine the significant efforts of German missionaries in formulating and implementing dalit emancipatory initiatives and movements in colonial Andhra. The main focus of this paper will be on German-Telugulogy and it will also analyse the scholarly and intellectual interaction between German missionaries and Telugu society in the modern period. It will also probe into the German missionary legacy in a long-term historical and comparative perspective.

South India witnessed the advent of many Christian organisations since the early eighteenth century. The most important of them included the Tranquebar Mission, the Leipzig Mission, the Church Mission Society, the Hermannsburg Mission, the London Mission Society etc. Some scholars have studied the contribution of certain Protestant missionaries towards socio-cultural change in south India in terms of religious conversion and the rise of a new consciousness, but the focus was mainly on the Anglo-American missionaries.

The first Danish-German Christian missionary station was established in the south east-coast port city of Tranquebar (Tamilnadu) in the early decades of the eighteenth century. The South Indian and German religious/cultural contact was established when the first German Protestant missionary Ziegenbalg set foot on South Indian soil in 1706.[6] Since then a number of dedicated missionaries carried out the propagation of Christianity and rendered valuable contribution to south Indian languages, literature and culture. Some of the devout followers of Ziegenbalg, like Benjamin Schultze made valuable intellectual and scholarly contributions to south Indian languages and culture. During the early 18th century the German missionary activities were mainly confined to the Tamil-speaking areas and the city of Madras. In fact, Madras was then predominantly a Telugu settlement inhabited by artisans, traders, fishermen, and lower castes people. It is a well-known fact that the Telugus were very closely associated with *Chennapatnam* since its inception and greatly contributed to its commercial, religious and cultural life. Among the early German missionaries Schultze was undoubtedly a unique personality for his outstanding contributions. He was the first German scholar who wrote a treatise on Telugu Grammar known as *Grammatica Telugica*. It amply illustrates the structure of the popular colloquial language spoken by the common people. It is interesting to note that he paid little attention to the written as compared to the spoken *Gentoo/Warugisch* language. Hence, he was able to capture the imagination of the local people and understand the functioning of the local and grass roots society. He was one of the earliest German missionaries who gave religious discourses in local languages i.e., Telugu/Tamil and also translated the Bible into them. He also produced the first Telugu Dictionary and wrote a bilingual (Telugu-English) textbook. The writings of Schultze provide many interesting facts and descriptions of the multifarious aspects of south Indian society in the early eighteenth century. In the popularisation of Telugu language his contribution was quite commendable and unparalleled. Indeed, the German missionaries were the foremost pioneers in propagating the Gospel in Telugu, the language to the local people.

Benjamin Schultze (1690-1760)

Benjamin Schultze was born on 7th January 1690 in Sonnenberg village, in present-day Poland. After schooling in Landsburg, he joined Frankfurt-on-Oder and Halle Universities for higher education. He studied Theology and Oriental Languages under the guidance of two professors, viz., August Herman Francke and Heinrich Michael. Since he had acquired a good command over oriental languages, besides Latin, Greek, and Hebrew he was sent as a missionary from Halle to South India in 1718. During the first half of the eighteenth century, the city of Halle was a famous centre of European Pietism, where professor Francke had established a missionary endowment, the Franckesche Stiffungen. It was regarded as an extremely progressive and socially committed institution of charity and philanthropy in the whole of Europe.[7] Being a multi-linguist, Schultze acquired a good command over the Tamil language and after a few months started preaching in it. During his stay at Tranquebar, between 1719-26 he translated many religious tracts into Tamil and published a hymn-book in 1723. Later, he also undertook the translation of the Bible into Tamil and completed it by November, 1725. He was of the opinion that "no task was more worthwhile than to provide the missionary church in South India with the Bible in its entirety". As a missionary at Tranquebar, Schultze rendered remarkable service to the cause of the spread of the Gospel and propagation of Christianity among the Tamils as well as authored several works in the local languages. However, due to some internal problems, he left Danish-Halle Mission at Tranquebar and joined the English Mission at Madras in 1726. As a gifted philologist, he mastered the Telugu language within a couple of months and began speaking and writing in that language. A native Telugu scholar also helped him to gain knowledge of it.

Madras, which was known to the Christian missionaries as

Madrasapatnam, was sought to be developed as the main centre for the spread of Christianity. A Christian missionary described the importance of Madras in the early decades of the 18th century thus: "*Madras* is a populous city, abounding not only with a vast number of *Malabarinas*, but also with many other Nations besides: so that next to *Batavia*, there is hardly a city so fit and conveniently placed for *propagating the Gospel of Christ* in India. And because more than twenty four distinct languages are spoken in this place, we may very much wish that the preaching of the word of the Lord may begin in that city; both and that from thence, as formerly from Jerusalem, the Gospel of Christ, both by sea and land, may go forth, and spread itself over all the Parts of *India*."[8]

Benjamin Schultze, "the Light Among the Gentiles" had the rare distinction of being the founder of the first Indian Protestant Church on English territory, viz. the English Mission of the Society for the Promotion of Christian Knowledge (SPCK) at Madras in 1728. He was encouraged by the Society in his religious and educational activities in the city of Madras and its neighbourhood. He said, "The English Nation and particularly the honorable Society have hitherto given sufficient proof unto the world of their Readiness to promote the great work of converting the Heathen."[9] After obtaining the official confirmation from London, Schultze established the church at Madras to spread the "word of God among the Heathen." Subsequently, he enlisted the support of the "English Gentlemen" of Madras which included the Governor and Chaplain Rev. W. Leake, in whom he found "a very good friend." With the moral and material help and support of Europeans in South India and outside he was able to carry out proselytisation work and religious propaganda among the native population. His role in building the English Mission stationed at Madras was appreciated by the members of the SPCK thus: "...he began this Mission, not withstanding many difficulties and impediments that occurred: with much pains and labour he fixed it, and he has hitherto conducted it with much prudence and circumspection. By the serpent's wisdom and the Dove's Innocency, he has merited the character of a worthy, just and Good man; by his long residence among and easy conversation with the Natives. Here, has gained love for his person and respect for his character..."[10]

The running of charity schools and literary works enabled Schultze to gain the confidence of the local inhabitants of the Black Town area of Madras city. He attracted Telugus from the beginning. Consequently he was able to convince many of them to change their religion. The first convert was a woman of 25 years, the daughter of an interpreter (*Dubashi*). The early converts into Christianity included a distiller, a carpenter, a cook, a labourer, a shoe-maker, an embroider of stockings, a grass cutter, a water seller and so on. From the available evidence it appears that "the first Indian Protestant Church at Madras was a congregation of lowly labourers and people who worked for Europeans."[11] Benjamin Schultze was the first German missionary who mastered the Telugu language and produced a number of works in it. He was an outstanding linguist and a multifaceted personality, who worked as a missionary for about a quarter of the century (1719-43) in South India.

About Schultze's efforts at founding the new station at Madras, the Secretary of SPCK remarked: "The Reverend Mr. *Schultze*, the Principal Missionary…made a Journey into the Empire of the Great *Mugul*; and thro'a long Tract of land of 150 Miles between *Porto Novo* and *Paliacattee*, preached the Gospel in above one hundred places. On his journey he went to Fort St. George, and there preached for some time to the Malabarians in the villages adjacent to that Town, and Fort St. David. And not only so, but at the earnest Desire of the Governor, and the *English* settlement at Fort St. George, he fixed there, hiring a House in *Madras*, and there opening a School and Church for those of the *Malabarie* Nation, in hopes, by these Means, of having an opportunity to instill into the Youth the principles of Christianity."[12] Schultze himself described his early works in Madras as follows: "I am engaged into self forth in laying down the first ground of an English Mission. Just as every new work by its first raising out of the dust will want a great deal more that when it is advanced to perfection; so like wife this English Mission will want many things which only the good providence of God is capable of to procure by exciting many Christian benefactors, well-wishes and friends, as well in Europe as here in East India. Since I began to move on the Missions work here, the number of Proselytes increases every month."[13]

Charity Schools

Among the German missionaries, Benjamin Schultze was considered to be an able worker, even though sometimes "slipshod"; but for his untiring labours the Madras station would not have been a reality. At Madras he was warmly received by the clergymen and the Governor. He requested the latter to permit him to start a school for "the Heathen Children." To begin with, Schultze hired a private house in the Black Town area. Thus he founded two schools: the Malabar (Tamil) School (1726) and the Portuguese School (1732). His school project was quite a success with the local inhabitants of Black Town, who came to him "from morning till late at night." He wrote to the higher authorities in London that "the Heathenish School, wherewith I begun, is now turned into a Chrstian one; Ten Boys I keep grain in the Mission, which proves a little beginning of a Charity School, for girls I can't yet find anyone to take care of them."[14] He also informed his superiors at Halle in Germany that his schools had received the enthusiastic support of the local people and that 12 pupils had joined the Malabar School. There had been seven students in the Portuguese school, subsequently the strength had gone up to 13. No fees were collected from the students. They were provided free boarding and lodging facilities in the church compound. Schultze spent about 600 *Varahas* (60 pounds) and purchased a House, and acquired land for the establishment of the church and school. The British Governor also sanctioned monthly grants to the schools established by him. The curriculum of the schools included an hour's instruction in Portuguese and an hour in English in the daily time-table. For the benefit of Telugu children, a Brahmin Pandit was appointed to instruct them in their mother tongue. Schultze was said to be the first European scholar who learnt Telugu well enough to bring out books in that language. To encourage enrolment in the school free tuition and scholarships were provided to the students out of the grants sanctioned by the British Governor. Perhaps Benjamin Schultze was the first European in India to have introduced the Grants-in-Aid system in educational institutions. He also produced religious literature in the local languages and delivered sermons in Telugu. These measures of Schultze increased the popularity of his schools. They were also used as centres for propagating Christianity and encouraging religious conversion. The financial assistance and free boarding and lodging for the school children had facilitated conversion of lower castes to Christianity. Consequently, the number of converts went up from 34 in 1728 to 206 in 1730 and to 618 in 1743.[15]

Telugu Works of Schultze

The popularity of Schultze's educational activities was mainly due to his close rapport with the native Telugu speaking communities (Malas/Parias) of Madras city, mainly in the Black Town area. He realised that it would be necessary for him to learn Telugu. This language which was then also called *Gentoo*, is related to Tamil, but is yet so different from it that a knowledge of one does not enable a person to understand the other. Yet Schultze compared them to German and Danish, and felt Telugu was not difficult to anyone who is at home with Tamil. During his stay in that city (1726-42) which was dominated by the Telugus in all spheres of its activity, he had acquired a very fair knowledge of the local languages and delivered religious discourses in them. Given his mastery over Telugu, he ventured into translations of original religious scriptures.[16] About his literary work during the first two years of his stay at Madras he wrote: "I have been much detained at Madras these two years [1726-28] making some other preparation, as the New Testament in the Warugian or Telugic Tongue, also a Dictionary for the Warugian and Malabaric Languages, and a Warugian Telugu grammar, which are all now complete."[17] He was considered to be the first European scholar who learnt Telugu well enough to bring out books in that language. In the very first few years of his arrival in Madras, he translated the short catechism and the New Testament, Garden of Paradise, True Christianity and other small tracts into Telugu. In order to carry out perfect translations he acquired good knowledge of Telugu grammar. In 1728, he produced a treatise on Telugu grammar known as the *Grammatica Telugica* in Latin. It was considered to be his *magnum opus*. It was also the first Telugu grammar book written by a European in India. It consists of eight chapters and an appendix which contains some parts of Bible translations. The book contains many phonetical rules, a detailed description of script and different writings of letters with their possible ligatures. Chapter one is about the Script and Alphabets; (2) Pronunciation; (3) Nouns; (4) Adjectives; (5) Pronouns; (6) Verbs; (7) Particles and (8) Syntax. Syntax is mostly explained by means of religious texts at the end of the Grammar. This manuscript Grammar book was printed in 1984 by the then East German Government. It is presently available in the Library of the Francke Foundation at Halle, Germany. The Grammar Book of Schultze was 80-90 years older than Telugu Grammatical works of William Carvey and Campbell. Thus Benjamin Schultze had the unique distinction of being the foremost-Europeans Scholar of Telugu Grammar. His grammatical work amply illustrates the structure of the colloquial Telugu language as spoken in and around Madras in the first quarter of the eighteenth century. This Grammar book is also a unique description of the language structure of that period. Unlike Ziegenbalg, for instance, Schultze paid very little attention to the written than the spoken language, hence his sermons were easily understood by the native people.

In addition to the Grammar Book, Schultze also translated the entire Bible, including the Old and New Testament into Telugu between 1728-35. It consists of 432 pages. The translation of New Testament was completed as early as 1728. Its Latin title is "*Vocabularium Telugo-Tamilo-Biblicum Novi Testamenti.*" He translated all the 260 Chapters of the New Testament and also gave Telugu and Tamil references. The translation of 659 chapters of the old Testament was completed in 1732. He informed the Secretary of the SPCK about his translation of the Bible into the Telugu language thus: "The translation of the Bible in the Gentoe Tongue in this very year [is] finished, for the benefit of that sort of heathens which use this language all there...Hitherto we have the Bible but in the Malabarian [Tamil] Tongue, printed at Tranquebar, but if we should have the pleasure to see them printed in a short time in the Gentoe Language too, according to the wish and desire of so many people, we doubt not, but to meet such an opportunity of communicating the Gospel more largely to a new kind of heathens, who for want of instructing are quite kept off from the knowledge of Jesus Christ."[18] By translating the Bible into Tamil and Telugu, Schultze also created a four language dictionary of English-Telugu-Tamil-Latin. This Bible-cum-Dictionary contains Telugu meanings for about 10,500 biblical words. However, these words are not arranged alphabetically but according to their place in the Bible. This Dictionary was an essential reference for all the German missionaries who came to South India from Europe. The four language Dictionary compiled by Schultze contains many local/colloquial words in addition to Biblical words. The influence of foreign languages like Arabic, Persian, Urdu/Hindustani on 18th century Telugu could be found through the vocabulary of the Dictionary. Some such examples are *Tainatu, Sharatu, Harramkoru, Jamedaru, Huzur, Wazir, Tahadilu, Subedari, Khajana, Majili, Bandikhana, Darwaja, Ladai, Gulapodu, Jumma*. During his stay in South India, Schultze had not only shown a keen interest in their languages and literature but also acquired many Telugu Palmleaf manuscripts. He also wrote religious songs, sermons on Palmleaves and distributed them among the local population. He collected nearly 167 Palmleaves and took them to Halle. Just like the Roman Catholic Missionary, Robert de Nobili, Benjamin Schultze also learnt the south Indian languages and tried to make use of them in missionary work and religious propaganda. He wrote the reason why he learnt Hindustani (Urdu) thus: "The main reason for me to learn this language was the following: There had been some people who wanted to become Christians. But I could not help them because I did not understand that language." His association with the Telugu language continued even after he left for Germany in 1743, after serving in Madras for about a decade and a half. He was aware of the fact that there were not many books of any sort printed in Telugu and hence decided to some elementary and basic works printed at Halle. During 1746-47 the following Telugu books were printed by Schultze, with Latin titles:

1. Catechismvs Telvgicvs
2. Vi Sive Ordosalvtis
3. Colloqvivm Religiosissimvm
4. Perspicva Explicatio

5. Mores Vitamqve Christianodignam
6. Conspectvs Litteratvrae Telvgicae Vulgo Warvgicae

In addition to these books he also wrote a bi-lingual (Telugu-English) work called Madras or Fort St. George. It contains a detailed description of the culture, tradition, religion, and socio-economic conditions of the local people in the form of 30 familiar dialogues. It was originally written in the "Waruga (Telugu) or Gentou language but afterwards translated into the English Tongue, for the benefit of some curious readers". Subsequently it was also translated into German and was printed in 1750, at Halle. This Book on Madras City in the East Indies Upon the Coast of Coromandel, provides a very interesting account of "the Genius, the Manners, the Carriage, the Behaviour and the very Character of the Natives; likewise their Trade and House-keeping; the Product of the Gardens"[19] etc. It also reflects an European's perspective on the nature of the country and the indigenous cultural practices. The writings of Benjamin Schultze helped many Christian missionaries to know more about the socio-cultural and religious conditions of south India in the eighteenth-ninteenth centuries. As we have noted above, Benjamin Schultze had tremendous zeal for language studies and was quite industrious. During the first two years of his stay (1726-28) in Madras, he had undertaken translation of religious scriptures and circulated them among the new converts. In addition to his translations he had daily oral practice of Telugu at the school. Everyday he used to spend at least an hour in conversation with the Telugu pupils. Having acquired a reasonable command over the language he gave daily sermons in Telugu and developed close relations with the local population. His literary work together with his school project facilitated the spread of Gospel among the local people, the Tamil and Telugu-speaking lower castes.

The running of charity schools and literary works enabled Schutze to gain the confidence of the local inhabitants of the Black Town area of Madras city. He attracted Telugus from the beginning. Just two years after his work in the city of Madras, he reported to Henry Newman, the Secretary of SPCK, that "53 citizens have been added to the true worship of God. I am fully persuaded that the time has come in which God hath most graciously decreed to visit the Gentiles at Madraspatnam, according to the Desires of all Good Christians for many years past."[20] Consequently he was able to convince many of them to change their religion. The educational and religious efforts of Benjamin Schultze in Madras had brought about considerable social and cultural change among the Telugu-speaking communities. For the first time the lower castes like the Parairs, Madigas and Malas were able to acquire modern education and a new consciousness. Many of the students of the charity schools became school masters and religious preachers. The mission schools acted as "cradles of awakening" for the untouchable communities.[21] Through modern education they could obtain material gains, social dignity and identity. Therefore, Benjamin Schultze could be considered a pioneer and an agent of socio-cultural change among the downtrodden castes in 18th century Madras.

August Mylius (1819-1887) and the Hermannsburg Mission

The work of Benjamin Schultze among the Telugus was continued by the Hermannsburg Mission in the nineteenth and twentieth centuries. During the 1860s the Hermannsburg Mission of North Germany sent a missionary called August Mylius –"Tough Man in a Hard Country"—to the southern parts of the east-coast of India.[22] Thus the Protestant German missionary activities were commenced mainly in the Telugu-speaking area of the southern coastal districts. He had earlier worked under Leipzig's Mission from 1847 to 1852 among Tamil-speaking communities. The Hermannsburg Mission established numerous stations and churches in Nellore, Chittoor and Cuddapah districts of the Andhra coast. In fact, several Anglo-American church organizations appointed several German missionaries in coastal Andhra to carry out proselytisation and evangelisation among the Telugus. For instance, the founders of Guntur (Father Heyer) and Rajahmundry Mission (Vallet and Groenning) were Germans by birth.

The first Hermannsburg Mission station was established by Mylius at Sulurpet on 28 Febraury 1865. For the next 22 years the mission reigns continued to be held tightly in his "iron hands."[23] Sulurpet was an important and flourishing commercial and administrative centre. Hence, it attracted his attention. Moreover, "the friendly reception of a law official who had been trained in a famous mission school and the willingness of the people to listen to the word of God preached to them persuaded Mylius to stay." Later he established few more stations at Nayudupet, Gudur, Vakadu, Kalahasti, Venkatagiri etc.[24] The first Baptism by him took place on 11 February 1866. The first convert, Rangaja alias Johannes, happened to be the caretaker of the travellers bungalow, Mylius's headquarters. Johannes became the first catechist of the Hermannsburg mission and worked for about 10 years. Under the guidance of Mylius, he evangelised a young policeman, who was baptised along with his wife and daughter. Thus August Mylius, the caretaker-catechist and his family, the policeman and his family and a Brahmin teacher of Mylius formed the first Holy Communion of the Hermannsburg Mission in Nellore district. Due to the hard work of Mylius, the early years of the mission were marked by significant success and many new stations were rapidly opened. Mylius, being a staunch adherent to the Lutheran confessions, was known for his sincerity, dedication and commitment to the cause of proselytisation. He never compromised on religious principles. It was said of him: "Mylius was as flexible as a railroad track. When he felt he was right, [he] was as conciliatory as a Russian at the UN." Yet he had "the deepest respect from everyone for his iron resolve to bend every ounce of energy towards preaching the Gospel. Those who did not agree with him nevertheless held him in high regard. He was a powerful preacher and an excellent evangelist and missionary."[25] As a result, after 10 years (1875) there were nine stations and 401 baptised persons, but by 1885 there were 1,275 baptised. Mylius was undoubtedly a keen and highly talented missionary. He spoke difficult regional languages like Telugu clearly and comprehensively. A colleague of Mylius remarked," Our Brahmin Teacher once said to me 'the Padda Dora speaks Telugu so beautifully and clearly that every old woman who can neither read nor write and every educated person not only likes to listen to him but also understands as they would their own people.'"[26] The

German missionaries were very impressed by the wonderful Telugu language, "the Italian of the East." Mylius was particular that every missionary must "learn well the Hindu religion, scriptures, fairy-tales, and superstitions, so that he will not needlessly offend the Indians." No wonder that many missionaries of the Hermannsburg Mission acquired reasonable command over the language and delivered their religious discoúrses in Telugu. They had also undertaken translations of religious texts into it. Mylius himself translated several biblical works like The First Milk (*modati palu*) into Telugu. Interestingly, the German missionaries were well-informed about the religious traditions, sects and philosophies of Hinduism. For example, in their conversations with the local people they freely quoted the verses of Vemana—the famous social revolutionary of medieval Andhra Desa. His verses denouncing the caste system and untouchability seem to be popular among them. A missionary translated it: "*Es gibt keinen Paria aus der welt, wer lught, der ist ein Paria, und wer sagt: du bist ein Paria, ist selbst der grosste Paria.*" [There is no Paria from[in] the world. Whoever tells a lie[lies] he is a Paria and whoever says to the other you are a Paria is himself the biggest Paria] (my translation). Such verses were used by the missionaries during their dialogues with the local people, "the Heathens."

Subsequent to the arrival of Mylius three more missionaries, Dahl, Petersen and Brunotte arrived and worked among the Telugus. The first mission-house was built in 1867 and the British Collector of Nellore District, Mr. Boswell, was instrumental in extending the activities of the German missionaries. They gradually spread their movement into several Andhra districts in South India. In the beginning, the Hermannsburg Mission started religious conversion movements among the upper castes i.e. Brahmins and established cordial relations with the local zamindars/landlords like the Raja of Venkatagiri. But they did not attract as many people as they had expected. Hence, they concentrated on the lower castes, and particularly the untouchable castes like Malas. Mylius remarked, "Our Christians belong to with the exception of one Sudra family in Tirupati to the Pariahs."

The German missionaries were able to attract the attention of the common, lower caste people because firstly, they used the Telugu language in their religious preaching and propaganda, and secondly, because the untouchable castes like the Malas were quite familiar and accustomed to travelling preachers (*Gurus*). "The missionaries had the added novelty of being white and were received with great curiosity and respect."[27] From the biographical accounts and field notes it appears that the missionaries were received "gladly and willingly" by the people of the south Andhra districts. Along with religious propaganda, the German missionaries also produced valuable Telugu literature in the form of religious tracts and translations for the benefit of religious preachers as well as the common people. Bible songs and Gospel messages were translated into the Telugu language. The tracts distributed by the missionaries were favourably received by those who could read. In particular, the priestly class among the untouchables known as the Mala Dasaris, who were literate and familiar with religious discourses were the earliest persons to be converted into the new religion. Most of them already had a fair education and previous religious experience as priests and poets. The first converts were "men of some education.". Among them were the best preachers and speakers that the Hermannsburg Mission had in its whole history. A German missionary described his encounter with a native convert: "Thirungulu requested me for books. I gave him our small Catechismus of Luther and a good booklet, *Modati Palu* (titled The First Milk) translated from Tamil by Provost Mylius. This he read through very largely. Learnt five main parts of Catechism by heart and often posed deep religious questions to me…Although he was only a Paria Priest he was sound, very well read and proficient in the religious writings of the Hindus. Large amount of the religious verse he had learnt by heart and had a lot of desire to argue / dispute with me. He visited me very often and listened attentively to my opinions. Very often he confessed that the biggest religion of India is not the true religion but Jesus Christ is the only Saviour of the World, whom he would also accept as his Saviour."[28]

A number of schools for boys and girls were established by Mylius at Sulurpet, Nayudupet and Gudur in Nellore district. Many of the lower castes were attracted by the educational programmes of the missionaries. The first school was started by him at Nayudupet for training the native workers. The missionaries needed catechists and liturgists, hence the best educated natives were given instruction. Many of the boarding schools served the educational and religious needs of the lower castes. It was found that the educational institutions of the missionaries were far superior to the native Telugu schools run by Brahmin and high caste teachers. Thus there was an increasing demand for missionary schools throughout the district towards the end of the 19th century: so much so that each congregation had an elementary school. Most of the early graduates of the missionary schools were appointed as teachers and preachers. Due to the religious and educational activities of the German missionaries the converts of the Mala untouchable community and other lower castes were able to acquire a new knowledge and consciousness, and change their livelihood conditions. Consequently, the spiritual and material life of these poor depressed communities had undergone a noticeable transformation.

REFERENCES

I am grateful to the Director of the Francke Foundation for awarding me the Fritz-Thyssen Visiting Fellowship for three months in 2002. During my stay at Halle, Germany I collected source material pertaining to the activities of German missionaries in South India.

1. G.A. Oddie (ed.), *Religious Conversion Movements in South Asia: Continuities and Change*, Curzon, 1997; *Religious Traditions in South Asia; Interaction and Change*, Surry, 1998; *Hindu and Christian in South-East India*, London, 1991; *Religion in South Asia*, Delhi, 1991; *Social Protest in India, Delhi*, 1979; "Protestant Missions", "Caste and Social Change in India, 1850-1914" in *The Indian Economic and Social History Review, (IESHR)*, Vol. IV, No. 3, 1969, pp. 259-91 (8) "Christian Conversion in the Telugu Country, 1860-1900: A Case Study of One Protestant Movement in the Godavari Krishna Delta", *IESHR*, Vol. XII, No. 1, pp. 61-79; D. Forrester, *Caste and Christianity: Attitudes and Policies on Caste of Anglo-Saxon Protestant Missions in India*, London, 1980; J.C. B. Webster, *A History of the Dalit Christians*

in *India*, Sanfrancisco, 1992; A. Copley, *Religions in Conflict: Ideology, Cultural Contact and Conversion in Late Colonial India*, Delhi, 1997; G. Viswanathan, *Outside the Fold: Conversion, Modernity and Belief*, Delhi, 1998. Y. Chinna Rao, "Writing Dalit History: A Note on Missionary Sources," (Memeo, 2004).

2. J. Worrlein, *Dreizehn Jahre in Indian* (German) Hermannsburg, 1884 and *Vierzig Jahre in Indian* (German) Hermannsburg, 1913; F. Wishan, *Missionar in Telugu Lande in Indien* (German) Philadelphia, 1891; J. Richter, *Die Deutsche Mission in Sudindien* (German) Gutersloh, 1902; E.R. Clough, *While Sewing Sandals: Tales of a Telugu Pariah Tribe*, New York, 1899 (Reprint); J.E. Clough, *Social Christianity in the Orient: The Story of A Man, A Mission and Movement*, New York, 1914; Martin Luther Dolbeer, Jr., *A History of Lutheranism in the Andhra Desa, 1842-1920*, New York, 1959; H. Grafe (ed.), *Evangalische Kische in Indien* (German), Erlangen, 1981.
3. A. Oddie Geoffrey, *Hindu and Christian in South-East India: Aspects of Religious Continuity and Change, 1800-1900*, London, 1991; Bugge, Henriette: *Mission and Tamil Society; Social and Religious Change in South India (1840-1900)*, Surrey, 1994; Kawashima, Koji, *Missionaries and a Hindu State: Travancore, 1858-1936*, Delhi, 1998; Robinson, Rowena: *Conversion, Continuity and Change: Lived Christianity in Southern Goa*, New Delhi, 1998; Studdert-Kennedy, Gerald: *British Christians, Indian Nationalists and the Raj*, Dehli, 1991; R.E. Frykenberg, "The Impact of Conversion and Social Reform upon Society in South India during the Late Company Period: Questions Concerning Hindu-Christian Encounters, with Special Reference to Tinnevelly", in C.H. Phillips and M.D. Wainwright, ed., *Indian Society and Beginnings of Modernization, 1830-1850*, London, 1976, pp.127-242.
4. C.S. Mohanavelu, *German Tamilology*, Madras, 1993; Dharampal-Frick, Gita: "*Indien im Spiegel deutscher Quellen der Fruehen Neuzeit (1500-1750)*", *Studien zu einer interkulturellen Konstellation*, (Fruehe Neuzeit; 18); Tuebingen, 1994. Jeyaraj: *Daniel: Inkulturation in Tranquebar: Der Beitrag der fruehen daenisch-halleschen Mission zum Werden einer indisch-einheimischenc Kirche (1706-1730)*, (Missionswissenschaftliche Forschungen, Neue Folge; (4). Erlangen, 1996; Michael Bergunder (ed.): "*Missionsberichte aus Indien im 18. Jahrhundert. Ihre Bedeutung fuer die europaeische*

Geistesgeschichte und ihr wissenschaftlicher Quellenwert fuer die Indienkunde", (Neue Hallesche Berichte; (1) Halle, 1999 ; Nehring, A.: *Orientalismus und Mission. Studien zur Repraesentation der suedindischen Kultur und Religion durch deutsche Missionare, 1840-1945*, Wiesbaden, 2003.

5. G.A. Oddie, "Protestant Missions, Caste and Social Change in India, 1850-1914" in *Indian Economic and Social History Review* (*IESHR*), Vol. IV, No. 3, 1969; G.A. Oddie, "Christian Conversion in the Telugu Country: A Case Study of One Protestant Movement in the Godavari-Krishna Delta", *IESHR*, Vol. XII, No.1, 1975; Susan Billington Harper : *In the Shadow of the Mahatma: Bishop V. S. Azariah and the Travails of Christianity in British India.* Grand Rapids; Michigan, 2000; C.B. Webster, *A History of the Dalit Christians in India*, Sanfranscico, 1992; H. Grafe, (ed), *Evangelische Kirche in Indien: Auskunft und Einblicke*, Erlangen, 1981; Grafe, Hugald: "Die Arbeit in Indien" in Ernst-August Luedemann (Hrsg.): *Vision: Gemeinde weltweit. 150 Jahre Hermannsburger Mission und Ev.-luth. Missionswerk in Niedersachsen, Hermannsburg*: Verlag der Missionshandlung, 2000, pp. 357-420.
6. Mohana Velu, *op.cit.*, Chapter-II. E. Arno Lehmann, *It Began at Tranquebar*, Madras, 1958.
7. Rich and Gawthrop, *Pietism and the Making of Eighteenth Century Prussia*, Cambridge, 1993.
8. Quoted in D. Jeyraj, *Inkulturation in Tranquebar* (German), Erlangen, 1996, p. 24.
9. Letter from Benjamin Schultze to the Hon'ble Society in London, dt. 10-12-1728, SPSK Archives, Micro Film Collection UTC, Bangalore.
10. Letter from the Correspondents of SPCK to the Secretary, SPCK, London, dt. 25.1.1735/6 in Francke Archives, F.No.II G 11.
11. H. Grafe, "Benjamin Schultze and the Beginnings of the First Indian Protestant Church in Madras" in *Indian Church History Review*, Vol. III, No. 1, 1969, pp. 46-47.
12. Circular Letter of SPCK dated 26 December, 1730.
13. Letter of Benjamin Schultze (not dated), Francke Archives File II h 3:5.
14. Letter from Schultze to Newmann, dated 17.10.1729.
15. Letter from Schultze to Newmann, dated 24.8.1732.
16. J.F. Fenger, *History of the Tranquebar Mission*, Madras, 1906, pp. 108-09.

17. Letter from Schultze to Newmann, dated 17.12.1728.
18. Letter from Schultze to Newmann, dated 24.8.1732.
19. B. Schultze, *Madras Or Fort St. George*, Halle, 1750.
20. Letter from Schultze to Newmann, dated 26.2.1728.
21. Martin Luther Dolbeer, Jr., *A History of Lutheranism in the Andhra Desa, 1842-1920*, New York, 1959; Grafe, Hugald: "Die Arbeit in Indien. In: Ernst-August Luedemann" (Hrsg.): *Vision: Gemeinde weltweit. 150 Jahre Hermannsburger Mission und Ev.-luth. Missionswerk in Niedersachsen*, Hermannsburg: Verlag der Missionshandlung, 2000, pp. 357-420.
22. L. Hesterman, *Missionary Pioneers of the American Lutheran Church*, Minneapolis, 1967, p. 16.
23. *Ibid.*, p. 17.
24. *Ibid.*
25. J. Worrlein, *Dreizehn Jahre in Indien* (German), Hermannsburg, 1884 and *Vierzig Jahre in Indien* (German), Hermannsburg, 1913; F. Wishan, *Missionar in Telugu Lande in Indien* (German), Philadelphia, 1891.
26. *Ibid.*
27. Martin Luther Dolbeer, Jr., *A History of Lutheranism in the Andhra Desa*, 1842-1920, New York, 1959.
28. J. Worrlein, *Dreizehn Jahre in Indien* (German), Hermannsburg, 1884 and *Vierzig Jahre in Indien* (German), Hermannsburg, 1913; F. Wishan, *Missionar in Telugu Lande in Indien* (German), Philadelphia, 1891.

9

Upper Caste Violence Against Dalits in Andhra Pradesh, 1947-1985

In recent years, incidents of murder and large scale arson perpetrated against dalits by upper caste Hindus across the country have been growing. While this indicates a complex and diverse pattern, one thing is clear: the growing assertion and awakening among dalits about their rights has become intolerable to the dominant castes/classes. The growth of socio-political consciousness of dalits in Andhra Pradesh can be traced to the early decades of the 20th century. The formation of the Adi-Andhra Mahasabha in 1917 under the leadership of Bhagyareddi Varma, Kusuma Dharmanna, etc., was a landmark in the history of dalit liberation in modern Andhra Pradesh. For the first time dalits were organized and mobilised by organic intellectuals. The movement grew independently and inculcated a new consciousness among them regarding their rights and safe-guards.

The founding of the Adi-Andhra movement which predated the Gandhian programme of "Harijan upliftment" was a pronounced act of consciousness of the dalit masses. It sought to articulate their sufferings and misery within the context of growing mass nationalism and the anti-colonial struggle. The emancipatory ideology formulated and articulated by dalits was independent of the nationalist discourse.[1] The dalit intellectual articulation represented by Babasaheb Ambedkar exposed the inadequacies, limitations and gaps in the Gandhian paradigm of dalit liberation and forcefully contested the hegemonic nationalist ideology propounded by the upper caste intelligentsia. The growing movement of dalits for self-respect, social justice, dignity and egalitarian social order necessitated a serious reflection and resolution of the problem of caste and nation. The issues raised during the pre-independence period regarding their emancipation continued to pose a serious challenges to the post-colonial state in India. Instead of resolving the problems of caste discrimination, untouchability and caste violence, the political leadership in India is subverting the constitutional and administrative machinery. The recent spate of upper caste violence against dalits is proof of this.

As far as Andhra Pradesh is concerned, caste Hindu atrocities on dalits intensified on the eve of independence and the emergence of the republic. In this chapter, an attempt is made to study the socio-political context and the social roots of caste violence during the post-independence period. It describes some incidents of caste Hindu attacks in coastal Andhra and analyses the structural dimensions of caste and class. Further, this chapter will discuss factors such as social/caste stratification, reinforcement of socio-economic inequalities, the culture and ideology of repression, and the active promotion of caste tensions.

Although perpetration of upper caste violence against dalits in rural Andhra not a new phenomenon, its extent and intensity began to grow since the 1950s. The culmination of caste antagonism was the ghastly massacre of dalits in Karamchedu and Chunduru.[2] Recent studies by various civil liberties organizations and the Dalit Mahasabha have analysed the multidimensional aspects of these attacks in Andhra Pradesh, but little is known about the pre-Karamchedu (1985) caste violence. Hence, in this chapter an attempt is made to highlight some aspects of the caste violence of the pre-1985 years.

Incidents of Caste Violence

It is ironic that when the entire free Indian nation was celebrating the dawn of the Republic in 1950 with pomp and show, the dalits of some coastal Andhra villages were being subjected to caste oppression and discrimination. A negation of the spirit and letter of Hinduism occurred in the north coastal Andhra district of Vishakhapatnam. In the two villages of Haribanda and Makannapuram of Sompet *taluk*, dalits were attacked thrice by caste

Hindus in April-May, 1950.[3] The reason for the attack was that on the so-called "Harijan Day", dalits of these villages drew water from the common well. In fact, the government declared that the 30th day of each month throughout the year would be observed as "Harijan Day." Legislation had been passed prohibiting discrimination against dalits, and in order to place them on an equal footing with the rest of the country in enjoying the rights of citizenship. The government desired that every effort be made to educate the public and enthuse them to remove social disabilities. Government servants, Congress organizations and Harijan Seva Sangams could play a prominent part in the great work of spreading propaganda and promoting work for the reformation of society. The government indicated the great importance it attached to the eradication of untouchability by directing the District Collectors to commemorate the day by organising celebrations, meetings, etc. As a part of these festivities, dalits and Savarnas were brought together and inter-community activities were encouraged. But after the celebrations were over and the officials had left the villages, the caste Hindus imposed a social boycott against the dalits and physically attacked them for having violated "caste norms." The terrified dalits fled the villages and took shelter in neighbouring places. In spite of repeated appeals to the government, nothing was done to safeguard their interests and protect their property and lives. Neither the officials nor the ministers bothered to visit the affected villages and console the victims of caste oppression. The promises made by concerned persons in the government remained unfulfilled. Ultimately, local leaders had to resort to Satyagraha and fasting in order to exert pressure on the government to protect and safeguard the constitutional rights of dalits. In the same year (1950), similar incidents were reported from several villages in the coastal districts of Guntur and Krishna.[4] In the prosperous Appikatla village (Guntur), dalit agricultural labourers were attacked by the upper caste rich peasants. In Kasukurru village (Krishna), a dalit couple (medical doctor), was prevented from participating in a marriage procession along the streets. When they persisted, they were dragged out of their car and beaten up. In Anamanapudi village, caste Hindu landlords attacked dalit agricultural labourers. In Kalvacherla village (West Godavari), a dalit woman—Nangalamma—was tortured by the brother of a village officer for drinking water from a public well. The editor of *Navajeevana* (a dalit weekly) questioned the atrocities on dalits and asked, "whether it is enough to just celebrate independence? Why do we need freedom without security to (dalit) people? Why the popular ministries?"[5] The feelings of the dalit masses about the achievement of independence and its relevance were well articulated in papers and journals. It was felt that the fruits of freedom were enjoyed by upper castes, while dalits continued to suffer from age-old socio-economic disabilities. The grant of political freedom did not make any difference to the vast majority of dalits in the villages. Such sentiments and opinions were expressed by many dalit intellectuals and leaders.

After the formation of Andhra Pradesh in 1956, several instances of caste Hindu violence against dalits were reported from the Rayalaseema and Telangana regions. In the Sambavaram village of Kurnool district, 16 dalits were injured, four of them seriously, and about 60 huts were set on fire.[6] The reason for the atrocity was that the caste Hindus objected to the construction of a community hall in the dalit locality which was close to a public pathway. In the attack, a dalit was killed and a couple of hay stacks were burnt. The report of the Commissioner for SCs and STs, 1960-61, mentioned that in a village in the Hyderabad district of Andhra Pradesh, due to caste prejudice, the caste Hindus left nearly 200 to graze in the fields that were ready for harvest and which belonged to dalit farmers.[7] In the Khondapalli village of Cuddapah district, houses of dalits were set on fire and destroyed by caste Hindus because a dalit cut grass in the field of a caste Hindu. Likewise, in Gandapalli village of the same district, 47 houses of dalits were burnt by caste Hindus, because a buffalo belonging to a dalit was seen grazing in one of their fields. Another report in 1964-65 mentioned that in some villages of Ananthapur district untouchability was being practiced. Dalit students in schools were made to sit separately when schools were run in private rented building of temples and *Dharmasalas*. In still another incident a dalit sarpanch (village head) and two other dalits were killed in a village in Guntur district, because the dalits used the village tank for drinking water. The "influential villagers" armed with axes, crowbars and other deadly weapons attacked the dalits and imposed a social boycott on them.[8] Apart from referring the matter "to the concerned authorities" nothing had been done to protect them. A dalit woman was beaten to death in the Govindpet village of Nizamabad district for suspected robbery. In another village in East Godavarai district, when the dalits wanted to enter a temple, one of them was killed and six others severely injured in a brutal attack by caste Hindus. A dalit boy was beaten to death by a group of five caste Hindus in Atmakur Village for an alleged theft of toddy from palm trees. In Nimmakur village, two dalit youths were tortured to death on suspicion of theft. This ghastly incident was reported in the Deccan Herald thus:[9]

> "Two SC youths were murdered after seven hours of torture by residents of Nommakur village in Krishna District on June 15... The boys walked seven miles to Nimmakur, the native village of film star NT Rama Rao to see him, they stood on a big house in the village where the rich Kamma are landlords. Suspecting them to be thieves they overpowered the boys, tied their hands with a rope, took them to the cattle shed and tortured them. They were then brought to the street, tied to electric poles and mercilessly tortured by 22 persons from 4.30 to 11.30 pm., and they were tied in gunny bags and thrown into the Bandar Canal."

When dalit agricultural labourers of Ramannapalli village of Cuddapah district refused to work at low wages, and demanded an increase in their wages, 500 armed caste Hindus raided the dalit colony and indiscriminately beat the men, women and children with various types of sharp weapons. They also used hand grenades and burnt the entire locality of 109 households. In the China Ogirala village of Krishna district, one dalit was murdered and 20 more injured by the caste Hindu landlords, because government wastelands were allotted to 108 dalit families. Similarly, in another village in Kurnool district, 30 huts belonging to dalits were demolished by the upper caste landlords, because land measuring 711.73 acres was granted by the government for house sites to dalits. The Illay Perumal Committee on Untouchability also reported numerous instances of caste discrimination in different parts of Andhra Pradesh. To quote a few of them:[10]

> "SCs are not allowed to go through the village, wearing shoes or chappals" (Padmagalai village, Anantapur)..."The SCs are not allowed to sit in a cart, when it passes through the streets inhabited by caste Hindus" (Anantapur)..."The SCs are not allowed to sit in boats along with caste Hindus" (Vijayawada)..."The SCs are not allowed to fetch water from the public drinking water wells" (Kaumabaripalem, Warangal) "In tea shops, separate glasses were kept for serving tea to the SCs which were to be cleaned before and after use by SCs themselves and kept by them separately" (Jankampet, Nizamabad)..."SCs are not served in plates in hotels" (Banagaripalyam, Chittoor)..."The scheduled caste children were not allowed to sit with the children belonging to other communities" (Cheekatim Anipally, Anatapur).

A sample survey conducted during July-August 1973, in six villages of Hyderabad, Guntur and Chittoor districts revealed the prevalence of acute untouchability. It was found that dalits were not permitted to use the public wells or allowed to enter temples in any village in the caste Hindu localities. They were also not served by the washerman and barbers. Nor were they allowed to enter tea stalls, but served tea in separate tumblers outside the stalls.[11] *The Hindu* reported on October 7, 1977, that in Mallaram village of Nizamabad district,

> "SCs were boycotted by the caste Hindus. Untouchability is observed everywhere in the entire Nizamabad district. Demand of SCs is to end segregation against them in village tea shops and stopping of serving tea to them in tumblers kept separately for SCs...Caste Hindus were fined for talking to SCs. On Independence Day representative of 40 Harijan families in Mallaram were allowed to climb the Hanuman temple platform to garland visiting politicians. Afterwards caste Hindus boycotted the SCs and imposed a fine of Rs. 5 on non-SCs who speak to SCs."[12]

The Scheduled Caste Employees Association of Hyderabad submitted a memorandum to the President of India on August 8, 1973, stating instances of atrocities murders, arson, rape and false implication in cases committed on dalits in a number of villages in the districts of East Godavari, Anantapur, Cuddapah, Chittoor, etc. It listed the instances of wanton attack on dalits, destruction of property and molestation of dalit women. The association remarked:

> "The only fault of the SCs was to demand higher wages and wasteland. Trivial offences alleged against the SCs, like theft to of toddy from palm trees, were enough to instigate the most inhuman treatment against them."[13]

The Kanchekacherla episode was the most brutal caste Hindu attack on the dalits during the pre-Karamchedu period. Koteshu, a dalit boy, was cruelly burnt to death on the suspicion of theft of some brass vessels. Hence, Kanchekacerla had come to be known as a village that, "parted with its conscience" and the incident of a dalit youth "who was roasted alive" shocked the people in the entire state. It also signified the growing upper caste rage and fury against the dalits. *The Indian Express* reported: "A SC boy was caught by the caste Hindu villagers who took him to a *pandal*, tied him to a pole, beat him and set fire to his clothes which resulted in extensive burns. He died in the hospital... ."[14] Similarly, a fourteen-year-old dalit boy was brutally beaten to death by caste Hindus for an alleged theft. In the same village, a dalit farmer was attacked with axes and spears and killed by the upper caste rich peasants in connection with a dispute over the grazing of cattle.

The above incidents clearly reveal that in post-independent India, dalits have had to pay a heavy price for asserting their civil and constitutional rights. Most of the caste Hindu atrocities on dalits centred around the right of access to public wells, tanks, educational institutions, social dignity and equality (marriage processions along the streets, wearing neat clothes, chappals, etc.). Caste violence was also related to agrarian relations, i.e., access to grazing land, grants of government wastelands, demand for an increase in wages, etc. The life of dalits was thought to be value less and hence they were put to death on the mere suspicion of a theft. The Dalits accused were not even allowed to prove their innocence or exercise their legal/constitutional rights. The dominant upper castes brazenly took the law into their own hands and meted out punishments to dalits. The extra-legal/ constitutional authority of the upper caste rich was demonstrated in order to force the dalits to accpet and respect their dominance in the villages.

Social Roots of Violence

The growing antagonism between dalits and upper castes in rural Andhra must be understood in the overall context of the changing agrarian relations and social transformation during the post-1947 period.[15] The caste system in Andhra Pradesh was undergoing a profound change in terms of the formation of new social classes and power relations. The traditional caste hierarchy closely corresponded to the broad class divisions within society: the landlords and rich peasantry in Andhra were mostly drawn from among the non-Brahmin upper castes such as the Reddy, Kamma, Kapu, Velama, etc., while the poor peasantry/tenants/agricultural labourers belonged to dalit communities. The post-colonial socio-economic development process led to the decline of parasitic old absentee feudal landlord classes. They lost their predominant position and grip over the economy and polity. Such a decline was also due to the abolition of the zamindari system and the shift of landholding from absentee landlords to cultivating/enterprising peasantry, mainly belonging to the Reddy, Kamma, and Kapu castes. Available evidence clearly indicates that during the post-1950 period the agrarian society of Andhra Pradesh witnessed the crystalisation of a progressive/dynamic peasant bourgeois class, which had taken advantage of new economic opportunities like commercial farming, the green revolution, the growth of agro-based industrialization, etc., and consolidated its position as a dominant socio-political class force. Also, the drastic decline and disintegration of absentee landlordism, represented by old zamindars and Brahmin *inamdars*, paved the way for the consolidation of a dynamic rural rich in the countryside. In caste terms, most of the neo-rich "Kulaks" belonged to the dominant upper castes. It may be pointed out that the rich peasantry among the Kammas could maintain and improve upon their lands primarily because of their attachment to land and the extraordinary care they took in agriculture. In areas where they numerically preponderant, as in some of the coastal districts, by virtue of their wealth they emerged as the dominant caste and class in the socio-economic and political fields. A similar case can be made for the Kapus and Reddies.

The strategies for rural development pursued by the state government, like the cooperative credit system, the Panchayati Raj institutions, etc., also provided immense opportunities for the rural rich to augment resource mobilisation and accumulation. Possession of considerable landed property and accumulation of surplus by the upper caste rural rich further intensified the process of stratification within the peasantry, which resulted in the alienation of the lower castes and Dalits from the land. A recent study on labour relations in Andhra noted that "the proportion of agricultural labourers in the total agricultural population had increased steadily and continuously from 27 per cent to 53 per cent between 1951 and 1981." Micro-level village studies of the post-1960 period also revealed that a considerable section of the lower Sudra castes and dalits did not possess land. Thus, they constituted the rural poor in the Andhra countryside. Census data on caste and occupation indicates that the Mala and Madiga communities accounted for the bulk of the agricultural labour class and worked as farm/field servants, *Paleru* and casual workers. Very few of them possessed land. The employment of the entire family (men, women and children) in the various agricultural operations is a unique feature of dalit communities. Hence, in the case of dalits, caste and class positions have closely converged.

The dominant upper caste, as landowners and employers of labourers, thus exerted considerable power over the dalits. In the villages, a majority of dalit agricultural labourers and poor peasants/tenants were dependent upon the rich Kamma and Reddy peasantry. Whenever class demands like wage increase were articulated by dalit communities, they were subjected to caste oppression like social boycott and denied access to village economic resources. The dominant rich peasantry did not tolerate any upward mobility among the dalits. Whenever dalit families acquired some wasteland, house-sites and other land grants from the government, the caste Hindu rich peasantry subjected them to physical attacks.

Hence, the struggle for wage increase and land distribution by dalits resulted in retaliation from the dominant caste peasantry in the form of abuse, harassment, molestation of dalit women and destruction of property. Dalits had become easy targets for trivial accusations of theft and witchcraft. There is no dearth of instances of caste discrimination in terms of preventing their entry into temples, taking drinking water from public wells and tanks, denial of sharing of cups in tea shops, etc. The perpetration of caste sharing of cups in the upper castes is closely related to the socio-economic and political domination of the rich peasantry in the countryside. The growing assertion of dalits for the actualisation of the concept of citizenship of mass literacy as the basis of new civil life and social/spatial mobility as a new principle of social life invited victimization by the dominant caste peasantry. The concern of the dalits for social mobility, education and diversification of occupation was consciously negated by the dominant castes. The unabated caste violence against dalits in the Andhra countryside is clear proof of this.

REFERENCES

1. For account of dalit liberation movement during the pre-independence period, See A. Satyanarayana, "Dalit Protest Literature in Telugu: A Historical Perspective", in *Economic and Political Weekly,* Vol. XXX, No. 3., January 1995, pp. 171-75, and "Dalit Identity and Consciousness in Colonial Andhra, 1917-47", in Vikalp, Vol. VI, No. 2, 1998, pp. 41-57, Y. Chinna Rao, *Dalit Struggle for Identity*, New Delhi, 2003.
2. K. Padma Rao, "Social and Philosophical Movements in India", *Ponnur*, p. 12; K. Balagopal, "Post-Chundur and other Chudurs", in *EPW*, October 19, 1991, pp. 2399-2404.
3. *Navajeevana*, July 30, 1950, pp. 7-8.
4. *Ibid.*, p. 1.
5. *Navajeevana* (Editorial), October 26, 1947.
6. *Deccan Herald*, August 5, 1958, cited in N.D. Kamble, "Atrocities on Scheduled Castes", New Delhi, 1980, p. 3233.
7. Quoted, *Ibid.*, p. 43.
8. *Ibid.*, p. 63.
9. *Ibid.*, pp.127-28.

10. *Ibid.*, pp. 138-39.
11. *Ibid.*, pp. 236-37.
12. *Ibid.*, p. 271.
13. *Ibid.*, p. 265.
14. *Ibid.*, p. 100.
15. For an analysis of agrarian relations during the post-1947 period, see. A. Satyanarayana, "Caste and Class in Rural Andhra: A Historical Perspective", in K.L. Sharma, (Ed.), *Caste and Class in India*, Jaipur, 1994, pp. 376-93.

10

"Birds of Passage" Migration of South Indian Laborers to Southeast Asia

This chapter deals with the migration of south Indian manual and unskilled workers to Southeast Asian countries in the nineteenth and twentieth centuries. It presents an analysis of the pattern of mobility of the laboring classes who crosse the seas and sought to develop a migration paradigm that encompasses the various dimensions of the different types of intra-Asian migrations. The author argues that south Indian laborers who migrated to Burma and Malaya experienced both free and unfree migration situations during the colonial period. Different types and streams of migration coexisted and depending upon the changing strategies of employers, government, and laborers themselves the migrants were free and unfree at the same time. Hence, it is suggested that an a priori distinction between free and unfree labor migration is difficult to substantiate, at least in the case of south Indian labor migrations. In this study migration is conceptualized as an integrated and continuous process. For the lower castes and communities out-migration meant an opportunity to better their material conditions and to overcome social and caste oppression. In other words, migration to foreign countries certainly provided them avenues for social mobility that was denied in their native land.

This chapter examines in a long-term historical and comparative perspective the course, nature and effects of migration to Burma and Malaya by members of Telugu and Tamil-speaking communities, called *"Madarasi"* / *"Coranghees,"* from south India.[1]

The chapter discusses the historical formation of south Indian immigrant labor communities and classes within the unorganized and unregulated sectors of employment in these two Southeast Asian countries. It also explores the constitution of an immigrant community and its interaction with and contribution to these two host societies. The study attempts to develop a comprehensive perspective on migration, and settlement patterns, and a migration paradigm that encompasses the dimensions of both free versus indentured migration and of voluntary versus forced migration outside the experience of the West during the nineteenth and twentieth centuries. Also addressed are issues related to the types of migration, systems and methods of labor recruitment and control, and the motivations, perceptions, and aspirations of the migrants, as well as the forces and factors that shaped the process of migration and the social origins and caste-community backgrounds of the migrants.

Historiographical Comments

In the historiography of Indian labor migration, various scholars have expressed conflicting interpretations and divergent views in recent years. One group of scholars, called the "nationalist," "anti-colonial," or "neo-Marxist" school,[2] maintains that the migration of Indian labor abroad under the indenture system was a "new system of slavery" and that it promoted the image of the migrant as a victim of various forms of greed, deception, and colonial coercion and manipulation. The absence of freedom, these scholars argue, is the distinguishing character of indenture inasmuch as workers were unable to withdraw their labor power or to bargain or negotiate over the terms of their contract for better wages and living conditions. Scholars who adhere to the "coercion" point of view stress the ignorance of the workers and argue that they were misled and misinformed by recruiters regarding the nature of plantation work and were even made captives and transported to foreign countries against their will. In these cases, they contend, migration cannot be defined as a "free choice." Workers were often drawn into debt bondage by the labor recruiters, and the contractual relations between the employers and the employees were not really voluntary. Scholars from this school emphasize that the employers used extra economic and penal methods to control labor and forced the workers to live in a state of virtual bondage. In contrast, scholars of the "modernization," "imperialist," "colonialist," and "revisionist," schools suggest that "migration" was economically beneficial." To quote Emmer, a leading "revisionist,"

> "new research concerning the government-supervised, long-distance migration movements of indentured Indians has clearly revealed that the considerable improvement achieved over time in living and working conditions made this migration stream a small but important escape hatch for migrant laborers from India."[3]

Further, he also argues

> "that indentured emigration from India to overseas colonies was the result of rational and deliberate choice on the part of migrants, prompted by hopes of bettering their future."[4]

In my opinion both these approaches tend to view the emigrant as an object of sympathy or pity, neglecting to take into account the personal and cultural considerations involved in the complex migration process. These scholars emphasize either "subsistence-oriented" push factors or "betterment oriented" pull factors as the determinant of emigration. The proponents of the "new slavery," theory for instance, have ignored the fact that over a period of time migrant laborers became familiar with the conditions abroad through relatives, friends, and neighbors and that the choice of a destination by a prospective migrants also depended on migration patterns and strategies based on networks of kith, kin, family members, fellow-villagers, and friends, who provided vital information and paid for the migrants' passages. For example, newcomers arriving in Burma were given surety by relatives and/ or friends. They were also provided shelter and accommodation for a few days till they found regular employment. Although the laborers moved across the Bay of Bengal they did not sever ties with their networks. These ties channelled migrant into specific segments of the labor markets and into specific regions of the host society. This trend also kept migrants within communities of fellow-villages and people of the same caste. For instance, coastal Andhra women in domestic service and prostitution in Burma invited other women from their villages and neighboring areas to come and offered to help them find jobs once they arrived. Port towns like Cocanada also played a significant role in this type of migration. Likewise, Dalit and lower-caste men increasingly brought others to work and earn money. Revisionist scholars like Emmer tend to highlight the pull factors and equate colonial migration with that of European migration to America, thus neglecting to account for the suffering and sacrifices of the earlier generation of emigrants to plantations. As Carter states,

> "a central flaw of both theories is their failure to analyse crucial changes in recruiting strategies which helped to maintain the dynamism of overseas labor mobilisation."[5]

Recent research has clearly shown that the debates about whether or not the emigrants were free or unfree ignore a complex and multidimensional historical reality and reduce the whole migration process to an overly simplistic set of alternatives.[6] Forgotten is the fact that migration of labor under colonial conditions was varied and mixed. No unilinear pattern of transition from unfree to free labor can be discerned in the case of south Indian migrations. As I show below, south Indian coolies were in some respects free and in other respects unfree at the same time, as a result of the changing strategies of employers, governement, and laborers themselves. For instance, in the case of emigration to Malaya, though the indenture system was adopted between 1860 and 1910, the recruitment of free laborers through middlemen called "kangany" also took place in the same period and in fact became quite popular. Similarly, migration to Burma was free, private, and unassisted, that is, without any government regulation, supervision, or control, yet elements of debt-bondage and coercion were very much present. Free and unfree types of migration were also socially conditioned. In the case of south India, upper-caste merchants and professionals migrated freely and voluntarily. By and large these people were more influenced by the pull factors, for they were enterprising and self-seeking individuals who took advantage of opportunities abroad to improve their career prospects and business profits. But the vast majority of dalit and lower sudra castes were subjected to debt-bondage and hence their migration was forced and involuntary, that is, the migrant laborers were more pushed than pulled. Therefore, it is necessary to investigate the sociohistorical context of the process and patterns of migration, and to situate the freedom or unfreedom of laborers and the role of push and pull factors within a proper historical perspective.

In this chapter I argue that it is impossible to make any fundamental and clear-cut distinction between free and unfree migration and that any definition of migration would be incomplete if it does not encompass both free and unfree types, as the Lucassens have argued elsewhere.[7] In other words, a prior distinction between free and unfree labor migration is difficult to substantiate. Thus, in this essay I conceptualize migration as an integral and continuous process, although the motives and aspirations of individual migrants and social groups varied substantially. I suggest that within the context of push and pull factors the prospective migrants had reasonable choices and decision-making power over their life-conditions, though their choices were subject to severe socio-economic constraints. I also want to emphasize that particularly for the lower social groups and castes migration meant opportunity, equality, and emancipation. Thus the history ofs south Indian labor migration has also been the history of social reform in south India in the modern period.

This paper is divided into four sections. The specific historical context of labor migration from south India in the nineteenth century, as well as patterns, various forms, and the nature of migration are discussed in the first section. The second section deals with the systems of labor recruitment and labor control. The third section contains details about wages, and working and living conditions of workers in Malaya and Burma during the period under study. In the fourth section I provide an account of the social background of the migrants and the effects of migration.

Context, Pattern, and Nature of Migration

Historically, relations between lower Burma and India's northern Coromondal Coast (viz., parts of present day Orissa and Andhra Pradesh States) go back to a few centuries before the birth of Christ.

For the *Telugus, Burma* was known as the *Swarna Bhumi*– the golden land of plenty. History tells of the local rules of the ancient Andhra country of Kalinga conquering the natives in Burma and establishing authority over and trading relations with the Talaings, as the inhabitants of lower Burma were called. In 1883 Arthur Purves Phayre observed,

> "From tradition and such scanty historical notices as have survived, we are led to look to the east coast of India especially to the country on the lower courses of the Krishna and Godavari, with the adjoining districts, in other words ancient Kalinga and Talingana, as the countries which at a very remote period, traded with and colonized the coast of Pegu. The people of Pegu are known to the Burmese, to the Indian influence to Europeans by the name of Talaing."[8]

Farther to the south, the Indian influence began to penetrate the Malayan region very early in time. "An Indian Era of Malay history" existed in Malaya until about the beginning of the sixteenth century. [9] Most of the south Indians who migrated to the Malayan peninsula in the pre-colonial period went in connection with trade and commercial activities. These early migrants were basically drawn from the traditional trading communities of south India like the Chettis and Komatis; in contrast, south Indians who emigrated to Malaya during the nineteenth century, when the plantation economy emerged, were chiefly "illiterate, cheap docile" laborers.

> A Telugu folk-song reads thus (my translation):
> It was in the early nineteenth century; we [Telugus] arrived in Malaya
> Those were the days of British rule over the Malaya peninsula
> The days of flourishing rubber and coconut plantations
> The Telugu from Andhra country were brought by the British to work in the plantation.
> We cut the forests, cleared the land for plantations
> We labored hard to make the country [Malaya] green and prosperous.[10]

The growth of transport and communication facilities between Burma and Malaya and the east coast of India, as well as the increasing demand for manual labor in the agrarian, plantation, and urban economies of these countries, brought successive waves of south Indian immigrants, particularly since the late nineteenth century. In fact, the colonial government needed large numbers of south Indian manual laborers for building roads, railways, harbours, bridges, and the like. In the beginning they were very important and were in special demand by the government more than by the planters. Thus employment by government was an important source of livelihood in Malaya for the Tamil laborers. Although the Coromandal coast had regular trade and commercial contacts with lower Burma and the Malayan peninsula during the pre-colonial period, it was only after the 1870s, when regular steamer services were introduced, that the number of people who emigrated from south India increased greatly. The principal role of south Indians in the plantation economy of Malaya had been that of laborers. south Indians and the estate economy were considered almost synonymous in Malaya between the 1870s and the 1940s.

The growth and distribution of the south Indian population in Malaya was closely related to the expansion of sugar, rubber, and oil palm plantations. For instance, the acreage under rubber jumped from about 350 acres in 1877 to about 20,000 in 1914 and to 43,000 acres in 1910. By 1940 it had reached over 2 million acres, making Malaya by far the world's largest producer of natural "Raja rubber." In 1918, exports of rubber from Malaya amounted to about 50 per cent of the world's total rubber consumption.[11] Thus demand for south Indian labor developed mainly in the context of the extensive growth of export crops and the exploitation of colonies as sources of supply of raw materials for production in the metropolitan countries of the West. In fact, during the late nineteenth century considerable quantities of European capital began to flow into the commercial and industrial sectors of Malaya and Burma. Among the plantation crops, rubber – 'white gold' created a massive demand exclusively for unskilled and manual laborers. The 'rubber rush' of the early decades of the twentieth century also attracted capitalists seeking fabulous profits and fortunes. By 1913 British capital investments in Malaya amounted to 40 million; by 1923 it had increased to a total of $100 million.[12] In addition to rubber, other plantation crops like sugar, coffee, tea, and palm oil were equally demanding with regard to labor requirements, while the construction of railways, roads, and bridges by the colonial government needed thousands of laborers each year. Since the indigenous Malayas did not come forward to work as laborers in the plantations for fixed hours of daily work, the planters looked toward south Indian laborers, particularly the untouchable and low-caste Madrasis and Adi-Dravidas, who were considered to be 'ideal laboring material for the furtherance of capitalist endeavours in Malaya'.[13] With their experience of south Indian labor in Ceylon, most of the planters considered the Madrasis and Adi-Dravidas to be the most suitable and satisfactory type of laborer, especially for the simple, repetitive and routine tasks. Hence they became the mainstays of plantations. It was said that the south Indian laborer was 'malleable, worked well under supervision and was easily manageable'; he was the most amenable to the comparatively lowly paid and rather regimented life of estates; he had fewer qualms or taboos than his Northern fellows, and cost less to feed and maintain. Similarly, a number of government officials and public works contractors also preferred the Madrasis because they were the ' best metal breakers' and were especially adept at road-making and railway construction. If the plantation economy of Malaya was the main attraction for south Indian Tamil-speaking laborers, in the case of Burma, the non-plantation sectors increasingly drew the largest number of Telugu-speaking dalit and lower sudra peasant castes. A long-standing British-India steamer circuit, Cocanada-Vizagapatnam-Gopalpur-Rangoon, contributed greatly to familiarizing the people of coastal Andhra with Burma and thus stimulated the emigration flow. Burma's industry and commerce were so diversified at the turn of the century that the demand for labor was steadily increasing. As the indigenous population was unable to meet the growing demand, employers of labor drew their supplies mostly from south India and Andhra on account of its close proximity and advantageous terms. A prominent labor leader of Burma pointed out that "under British control the industrial expansion of the Province has been so rapid that it has already attained prominence as centre of great industrial and commercial activity during the period from 1915 to 1928, the number of factories had almost doubled while the number of persons employed had gone up by 152 p.c. [per cent]."[14] Rice field, paddy-processing industries, mineral oil and refineries, saw mills and timber yards, ports and harbours, and railways were among the main sources of employment. It was largely south Indian laborers who reaped the harvests, manned the industry, dealt with transport, cleared the streets and cleaned the sewers in Burma's cities. As the census Commissioner of Madras (1931) put it, "He [the south Indian laborer in Burma] tills the paddy fields, mans the railways, handles cargoes at Rangoon. He functions largely in the domestic service, clerical employment claims him and there is nothing to which he cannot put his hand with acceptance."[15] He was indeed "the toiler and the drudge" and in all those occupations labelled "disagreeable and disrespectful" and forsaken by the local Burmese the immigrant laborer did the work uncomplainingly. As Narayana Rao remarked: "Burma could never have built her splendid Railway systems, cleared her inaccessible forest domains and transformed them into smiling fields, operated her factories amidst fumes and high temperature for a miserable poor wage but for these patient, long suffering, obedient, faithful and grateful but much maligned sons of India."[16] Whereas in Malaya the Madrasi was, as it were, a specialist, in Burma he fulfilled a wide variety of functions. The vast majority of the Telugu laborers, around 90 per cent, were engaged in unskilled jobs. In fact, they constituted the single largest group (more than 50 percent) of unskilled laborers in Burma in the 1920s and 1930s. However, they worked mainly in the rice and saw mills, oil wells and refineries, harbours, shipping companies, and in harvesting. In some fields and sectors they were the dominant group. To name but a few: rickshaw (*lanachas*) pulling, sweeping and scavenging, and labor in rice mills, harbours, and ports. A report in *The Rangoon Gazette stated*:

> "In Rangoon alone about 80,000 Indian laborers find employment in various industries. Of this number about 55,000 are Telugus. The sweepers and *mehters* are Telugus. These classes are absolutely necessary as under no conditions would the Burmese agree to carry out the work of the *dhobis*, sweepers and *mehters*."[17]

A definite regional and linguistic pattern could be observed in the emigration of south Indian laborers to Southeast Asian countries in the nineteenth and twentieth centuries. Migration to Burma was basically a Telugu and Circars phenomenon. That is to say, the mainstream of emigration to Burma was from the northern coastal districts of Ganjam, Vizagapatnam, Godavari and Kistna. Together they contributed 70 per cent of labor migrants from the Madras Presidency in 1921; the rest came from the Tamil districts in the extreme south. Available data also shows that immigrants from the Telugu districts were by far the largest group among unskilled laborers in Rangoon, which was primarily a city of immigrants. Burma was certainly an important factor and feature in the ordinary life of the laboring classes of Andhra's northern coastal districts. The Indian population at Rangoon increased from 26.5 per cent of the city's population in 1872 to 51 per cent in 1901, accounting for 75 per cent of the unskilled and 70 percent of the skilled workforce in the Burmese capital.[18]

Among all the Telugu districts, Ganjam sent the largest number of laborers to Burma in any given year; in 1921 Ganjam accounted for more immigrants in Burma than any other Indian district, except Chittagang. Approximately 5 per cent of the population of Ganjam, and 3 per cent each of Vizagapatnam and Godavari districts were working in Burma, according to the Burma Census Report (1921).[19] The only district of coastal Andhra in which the population decreased was Ganjam, where it fell by nearly 2 per cent during the ten years from 1911 to 1921, mainly due to emigration. Burmese developments had a profound influence on the coastal Andhra region: the presence of about 300,000 Madrasi in Burma in the 1930s was an indication of the importance of migration movements. In fact, the largest number of Telugu-speaking persons outside the coastal Andhra districts lived in Burma during the pre-1947 period. According to the Burma Census Report (1931), the total Indian resident population was 522,000, of whom Telugus were 13,200 (about 25 per cent).[20] Despite the unfavourable conditions in the 1930s—the lack of employment due to depression and anti-Indian troubles and riots—the Madras-born population in Burma had increased by 25,000 since 1921, indicating the hold that Burma had upon Madrasi labor. The difference between Burmese-born Indians in Madras and Madras-born in Burma in 1931 was 294,000 in favour of the latter as against 271,00 in 1921: the percentage of increase in this difference was 8.52.[21]

Although emigration to Malaya was essentially a Tamil phenomenon, though not so pronounced as in the case of Ceylon, a few Telugu districts like Ganjam, Vizagapatnam, Godavari, and Chittoor also regularly contributed their laborers. Telugus constituted the second largest ethnic group among the Indian immigrants in Malaya in the 1920s. In 1921, for instance, they accounted for 8.5 per cent of the Indian population and 9 per cent of the total number of south Indians living in the Malayan Peninsula.[22] In Malaya, the Telugu coolies were conspicuous by their overwhelming presence in the rubber plantations on the West Coast – the lower Perak region, for instance. Nearly 90 percent of coolies in Malaya were from the southern districts of Madras Province. The number of Madras-born persons in Malaya increased from 366,000 in 1921 to 583,000 in 1931.[23] Trichinopoly, Tanjore, Salem, and the south and north Arcots districts accounted for the bulk of emigrants to Malaya. Available census figures for 1921 show that 19 per cent of those born in or associated with Trichinopoly migrated from their district. For Pudukottai, the number was 13 per cent; for Tanjore, Ramnad, and Tinnelvelly, 7 per cent each. Although the volume of migration might look insignificant in terms of the whole of the Madras presidency, for the specific districts and groups of people the numbers were indeed very important. The three coastal Andhra districts and the Kaveri Valley and delta districts in the south accounted for the greater incidences of migration. Similarly, for the lower castes, that is, Adi-Dravidas and Adi-Andhras, migration abroad was central to their economy and life-conditions. In fact, from an economic point of view the most important streams of emigration from Madras Province were those to Ceylon, Burma, and Malaya. Emigration to these areas acted as a 'safety valve,' especially in times of land scarcity, natural disasters, and the loss of livelihood and rural employment in the Madras Presidency.

South Indian migration to Southeast Asia was not a new phenomenon; it went back centuries. Since the late nineteenth century south Indian labor contributed heavily to the industrial prosperity of Malaya and Burma. Nevertheless, the most important and noticeable features of south Indian labor migrations to Malaya and Burma were that they were steady, seasonal and cyclical. (See Tables 1-2).

Table 1
Arrivals and departures of South Indian laborers, Burma, Selected Years, 1888-1929

Year	*Arrivals in Burma*	*Departures From Burma*
1888	38,018	N.A.
1889	34,048	N.A.
1890	33,048	N.A.
1891	43,717	N.A.
1892	43,881	N.A.
1893	54,574	N.A.
1894	49,281	42,672
1895	38,978	35,888
1896	61,020	35,517
1897	71,190	36,554
1898	71,113	44,427
1899	78,452	47,336
1900	99,038	50,745
1901	84,329	54,488
1903	100,646	81,266
1904	100,622	83,721
1905	124,365	96,216
1906	152,207	135,354
1907	105,614	93,792
1908	119,742	89,516
1909	131,587	112,827
1910	133,495	125,984
1911	144,503	109,328
1912	116,610	112,061
1913	130,725	N.A.
1914	79,757	105,382
1921	117,449	N.A.
1922	117,578	112,658
1923	158,438	N.A.
1924	156,436	N.A.
1925	145,194	N.A.
1927	157,807	N.A.
1928	151,354	N.A.
1929	149,799	N.A.

Source: Compiled from the Emigration and Immigration Reports of Madras Presidency. N.A. = Not Available.

Table 2
Arrivals and departures of South Indian laborers, Malaya, selected years, 1888-1935

Year	*Arrivals in Malaya*	*Departures From Malaya*
1888	22,299	N.A.
1889	19,800	N.A.
1894	15,016	14,012
1895	16,162	14,843
1896	20,474	13,163
1897	21,141	17,143
1898	15,539	14,880
1899	20,266	13,876
1900	39,585	14,263
1901	27,950	16,040
1903	22,960	N.A.
1904	28,249	21,173
1905	40,900	21,173
1906	52,306	N.A.
1907	62,537	32,503
1908	58,773	30,571
1909	48,719	30,745
1910	85,015	N.A.
1911	109,189	51,268
1912	107,842	60,992
1913	117,783	N.A.
1914	49,028	59,038
1920	95,720	55,481
1921	45,627	61,551
1922	59,169	34,475
1923	57,684	45,733
1924	62,001	37,326
1925	88,678	52,286
1926	159,061	N.A.
1927	145,181	N.A.
1928	52,599	N.A.
1929	101,517	N.A.
1930	55,360	N.A.
1931	19	N.A.
1934	28,639	N.A.
1935	13,267	N.A.

Source: Compiled from the Emigration and Immigration Reports of Madras Presidency. N.A. = Not Available.

Laborers migrated to Burma between the months of October and December, and returned again during the months of March through May. The cyclical character of the migration was due in part to monsoon conditions and the demand for seasonal labor in agriculture and the rice mill industry. The vicissitudes of seasonal and labor in agricultural conditions in their places of origin—and not conditions in Burma—heavily affected the labor migrants. During favourable seasons people generally did not migrate and Telugu labor migration to Burma mostly took place during the harvest period. Migration to Malaya from the southern districts was predominantly a hot weather phenomenon; it was greatest from April to June and least from October to March during the year.

Nearly 80 per cent of south Indian laborers did not migrate with a view to settling down. They intended to stay only temporarily, for two to three years, though many returned for subsequent spells on the plantations and in the rice fields and mills. Labor emigrants consisted mostly of single adult males aged between 15 and 40 who migrated for comparatively short periods of time, intending to return home as soon as possible with their earnings. Hence, they were "birds of passage." This male-centred migration caused a tremendous imbalance of sex ratios in Burma. Telugu male emigrants outnumbered Telugu female emigrants by four or five to one. The average number of females for every 1,000 males in Burma during the period 1921-31 was 208, compared to 430 among Tamils.[24] The proportions of females among all migrants was very low among the communities from coastal Andhra districts. In fact, Ganjam district, which had sent the largest number of laborers to Burma in 1921, contributed the least number of females: 1,366 females, compared to 21,907 males. Surprisingly, Telugu migration to Malaya was more family-oriented than was the case with Tamils: 717 women for every 1,000 males, compared to 515 among Tamil laborers in 1931.[25] This sort of enforced system of celibacy quite often resulted in the widespread practice of keeping mistresses and concubines. For Malaya, 'a certain number [Tamil females] were regularly received for prostitution in the new labor settlements.' One colonial official remarked that 'no Tamil women can go to the Federated Malaya States and return with a rag of reputation left.[26]

The fact that Telugu women went in large numbers to work as prostitutes is confirmed by various accounts in official documents, contemporary writings, and the local vernacular press. The Manual of Madras Administration mentioned that:

> "women go in numbers for the purpose of prostitution, and stay some years. A temple was recently built at Coringa in the Godavary district at a cost of Rs. 10,000 by a woman of this class who had saved money and returned."[27]

A Telugu press report stated that nearly 50 per cent of the female laborers in Burma worked as prostitutes and the rest as domestic servants and other menial workers. Most of them were drawn from the professional caste of Devadasis, known as Kalvantulu or Bhogam, and from other lower sudra and 'untouchable' castes.

> "Many of the low-caste Hindu women found in Burma, particularly those from Oriya-and Telugu–speaking areas, were prostitutes who thrived in the slums of Rangoon, where large numbers of single, young males were crowded into squalid tenements with little to divert them after long hours of hard labor."[28]

One contemporary observer remarked that:

> "the moral conditions of the laborers are no less pitiable than the civil conditions. The proportion of women to men is so small that it is far less than that which shocked me so much in Fiji. For here, in Burma, the proportion of women, which goes over [sic] on the ships, is less than one to five. Gangs of dock laborers employ a single woman to cook their food for them, and use the same women for the purpose of prostitution. These things are told to me openly, shamelessly; they are published in pamphlets and newspapers and not contradicted. They are not contradicted, because they are true."[29]

Many factors account for the temporary, seasonal, and long-distance migration of working adults from south India. No single factor was predominant—neither the push of poverty nor the pull of high wages. Growing pressures on land, poverty, unemployment, adverse seasonal conditions, natural calamities, and the proximity of prominent trading routes and ports all undoubtedly stimulated emigration. Data show that sudden natural calamities like famines, floods, and cyclones also had a significant correlative effect of migration—especially at the local and district levels. The Madras Census Report of 1921 described the situation in a prominent Telugu district that contributed a regular flow of laborers to Burma:

> "The only district in which the population has decreased is Ganjam where it had fallen by nearly 2 per cent of during the decade 1911-21. This decrease is due to emigration on account of the famine which visited the district in 1918-19."[30]

The annual emigration and immigration reports of the Madras government give evidence of the role of local conditions and external demand in the emigration of labor communities abroad:[31]

- "The large increase from Tanjore district is ascribed to a greater demand for labor in Burma" (report for 1898);
- "The increase is chiefly contributed by the Ganjam and Vizagapatnam districts, which is due to the great demand for labor in Rangoon and to the liberal wages received there by the coolies and also partly due to the unfavourable character of the season in the district" (report for 1899);
- "The increase in the number of passengers to the Straits Settlements is attributed to larger demand and better wages for cooly labor in the rubber plantations" (report for 1913);
- "The special feature of the year was the failure of the north-east monsoon in the chief recruiting districts which resulted in a large increase of emigration in the cold weather, usually the slack season owing to harvest time" (report for 1923).

Recent studies have also indicated that the "pressure to migrate, in the economic sense, has always been great enough to provide a stream of immigrants".[32] Adas, in his study of Burma, states:

> Although the movement of Indians between the subcontinent and Burma was influenced by a combination of "push" and "pull" factors, specific events in India were largely responsible for fluctuations in the volume of net migration. As early as 1865-66, and again in 1899, large-scale emigration from Vizagapatnam to Lower Burma averted the spread of famine from neighbouring

areas into that district. In 1896-97 the number of emigrants from Ganjam to Burma doubled and those from Vizagapatnam tripled as a result of widespread famine in these districts.[33]

Recruitment of Labor: *Maistry and Kangany Systems*

Labor recruitment for the growing number of mills, factories, and plantations in the Southeast Asian countries was concentrated in the rural areas of south Indian coastal districts.[34] Labor recruiters performed the most important and crucial function of linking the rural society of India with the plantation and urban economy of Malaya and Burma. Rice and saw mills, petroleum refineries, and transport were some of the principal industries in Burma in which Telugu and Tamil laborers were employed. Planters in Malaya and mill/factory owners in Burma rarely engaged the labor they needed directly. Instead, they delegated the task of labor recruitment to a special class of people called the maistry in the Telugu districts and the Kangany in the Tamil area. The employers contracted with these labor recruiters to secure an adequate and regular supply of labor for their mills and plantations. For their services, the employers paid them a premium of 5 to 10 rupees per person supplied or recruited. Since these middlemen belonged to the rank and file of the grass-roots or local society from which the laborers came, they were empowered to engage, discipline, and control the laborers, as well as to provide them with elementary knowledge about the tasks to be performed in the factories and plantations. These middlemen jobbers frequently visited the rural areas and lured economically and socially vulnerable villagers by narrating or painting plantation life in bright colors and offering them travel and other expenses as an additional inducement. Their personal approach and standing in the local society enabled them to influence the decisions of the prospective emigrants. Since the factory and plantation owners delegated to them the distribution of much sought after and highly regarded employment opportunities the maistries were able to build up a position of considerable strength. The relationship between the laborers and the maistry and his agents was of mutual but unequal interdependence that could be described as a form of patronage and exploitation. The employment relationship then was essentially between the maistry Kangany and his laborer.[35] The maistry or contract system of recruitment of Telugu labor for Burma was in essence comparable to other systems like kangani, sirdari, and jobber. The system of advances, the initial indebtedness of the laborers, the subordination of labor to the middlemen, innumerable illegal deductions from the wages of workers, underemployment, and the compulsory contribution of free labor were the main features of the maistry recruitment. The maistry system was also graded and hierarchical, as Kondapi explains:

> The labor contractor, the Head *Maistry*, the Charge *Maistry* and the Gang *Maistry* constituted the hierarchy of middlemen employers. A man in charge of a small gang of between 10 and 20 laborers was a Gang *Maistry* and *maistry* having under his control several such gangs was a Charge *Maistry*. A *maistry* in charge of the entire labor organization of a particular firm or company was the Head *Maistry*, while the Labor Contractor was a superior individual who was under a contract to supply and maintain the necessary labor force as stipulated in the contract. Hence the Labor Contractor was usually a man of financial standing and influence.[36]

Therefore, under the maistry system the laborer was indeed the servant of his contractor and not of the factory or plantation.

The contract maistry system of recruitment of Telugu labor for Burma began in the last quarter of the nineteenth century, particularly in the context of the growing demand from Europe for Burmese rice and the establishment of steam mills. Indians were considered to be the "backbone of the labor force in the rice mills." [37] The failure of local government authorities to tap the indigenous labor from upper Burma districts led to persistent efforts from 1874 onward to attract Indian emigrants both as agriculturists and laborers. In 1876 a Labor Act was enacted that provided for the appointment of a recruiting agent for Madras labor in India.[38] Between 1876 and 1878 approximately 15,000 Indians migrated to Burma as free settlers. By 1883 the number of emigrants had increased to 83,000 due to the operation of the maistry system in the Telugu district of south India.[39]

Shipping companies like the British India Steam Navigation also recruited Telugu laborers to Burma through their commission agents. To increase their income and profits from commission they

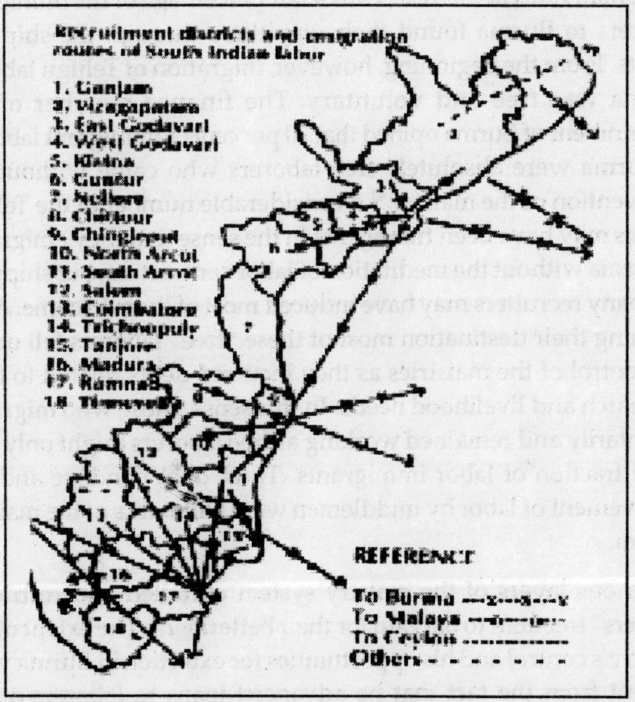

Map of Southeastern India showing recruitment districts and emigration routes of South India labor. (Adopted from a map based on M. W.M. Yeattas, Census of India, 1931, Vol. XIX, Part 1, Report, Madras, 1932, p. 93)

got for each laborer they booked and recruited, unscrupulous agents of the shipping companies stationed a large number of subagents at port towns like Gopalpur, Baruva, Kalingapatnam, Cocanada, Bimilipatnam, and Vizagapatnam, and sent them into interior localities to influence and lure as many people as possible to go to Burma. They also visited village fairs and pilgrim centres, promoting the advantages of emigration to Burma by word of mouth and tom-tom. They described exaggerated success stories and passed out leaflets, among other ingenious practices. Illiterate and ignorant village folk, enticed by rosy and bright pictures of Burma, tended to fall prey to such overtures. To pay for their transport and other expenses they borrowed the necessary funds from village moneylenders and/or the recruiting agent himself at exorbitant rates of interest. Thus a fair percentage of the immigrant laborers to Burma found their way there through the shipping agents. From the beginning, however, migration of Telugu labor to Burma was free and voluntary. The finance member of the Government of Burma opined that 70 per cent of immigrant laborers in Burma were absolutely free laborers who came without the intervention of the maistry.[40] A considerable number of the Telugu coolies may have been free agents in the sense that they emigrated to Burma without the meditation of labor contractors, but shipping company recruiters may have induced most of them to come. After reaching their destination most of these "free" laborers fell under the control of the maistries as they incurred debts related to their job search and livelihood needs. In this sense, those who migrated voluntarily and remained working as free laborers might only be a small fraction of labor immigrants. Thus, debt bondage and the enslavement of labor by middlemen were hallmarks of the maistry system.

Various layers of the maistry system curtailed and restricted laborers ' freedom to bargain for their betterment. The extent of the maistry's control and his opportunities for extortion in Burma were evident from the fact that he advanced loans to laborers on an inducement to immigration, regulated the laborer's employment, controlled the disbursement of wages, and had an arbitrary power to select and dismiss laborers.

The employment of south Indian labor on Malayan plantation began around the 1830s. Initially Tamil and Telugu laborers were brought to work on sugar plantations under the indenture system. The organization of labor recruitment for the Malayan peninsula was unique, for both the indentured and the Kangany systems coexisted for about half a century. The Kangany system, which was basically a Tamil phenomenon, seems to have originated in the late 1860s. Indeed, the Kangany system of labor recruitment started to function nearly half a century after the indenture system came into being. After the abolition of indenture in 1910, Kanganies recruited most of the laborers for Malayan plantations. Subsequently various other forms of labor recruitment coexisted with the kangany system. Compared to Burma where free and voluntary forms of labor migration coexisted with the maistry system, in the Malayan peninsula indenture, Kangany, and voluntary forms of labor recruitment were followed. The Kangany system in Malaya was closely linked to the growth of the plantation economy because from 1865 to 1897 nearly one thousand recruits were brought to Malaya annually.[41] The growth of the Kangany system was also linked to the changing nature of the plantation economy. Most of the south Indian laborers on the sugar plantations came as indentured laborers, but with the expansion of coffee plantations in the 1880s and 1890s the planters preferred and encouraged the Kangany system of recruitment. Later, when rubber displaced most of the sugar and coffee plantations in the early decades of the twentieth century, the Kangany system gained in importance and popularity and won the support of the Malayan government. The acreage under rubber increased in Malaya from 50,000 in 1900 to 543,000 in 1910. Much of this acreage was in small holdings as well as in the plantation sector. The rubber plantations depended heavily on laborers recruited by the Kanganies. The increasing number of these recruits shows that the Kangany system had become the maistry of labor recruitment for rubber plantations. Heidemann wrote: "From 1903 to 1906 their number of Kangany recruits almost doubled every year: 1,858 in 1903; 3,375 in 1904; 7,729 in 1905; and 19,177 in 1906.[42] More than 62 per cent of the total assisted-labor migration and nearly 44 per cent of all labor immigrants into Malaya were estimated to have been recruited by kanganies.[43]

Kanganies themselves worked on the plantations as foremen and even as laborers with some influence and standing. A considerable number of the Kanganies who were not foremen were elderly laborers who had worked on the plantation for some time. They were said to be "generally of good caste and had preferably to be heads of large families and persons of influence among others and subordinate castes in the village... The *Kangany* had to be a person who could command the respect of as wide a sector of the community of his village and district as possible."[44]Available evidence suggests that the Kangany, like the maistry, played a role in the south Indian countryside. He was a combination of patron, patriarch, businessman, ambassador, and self-appointed welfare officer. One newspaper report at the time wrote:

> The kanganies are easily believed by the simpletons because he...shines like a tin-god clothed in gorgeous velvet coat and lace turban and bedecked with costly jewels in his ears and his fingers...he is passed by all as [a] real and sympathetic gentleman... He shows he does not care for money and gives any amount to his newly acquired friends... He takes an interest in all matters concerning the welfare of the village or town he resides in... Soon he becomes popular with all and is generally invited to all social and public functions... His gold attracts like magnet everybody, and his position is envied by many. He instills in the mind of these ignorant seekers of fortune that Malaya...[is an] E1 Dorado...where they could become very rich in the course of an [sic] year or two... Thus the ignorant people of the village are entitled away from their homes. Husband and wife are separated, young girls kidnapped...[and] boys are spirited away from their...parents.[45]

Right from the beginning the Kangany system of labor recruitment was defective: their recruiting practices indulged in coercion, fraud, malpractice, and other abuse: they kidnapped minors and ensnared recruits at the weekly *shanties* (markets); they seduced young men with the promise of getting them married in Malaya; they took advantage of petty domestic quarrels between sons and fathers, and husbands and wives, inducing them to leave their homes; they matched strangers as brothers, fathers and sons, brothers and sisters, and husbands and wives in order to take advantage of immigration rules that allowed family members to immigrate together; they misrepresented the nature of the work and the rates of wages on the estates; they substituted one person in the place of another duly passed by the village munsiff (village headman) and forged the village munsiff's signature on the license; they booked passage for recruits as ordinary passengers or as non-emigrants; they obtained laborers from professional recruiters, brokers, and hotel-emigrants; they obtained licenses signed by munsiffs of villages (the recruits did not come for having the munsiff's signature forged on the license).[46] In many instances the Kanganies colluded with corrupt village officials and enticed ignorant villagers to emigrate. The monetary inducement, commissions, and premiums offered by estates to Kanganies tempted them to recruit labor unlawfully through fraudulent methods such as those named above. The planters willingly accepted the Kangany system, as one of them explained, "The Kangani or *mistri* system at its best is probably the best system evolved. It is strictly patriarchal. The men brought members of the family. The head Kangani is practically the father of the estate."[47] As Jain's study shows, after the decline of the indenture system, the Kangany became almost indispensable as a labor-recruiter, gaining more power over the labor force and importance among the planters.[48] The plantation managers supported Kangany recruitment with all its abuses and irregularities because they assumed that the Kangany, who was himself an immigrant who worked on the plantation, would exercise greater care in the choice of laborers. Moreover, in south Indian villages, the Kangany was known to the local community and spoke the language of the potential emigrants. Thus, villagers were more willing to volunteer as emigrants. In Malaya, the Kangany had subtle means of keeping laborers on a lead, attached to and dependent on him. As long as the power and authority of the Kangany kept laborers in check and facilitated the smooth functioning of the plantation economy, the management allowed the Kangany system to continue. Management gave the Kangany the authority to mete out severe punishment to the laborers. "The dominant and influential Kangany was rather free in establishing his own interests, values and ideas as the social norm. And he was free to choose the methods of social control, which ranged from paternalism to brutal arbitrariness. Therefore, there was a clear intersection between the planter and the worker", and the dominant Kangany was the undisputed master in the workers section.[49] The Kangany was not

> "a mediator of conflicts between labor and capitol; he was very much the agent of capital and his primary role was to subject labor to the rigorous discipline required by the plantation production system."[50]

Until the middle 1930s, when the Kangany system began to decline, the Kanganies played a significant role in the management of labor relations in the plantation economy of colonial Malaya.

Wages and Working Conditions

Manual and unskilled laborers were the most numerous immigrants in Burma and Malaya. The fact that the vast majority of south Indians in these two Southeast Asian colonies belonged to the working class makes the question of wages important. The Kangany and maistry systems were the bane of Indian labor, but cash advances and the prospect of making a fortune in these two countries acted as a powerful allure, enticing south Indian laborers to cross the Bay of Bengal. In spite of the fact that cash advances were not in the interest of the laborers and bound them in perpetual slavery to the middlemen-recruiters (maistry and Kangany), the money to be made in rice mills and on the plantations attracted the attention of many a laborer. Although it is difficult to get reliable or authentic comparable quantitative data on the standard and cost of living, or on income, wages, earnings, and expenses, information that is available indicates that plantation and factory work was well paid relative to comparable employment in rural south India. In the home and Southeast Asian settings, various surveys and statistical data provided in government and other reports reveal that by and large contract laborers. Burma obtained three to four times the wages they received in their native places. Table 3 shows the average cash wages paid to adult male agricultural laborers, which was almost wholly the occupation of the emigrants, in the south Indian districts from which they were recruited in large numbers.

Table 3
Average daily cash wages for selected agricultural work, for selected districts in South India, 1926

District	*Sowers/transplanters*			*Weeders*			*Reapers/harvesters*		
	Rs	*An*	*Ps*	*Rs*	*An*	*Ps*	*Rs*	*An*	*Ps*
Vizagapatnam	0	4	6	0	4	2	0	4	3
Chinglepat	0	6	2	0	5	6	0	6	1
North Arcot	0	5	11	0	4	6	0	5	3
Chittoor	0	4	9	0	4	1	0	4	5
Trichinopoly	0	6	3	0	5	0	0	6	0
Salem	0	4	10	0	4	1	0	4	6

Compare the data in Table 3 with that in table 4, which gives averages daily paid for comparable work in Burma.

Table 4
Average daily wages paid for selected kinds of labour in Burma, 1926

Description of Work	*Amount* *Rs - An - Ps*		
Stevedore/Dockyard: coolie	1	12	0
Burma Oil Company: coolie	0	15	0
Oil fields general labour	1	0	8
Rice mill: unloading/storing coolie	0	15	0

Sources for Table 3 and 4: Data contained in The Emigration and Immigration Reports of the Madras Presidency, 1926, p.3, and A. Narayana Rao, *Indian Labor in Burma* (Rangoon, 1933), pp. 170-71.

The average monthly earnings of unskilled labor in Burma varied between 20 and 25 rupees, while in south Indian districts it was between 6.25 and 9.50 rupees. Similarly in the case of Malaya, from the figures noted in Kanganys' recruiting licenses and from information gathered from return emigrants, it has been calculated that the average wages of a working adult man was 42 cents per day (in Malayan Straits dollars). Converted into Indian money this works out to be 10.5 anns, that is, more than double the wages obtained in south India.[51] Moreover, work was not available in India for the agricultural laborers throughout the year, but in Malaya work was fairly continuous (about 25 days per month). However, in comparing the wages in Malaya with those prevailing in India it must be noted that the cost of living in Malaya was about 40 per cent higher. The average monthly incomes of plantation laborers in Malaya ranged between 12 and 15 rupees.[52] So, the south Indian manual laborers in Southeast Asian countries received higher wages, but the cost of living was also higher in those countries. Hence there was a great rush of emigrants during the hot weather, partly owing to seasonal conditions and want of labor in the districts and partly owing to the greater demand in Southeast Asia for labor on the plantations and in dockyards and other sectors. The fact that south India plantation and factory workers could and did save money and send remittances home on a regular basis is also confirmed by the available data given below. (See Tables 5 and 6)

Table 5
Post office savings/bank accounts of Indians in Malaya, selected years, 1906-24

Year	*Amount (Malaysian straits $)*
1906	199,048
1907	208,000
1908	N.A
1909	278,508
1910	342,856
1911	400,848
1912	461,917
1922	476,917
1923	894,704
1924	166,443

Table 6
Amount sent from Malaya to India by money orders

Year	*Amount (Millions of rupees)*
1906	2.04
1907	2057
1908	N.A
1909	2.23
1910	2.82
1911	3.40
1912	4.29
1920	2.23
1921	5.07
1922	3.67
1923	3.35
1924	3.22

Sources for Table 5 and 6: Data contained in the Annual Reports on Indian Immigration into the Federal Malay States, for the years shown.

Although financial remittances cannot be taken as evidence of comparative prosperity, they certainly indicate that some of the immigrant laborers saved money. Evidence also shows that some of the returned migrants became well-to-do bought landed property and other assets in rural or urban areas. Whether remittances to the rural areas in south India were substantial or not is difficult to say. Labor leaders and administrators and government officials disagree about the benefits of migration to laborers, their actual conditions of life, and the degree of their indebtedness and exploitation by labor contractors.[53] There is not much dispute, however, about the rate of gross money wages paid to manual laborers in Burma and Malaya, although opinions differ greatly regarding net wages, savings, and surplus. Most of the colonial government's official reports tended to present an exaggerated and rosy picture of labor conditions on the plantations and in the factories. They emphasized the higher wage rates obtained by the workers, but neglected to take into account recurring hazards like disease, sickness, stoppage of work, withholding of wages, and indebtedness, which substantially reduced net wages and the possible accrual of surplus to the laboring poor.

The provision of loans by maistry and other labor recruiters was an important instrument of control over the labor force. It was also the starting point of the debt spiral because job-seeking migrants, who generally needed loans at the start, turned to contractors and/or their agents for work and loans. Kondapi writes:

> "The kangany and maistry systems of recruitment were based and reared on the indebtedness of the worker. While ordinarily everywhere lower wages led to indebtedness, in Malaya, Ceylon and particularly in Burma, the method of labor recruitment and control constituted the chief cause of indebtedness. The low wages and defective recruitment had a crushing cumulative effect in increasing indebtedness of the Indian workers in these countries."[54]

Laborers who arrived in Rangoon, for instance, did not possess much hard or ready cash, and they usually did not find work immediately upon arrival. Yet, they needed to make a living. In addition, they were obliged to pay the maistries some commission as the price of employment. Even after a job was secured, it did not solve the immediate problem of a lack of cash. Rice mill and other factory owners in Burma invariably paid wages only through the maistry. Consequently, in most cases, employment in a rice mill or a factory coincided with the laborer entering into a debt relationship with the maistry.

An investigation in 1925 of a number of laborers from Burma picked at random had shown that out of 163 laborers examined 61 or 37 p.c. [per cent] were found to be in debt to the extent of Rs. 15 to Rs. 1,000 borsrowed on interest at rates ranging from 1 to 25 per cent. per month. Illegal deductions, exaction and commissions varying from 35 to 50 per cent. of the wages, high rentals for living accommodation, drinking and extravagant expenditure on extras were found to be the other causes of debt.[55]

Similarly, in the case of plantation labor in Malaya the

> "kangani's money-lending activities constituted another important aspect of his paternal role. Money given on credit was recovered from laborers either by deduction from their wages or [by] enrolling them in a saving scheme...[A] study of two estates shows that in early twentieth century, the management paid the wages of the laborers to the kangani so that he could deduct a proportion of the debt owed to him. Laborer always paid their debts to the kangani due to their social dependence on him."[56]

Evidence shows that the majority of laborers did not receive their rightful wages. The minimum "standard" or "living" or "family" wage fixed by the colonial governments from time to time, both in colonial Burma and Malaya, was not in any way received by them.

In spite of being denied a decent wage the immigrant laborers continued to struggle to maintain a reasonable standard of living. The conditions under which they labored were quite inhuman; they were pathetic and miserable. Industrial laborers in Burma, particularly in Rangoon, were housed in barracks covered by zinc or iron sheets and in rented tenement houses, with each room or hall accommodating thirty to fifty persons. This overcrowding resulted in a choking and malodorous atmosphere, according to the Report of the Public Health Committee, Rangoon:

> Dark, ill-ventilated houses on sites perennially flooded with rain or tide waters or with stagnant pools of household sullage waste, with scarcely a ray of direct sunshine in the inner room, are inhabited by hundreds and thousands of the poor class of the

> community; and with their poor wages, in addition to drink and drug, squalor and filth surrounding their social life, form a tragic total climax of their slum life. There are thousands of houses, huts and hovels in our town, which are unfit for human habitation.[57]

Like their housing, the medical attention and facilities offered to laborers were also very unsatisfactory. The public health system had many defects and most of the hospitals on plantation estates in Malaya did not possess qualified medical and paramedical staff. Consequently many laborers on the plantations succumbed to disease. The condition of many sick or injured laborers worsened as a result of the hardships of their transport from rural estates to hospitals. Nor were conditions better during the passage to Malaya. Several government reports referred to many complaints received regarding inadequate medical aid and attention during such voyages. The journey by ship under overcrowded and inhuman conditions resulted in high morality.[58] Innumerable cases were reported wherein the very journey across the sea aggravated conditions that resulted in the death of laborers.

Social Composition of Migrants and Effects of Migration

The victims of disease, illness, deprivation, and exploitation on plantations in Malaya and in factories in Burma were the poor laboring populations of south Indian districts. The immigrant population in these two countries contained a considerable number of laborers. Therefore, it is pertinent to investigate the social background of the immigrant labor. Census and other reports throw abundant light on the social origins of the Tamil- and Telugu-speaking people who emigrated in the nineteenth and twentieth centuries. Available data shows that emigrants came mainly from certain social and economic groups. As we will see below, they belonged overwhelmingly to three caste groups, namely, agricultural or peasant castes, trading and commercial castes, and service/dependent, artisanal, and dalit communities of coastal Andhra.

Upper-caste Brahmins were conspicuous by their absence; indeed, they did not migrate in large numbers. Only a few went to Southeast Asian countries and worked as priests of temples (*purohits*) to non-Brahmin castes; others found employment as professionals (e.g., teachers, lawyers, doctors, journalists) or as clerks, managers, and superintendents in government and business. The figures in Table 7 show clearly that the Telugu peasant castes migrated in greater numbers than the dalits. However, in the case of Tamils, dalit castes like Parayas, Pallans, and Adi-Dravidas constituted about one-third or more of the total emigrants in 1930s.[59] In the case of Burma no such data regarding the caste representation of emigrants is available, but from descriptive accounts it appears that the emigrants were a mixed group. In 1840 the district Collector of Godavari stated that it was mainly barbers, washermen, tailors, and weavers who went to Burma, while the Vizagapatnam Collector mentioned (in 1863) that the majority of emigrants were weavers and that were not agricultural laborers.[60]

In the twentieth century, emigrants to Southeast Asia were drawn from the agricultural communities, including the dalit labor castes. Most of the migrants were not necessarily the settled *ryots (pattadars)*, but poor or middle peasants and agricultural laborers who were used to moving from place to place in search of employment. The internal migration of agricultural laborers in the coastal region was an acknowledged factor in the agricultural laborers in the coastal region was an acknowledged factor in the agrarian economy. Among the agricultural groups emigrating to Southeast Asian countries there were the non-Brahmin castes of owner-cultivators, tenants, sharecroppers, and landless agricultural laborers, including Kapu, Nayudu, Kamma, Reddy, Padayachi, Velala, Muthiraj, and Gavara. There were also agricultural laborers who belonged to the Adi-Andhra and Adi-Dravida dalit groups of the Mala, Madiga, Pallan, and Parayan, and Chakkilyan castes. The traders were drawn from particular castes like Komati, Chetti, and Balija. Castes such as Mangali (barber), Tsakali (washermen), Mera (tailor), Kummari (potter), Golla/Yadav (Shepherd), Sale (weaver), Gamandla/Settibalija (toddy tapper), Kamsali (goldsmith), Vadrangi (carpenter), and constituted the dependent and artisan groups. The cultivating castes were able to find work on the plantations and in the mills, while the trading castes opened grocery or provision shops around industrial, commercial, and urban centres. The dependent and artisan castes were able to pursue their traditional occupations, as their services were in demand. Those who were not able to carry on their traditional callings joined the ranks of manual and unskilled laborers. Interestingly, there was a broad correspondence between caste and occupation. For instance, barbers, washermen, goldsmiths, and carpenters were from the castes of Mangali, Tsakali, Kamsali, and Vadrangi respectively. Likewise, laborers who were engaged as scavengers, particularly in Rangoon, belonged to Adi-Andhra and Adi-Dravida castes, while the traders and shop-assistants came from castes such as Chettis, Komatis, and Balijas. The scope for occupational specialization, particularly in the service, dependent, and dalit castes, contributed to the perpetuation of caste-centred specialization and caste-oriented activities. Presumably, the majority of the emigrants from the service, dependent, and dalit castes would have been landless laborers and hence they worked as manual laborers. But it is also of interest to note that other agriculturists from high to middle levels in the caste hierarchy (e.g., Kapu, Kamma, Reddy, and Velama) also chose to migrate. It is possible that deteriorating conditions in agriculture (e.g., pressures on land) or natural disasters such as famines, floods, or cyclones were responsible for their migration. For them emigration became a habitual escape. Certain non-Brahmin lower sudras—castes like Agnikulkshetriyas (fishermen), Settibalijas (toddy tappers), and Gollas/Yadav (Shepherds), who migrated to Burma in considerable numbers—left their traditional occupations and worked as unskilled or manual laborers in paddy fields, rice mills, and water transport, among other work situations.

Table 7
Telugu emigration to Malaya, 1935-38

Caste Groups	*1935*	*1936*	*1937*	*1938*
Agricultural/Peasant	768	69	2213	72
Agricultural Labour	34	35	107	37
Trading/Commercial	25	N.A	300	N.A
Service/Dependent/Artisan	187	02	4789	31
Total	*914*	*106*	*7409*	*140*

Source: Emigration and Immigration reports of the Madras Presidency (Government of Madras), for the year shown. N.A. = not available.

In fact, rural south Indians resorted to migration to Burma and Malaya as a temporary measure to supplement their family income. Normally, single male emigrants were able to return after three to five years with some cash savings with which they tended to acquire some assets and property.

Though castes are known by their respective traditional occupations, all the non-Brahmin castes in Burma and Malaya were dependent on agricultural operations directly or indirectly. By and large it was only the service and dependent castes that stayed with their traditional work. Nevertheless, there was heterogeneity in the choice of occupations. This heterogeneity in the choice of occupations and occupational mobility in Burma and Malaya did affect the caste system. Dalit Adi-Andhra castes like Malas and Madigas or Adi-Dravida castes like Parayan and Pallan, though they pursued caste-related occupations like scavenging and menial jobs overseas, did not strictly speaking perform their traditional occupations like leather-work. Opportunities to diversify their occupations were plentiful. Although they worked predominantly as unskilled manual laborers either on plantations in Malaya or in rice mills or factories in Burma, their new occupations implied a break with traditional occupational specialization. Members of the service/artisan castes were also able to secure opportunities to practice other occupations besides or in addition to their traditional callings. The new occupational system prevalent in Burma and Malaya thus weakened caste rigidity and caused disjunctions between caste and occupation. Consequently, caste feelings and other manifestations of caste sentiment were also minimized. Yet the caste system did not disappear.

The magnitude of the migration had a noticeable impact both socially and economically. As one observer noted:

> "The returning immigrant brought new habits of life and new values. He was more self-reliant, and possessed more self-respect. The large proportion of untouchable castes also had a salutary effect on the operation of the caste system. They generally benefited from this change, and when they came back [they] did not submit to gross forms of discrimination against them."[61]

Emigration also increased socio-economic mobility inasmuch as

A. Tailor's family (Muslim) returned from Burma. [Photo taken by author in the "Burma colony" of Kakinada least Godavari district, Andhra Pradesh, India, August 1999.]

the emigrants returned with greater knowledge of agricultural operations and less willingness to abide by caste restrictions. A census Commissioner reported that at Nagapatam (a port of embarkation) a Brahmin once chided a *parayan* who barged into him on the way. The Parayan replaced: "I have taken off my caste at lest it with the officer. I won't put it on again till I come back."[62] The readiness of the lower castes to disregard traditional caste prejudices and restrictions shows that the effects of emigration were strong. One colonial official remarked:

> "I have heard of depressed classes or at least of depressed individuals evolving into substantial farmers with the aid of the money earned and saved in foreign countries."[63]

Most colonial officials held the view that emigration was beneficial to the lower caste laborers because after a few years' stay abroad the emigrants returned with hard cash with which they bought a plot of land to cultivate on their own. It was also felt that emigration in the long run raised the general level of prosperity and that the returned emigrants were much better off than they had been before. More than the economic and material benefits, emigration instilled a sense of independence, equality, self-respect, self-reliance, and dignity among people in the lower castes and classes who went abroad. In 1931, the census Commissioner of Madras said:

> A man who, little removed from praedial serfdom...finds himself treated on his own merits like every one else when he crosses the sea, paid in cash for his labors and left to his own resources, must in the majority of cases benefit from the change, and it is probably the existence of the emigration current that has contributed most to the growth of consciousness among the depressed classes... Laborers from well-run estates generally bring back to their village some of the ideas on cleanliness, food and comfort acquired while abroad. Evidences of this are to be seen in many a south India village and I have myself on several occasions had pointed out to me a house differing markedly from its neighbours as being that of someone who had been to Malaya.[64]

Concluding Remarks

In this essay, I have made an attempt to study the course, nature, and effects of migration by laborers from south Indian communities to Southeast Asia. I have also presented an analysis of the patterns of mobility of the laboring classes who crossed the seas. Most migration studies lack a comprehensive perspective and fail to link specific events with particular groups of migrants as well as with the areas of origin and recruitment. Scholars disagree strongly about whether labor migration under colonial conditions was free or not. In this study I have found that different types of migrations coexisted and that there was no unilinear pattern of succession of one kind by another. Drawing a rigid line or making a clear-cut distinction between free and unfree types of migration is difficult. To begin with, emigration to Malaya was based on the indenture system, but kangany-assisted free migration was also encouraged during the same period. Similarly, since its inception, migration to Burma was free and unassisted, but over the course of time the contract or maistry system of labor recruitment became dominant. I have shown that the contract labor system of labor contained many elements of unfreedom. Hence, I have suggested that no arbitrary distinction between freedom and unfreedom is possible in the study of labor migration. Both these aspects were present in labor relations throughout the nineteenth and twentieth centuries. For instance, the abolition in 1910 of the government-regulated indenture system for migration to Malaya did not necessarily usher in a free plantation labor force due to the introduction of the Kangany system. Lilewise unaided free and voluntary migration to Burma did not grant real freedom to laborers because the maistry system presented numerous possibilities for labor enslavement. Nevertheless, maistry and Kangany systems of labor recruitment represented unique caste and cultural arrangements. Interestingly, these labor intermediaries had an overwhelming presence in the landscape of capital-labor relations and acted as the chief mediators between the employers and employees. They were an integral part of the caste and clan system of local society in south India. They were also, indeed, the crucial links incorporating the rural economy of south India into the plantation and urban economies of Southeast Asia in the nineteenth and twentieth centuries. They undoubtedly acted as the important agents, making possible regular, continuous, and unbroken streams of labor migration.

The poor economic situation and unfavourable agricultural conditions of persons from lower castes and classes necessitated their emigration. General social dislocation and economic distress compelled them to migrate. It was a sort of "shoveling out of paupers." Especially for the lower sudra and depressed castes emigration also meant "fleeing from caste oppression". Migration to Southeast Asia provided them better opportunities and potential social mobility that were denied in their native places. As casual laborers and coolies in Burma and Malaya they were able to earn relatively higher wages. In many respects lower-caste labor communities were better able to respond positively to opportunities abroad. Many of them also emigrated because friends and relatives who had been to Southeast Asia told them of the higher wages obtainable there and assured them that employment could easily be found.

REFERENCES

This paper is a revised version of a CLARA Working Paper (No.11) published by the International Institute of Asian Studies (IIAS) and the International Institute of Social History (IISH), Amsterdam. I am thankful to the authorities of the Changing Labor Relations in Asia Programme (CLARA) for awarding me a short-term fellowship. I am also grateful to professors Jan Lucassen and Marcel Linden and Dr. Ratna Saptari for their help and encouragement as I wrote this paper.

1. The Telugu-speaking people in Burma were known as *Coranghees* to the local people as well as to the press and government. Since the Andhras migrated in earlier times from a port called Korangi in the present day East Godavari District of Coastal Andhra Pradesh in south India, they were identified with that place. The Telugu-speaking communities in the Malay Peninsula were identified along with the Tamil-speakers as *Madrasis.* The local population and the government tended to treat all south Indian people alike. The specificity of the Telugu language and culture was subsumed under Tamil identity.
2. See P.E. Baak, "About Enslaved Ex-Slaves, Uncaptured Contract Coolies and Unfreed Freemen", *Modern Asian Studies,* 33, No. 1 (1999), p. 124; H.Tinker, *A New System of Slavery: The Export of Indian Labor Overseas, 1830-1920* (London: Oxford University Press, Published for the Institute of Race Relations [London], 1974); R.P. Behal and P.P. Mohapatra, Tea and Money versus Human Life: The Rise and Fall of the Indenture System in the Assam Tea Plantations, 1840-1908, *Journal of Peasant Studies* (hereafter *JPS*) 19, No. 3-4, (1992), pp. 142-72; R.D. Gupta, "Plantation Labor in Colonial India", *Ibid*., 173-98; R.D. Gupta, "Structure of Labor Market in Colonial India", *Economic and Political Weekly* (hereafter *EPW*) 16, No. 44-46 (1981): 1781-1801; R.D. Gupta, "From Peasants and Tribesmen to Power and Proletarianization in North East India, 1850-1947, *EPW* 21, No. 4 (1986): 2-9; Gail Omvedt, "Migration in Colonial India: The Articulation of Feudalism and capitalism by the Colonial State", *JPS* 7, No. 2 (1980): 185-212; Jan Breman, *Taming the Coolie Beast: Plantation Society and the Colonial Order in Southeast Asia* Delhi and New York, 1989.
3. P.C. Emmer, "Was Migration Beneficial?" in J. Lucassen and L. Lucassen, eds., *Migration, Migration History, Old Paradigms and New Perspectives* Bern and New York, 1997, 123.

4. Cited in Behal and Mohapatra, *"Tea and Money"*, 143.
5. M. Carter, "Strategies of labor Mobilization in Colonial India: The recruitment of Indentured Workers for Mauritius", *JPS* 19, No. 3/4, (1992): 122.
6. Baak, *About Enslaved Ex-Slaves*, 151-53; Tom Brass and Marcel van der Linden, (eds.), *Free and Unfree Labor: The Debate Continues* Bern and New York, 1997, 11-41; Shahid Amin and Marcel van der Linden, eds., *Peripheral Labor Studies in the History of Partial Proletarianization* New York, 1997, 1-7.
7. Lucassen and Lucassen, *"Migration"*, pp. 12-19.
8. Arthur Paurves Phayre, *History of Burma: Including Burma Proper, Pegu, Taungu, Tenasserim, and Arakam, from the Earliest Time to the First War with British India* London, 1883; New York, 1969, p. 32; see also H.R. Spearman, ed., *"The British Burma Gazetteer"*, Col. 1 (Rangoon, 1880), 54-59.
9. Kernial Singh Sandhu, *Indians in Malaya: Some Aspects of Their Immigration and Settlement, 1786-1957*, Cambridge, 1969.
10. B. Nukaiah and V.K. Sharma, eds., *Proceedings Volume of the Second World Telugu Mahasabha* (Telugu), Hyderabad, 1981, 76-77.
11. See P. Ramasamy, "Labor Control and labor Resistance in the Plantations of Colonial Malaya", *JPS* 19, No. 3/4, (1920: 88-89; Sinnappah Arasaratnam, *Indians in Malasia and Singapore* (London and New York: Oxford University Press, published for the Institute of Race Relations [London], 1970). "The Acreage under rubber increased from about 50,000 in 1900 to 543,000 in 1911, and in 1938 it stood at 3, 272,000 acres," p. 29.
12. Sandhu, *Indians in Malaya*, p. 50.
13. *Ibid.*, p. 56.
14. A. Narayana Rao, *Contract Labor in Burma*, (Madras, 1930), 1-2; A. Narayana Rao, *Indian Labor in Burma*, Rangoon, 1933, 1-17.
15. *Census Report of India, 1931*, (Madras), Vol. 14, pt. 1, 82 (hereafter Census Report).
16. Rao, *Contract Labor, 94-95; The Royal Commission on Labour* (1931) noted, "Telugus, who show the highest percentage from outside Burma, contain a larger proportion of industrial workers than the others", p. 17.
17. Cited in Rao, *Indian Labor*, 61-62. "In Rangoon in 1928 there were said to be 7,000 Telugu rickshaw pullers, and 8,000 handcart pullers, who were mainly Telugus." See Royal Commission on Labour (1931), 430.

18. Michael Adas, *The Burma Delta: Economic Development and Social Change on an Asian Rice Frontier, 1852-1941* (Madison: University of Wisconsin Press, 1974), 99.
19. *Census of India*, 1921 (Madras), Vol. 12, pt. 1, p. 20.
20. N.R. Chakravarti, *The Indian Minority in Burma: The Rise and Decline of an Immigrant Community*, Oxford and New York, 1971, 24.
21. *Census Report*, 80.
22. Sandhu, *Indians in Malaya*, 56.
23. The Census Commissioner remarked: "Madrasis found abroad in census time were more numerous in 1931 than in 1921." *Census Report*, 32.
24. *Ibid.*, 79.
25. *Ibid.*, 87. "There was a more marked preference among Telugus to move as family units than there was among Tamils...The Telugus...are mainly plantation laborers. They came with families, and tended to settle permanently in this country from early on." Arasaratnam, *Indians in Malaysia*, 25 and 45.
26. Government Order (Public) 143, 16 February 1907 (hereafter G.O.); G.O. 568, 16 July, 1907.
27. *Manual of Madras*, 500
28. Adas, *Burma Delta*, 89-90.
29. *Indian Review*, (November 1924): 708.
30. *Census Report*, 1921-20.
31. Emigration reports for the years 1898, 1899, 1913, and 1923 included in G.O. 694-95, 21 June, 1899, 19; G.O. 29-30, 10 September, 1890, 16; G.O. 581, 12 June, 1914, 2; Government Order (Law General) 1890, 25 June, 1924, 2.
32. Kingsley Davis, *The Population of India and Pakistan* (Princeton: Princeton University Press, 1951), 99.
33. Adas, *Burma Delta*, 95.
34. Rao, *Contract Labor*; 14-23; C. Kondapi, *Indians Overseas, 1839-1949* New Delhi, 1951, 41-51.
35. For details see Frank Heidemann, *Kanganies in Sri Lanka and Malaysia: Tamil Recruiter-cum Foreman as a Sociological Category in the Nineteenth and Twentieth Century*, (Munich: Anacon, 1992), 50-61; Ravindra K. Jain, *South Indians on the Plantation Frontier in Malaya* New Haven, 1970, 199-218; Arasaratnam, *Indians in Malaysia*, 16-24.
36. Kondapi, *Indians Overseas*, 46.
37. Tinker, *A New System*, 35.
38. *Manual of Madras*, 501.

39. Kondapi, *Indians Overseas*, 48.
40. Quoted in Rao, *Indian Labor*, 28.
41. Sandhu, *Indians in Malaya*, 96.
42. Heidemann, *Kanganies*, 55.
43. Sandhu, *Indians in Malaya*, 96.
44. Arasaratnam, *Indians in Malaysia*, 17.
45. Cited in Heidemann, *Kanganies*, 59.
46. Emigration Reports for 1924 and 1926 in G.O. (Law General) 1598, 12 May, 1925, 5-6; *Ibid*. 1614, 8 May, 1926, 5-6.
47. Cited in Omvedt, *Migration in Colonial India*, 193.
48. Jain, *South Indians*, 199-218.
49. Heidemann, *Kanganies*, 70-71.
50. Ramasamy, *Labor Control*, 99.
51. Emigration Report for 1926, 3-4.
52. G.O. (Law General) 1614, 8 May, 1926.
53. *Ibid.*, 1877, 11 June, 1925; *Ibid.*, 1878, 11 June, 1925; *Ibid.*, 1916, 16 June, 1925.
54. Kondapi, *Indians Overseas*, 74.
55. *Ibid.*, 78.
56. Ramasamy, *Labor Control*, 99.
57. See Kondapi, *Indians Overseas*, 83.
58. 'Of the total of about 4,250,000 gross Indian emigration to Malaya between 1886 and 1957, nearly 750,000 were estimated to have died.' Omvedt, *Migration in Colonial India*, 189; Rao, *Indian Labor*, 126-27; G.O. 1496, 9 December, 1912; G.O. 759, 20 Junem 1913.
59. Arasaratnam, *Indians in Malaysia*, 26.
60. Cited in Dharma Kumar, *Land and Caste in South India: Agricultural Labor in the Madras Presidency during the Nineteenth Century*, Cambridge, 1965, 139.
61. Arasaratnam, *Indians in Malaysia*, 27.
62. *Census Report*, 1911, 26.
63. *Ibid.*
64. *Census Report*, 1931, 93.

Index